# Literacy for Learning

# Literacy for Learning

## A Handbook of Content-Area Strategies for Middle and High School Teachers

Gregory Berry, Ed.D.

ROWMAN & LITTLEFIELD
Lanham • Boulder • New York • Toronto • Plymouth, UK

Every effort has been made to contact copyright holders for permission to reproduce borrowed material. We regret any oversights that may have occurred and would be happy to rectify them in subsequent reprints of the work.

Published by Rowman & Littlefield
4501 Forbes Boulevard, Suite 200, Lanham, Maryland 20706
www.rowman.com

10 Thornbury Road, Plymouth PL6 7PP, United Kingdom

British Library Cataloguing in Publication Information Available

**Library of Congress Cataloging-in-Publication Data**

Berry, Gregory (Gregory Wayne)
  Literacy for learning : a handbook of content-area strategies for middle and high school teachers / Gregory Berry, Ed.D.
      pages cm.
  Includes bibliographical references and index.
  ISBN 978-1-4422-2711-8 (cloth : alk. paper) — ISBN 978-1-4422-2695-1 (pbk. : alk. paper) — ISBN 978-1-4422-2696-8 (electronic)  1.  Content area reading. 2.  Language arts (Secondary)  I. Title.
  LB1050.455.B47 2014
  428.4071′2—dc23                                                    2013035372

∞™ The paper used in this publication meets the minimum requirements of American National Standard for Information Sciences—Permanence of Paper for Printed Library Materials, ANSI/NISO Z39.48-1992.

Printed in the United States of America

# CONTENTS

## PART 3

## PART 4

# ACKNOWLEDGMENTS

I would like to thank all those individuals who have played a role in the creation and completion of this work. Thanks to my supportive and loving family members, as well as my friends and colleagues, for your encouragement. Special thanks to my editor, Susanne Canavan, for believing in this project and always being available to offer advice and suggestions. Also, special thanks to assistant editor Andrea Offdenkamp Kendrick, who provided invaluable help and patience during the manuscript preparation. Thanks to Rowman and Littlefield for offering me the opportunity to complete this work and bring it to publication.

Thanks also go to my colleagues in the Salem-Keizer School District, including Dr. Barbara Bamford, teacher Jennifer Harris-Clippinger, instructional coach Laurelin Andrade, and my colleagues in the English Department at South Salem High School. I am also thankful to Dr. Mark Girod from Western Oregon University, Dr. Susan Lenski from Portland State University, and all of the other professors and teachers who over the years have inspired and motivated me. Special thanks to authors Larry Lewin and Betty Jean Shoemaker for granting permission to use their material in this book. Additional thanks are extended to Mid-continent Research for Education and Learning (McREL) and the AVID (Advancement Via Individual Determination) Press for their contributions to this work. My additional grateful acknowledgments go to all the other individuals who offered advice and suggestions and reviewed the manuscript.

Finally, I would like to acknowledge all of the amazing teachers I have worked with during my long career, those who have continually inspired me, challenged me, and amazed me with their caring and dedication, and teachers everywhere who have dedicated themselves to the never-ending pursuit of excellence in this challenging but most noble of professions.

**PART ONE**
# GETTING STARTED WITH CONTENT-AREA LITERACY

After giving your class time to read the assigned textbook chapter, you attempt to lead a discussion about the material in the chapter. Hoping to hear your students' brilliant insights, instead you get expressions of frustration:

"I didn't understand it!"
"The chapter didn't make any sense to me."
"It had too many big words that I didn't know."
"This chapter was boring!"
"Why do we have to read this?"

Does this sound familiar? Students often express frustration when faced with reading material that may be significantly above their reading levels and that grows increasingly more difficult as students progress through secondary school. Cris Tovani, in her book *I Read It, But I Don't Get It*, points out that many students have mastered "fake reading" and have gotten through school by listening to the teacher and other students or copying the work of their peers. They may have mastered decoding, but they don't understanding the thinking and active involvement that reading requires. Thus, they don't comprehend or remember what they read (Tovani, 2000). In my many years of teaching high school English, I have always been frustrated when I observe students read stories, novels, articles, and other classroom materials, only to realize later, in the course of discussion, that students did not understand what they were reading or missed the point altogether. These students also had no idea what to do when they recognized that they were not understanding. They may have had very little understanding of the content-rich vocabulary they were encountering, and they could not effectively write about what they had read or compose a summary of the material.

To complicate matters, with the implementation of the Common Core State Standards (CCSS), students are expected to read and comprehend a variety of materials at much higher levels of text complexity, both literary and informational. The CCSS describe good readers as those who:

- engage in close, attentive reading;

- perform critical reading of informational material;

- thoughtfully engage with high-quality literary and informational material; and

- demonstrate thoughtful reasoning and use of evidence (Council of Chief State School Officers and National Governors Association, 2010).

Most of our students in secondary schools today have a long way to go to meet the level of rigor called for by the CCSS. Good literacy strategies can provide them the tools needed to read and comprehend more complex texts.

The National Assessment of Educational Progress found that over 60 percent of twelfth graders scored below proficiency in reading level, and 27 percent scored below basic reading achievement (National Center for Education Statistics, 2011). Yet in the world today students need ever-higher levels of literacy skills to understand complex written texts and use information for problem solving. Most students have been taught that reading means you start at the beginning of the book or chapter and read through to the end, regardless of whether you comprehend what you are reading. But good reading is not just a matter of decoding. Decoding does not automatically mean comprehending. Students also assume that good readers can comprehend automatically, and that, therefore, they themselves must not be good readers. Some students may have been encouraged to stop and reread if something wasn't clear to them, but very few students have been taught how to read actively, how to monitor their comprehension, or how to effectively use tools of active reading such as asking questions, summarizing, or text marking. Furthermore, most content-area teachers do not know what to do to help students, beyond using a few end-of-chapter discussion questions or focusing on summarizing the text. Numerous easy and useful strategies are available for teaching students to engage in active reading, many of them equally effective for both fiction and non-fiction texts. There are also many excellent strategies to help you easily incorporate writing and vocabulary instruction into your teaching, and they help us to meet both state standards and CCSS.

One of the strategies introduced later in this book is called the Anticipation Guide. Before reading any further, take a moment to complete the following anticipation guide to reflect your own opinions on content-area literacy. Mark each statement as "Agree" or "Disagree":

|  | Agree | Disagree |
|---|---|---|
| 1. Students shouldn't have to read in content-area classes. | _____ | _____ |
| 2. Teaching reading is the English teacher's job. | _____ | _____ |
| 3. I should teach reading only in the context of my subject area. | _____ | _____ |
| 4. If elementary teachers had done their jobs, we wouldn't have to worry about teaching content-area reading. | _____ | _____ |
| 5. I don't have enough time to cover content and reading strategies. | _____ | _____ |
| 6. Students get enough reading in English classes. | _____ | _____ |
| 7. Teachers need to help students organize and visualize information. | _____ | _____ |
| 8. Teachers learn best by thinking critically about their own practice. | _____ | _____ |
| 9. Reading strategies can help students become better at working out their own understanding of the material. | _____ | _____ |
| 10. Reading is a constructivist process: students explore and make meaning from the text they are reading. | _____ | _____ |
| 11. The only prereading strategy students need is opening their books. | _____ | _____ |
| 12. Vocabulary is an integral part of comprehension. | _____ | _____ |

If you marked "Agree" to numbers 3, 7, 8, 9, 10, and 12, you are doing very well. You are already aware of the importance of literacy learning across the curriculum. Now perhaps you are just looking for some really good strategies and ways to incorporate literacy into your content area, which this book will provide you. If you marked "Agree" to any or all of the numbers 1, 2, 4, 5, 6, or 11, then you can really benefit from reading this book. You have yet to be convinced of the important role that content-area teachers play in promoting student literacy. I want to help you understand that reading and writing are important in all content areas, that you can cover both content and literacy at the same time, that students currently do not spend enough time reading and writing in their classes, and that there is a huge variety of practical and useful strategies you can use to help you improve your teaching and your students' learning.

Literacy is the single most important skill adolescent students need to be successful academically. A report by the Alliance for Excellent Education notes that poor reading and writing skills "seriously constrain graduates' options in selecting a pathway to a sustainable future," regardless of widespread agreement among researchers about what constitutes good literacy education from the earliest years through high school (*Confronting the Crisis*, 2012, p. 3). Literacy is the key to learning in all content areas, and therefore, it is the responsibility of all secondary teachers to play a part in building and improving students' literacy skills. Doing so pays off for every teacher because it means that your students will better understand and retain the subject matter you are teaching, whether it is science, math, history, English, fine arts, business, career and technical education, or other electives. Building student literacy involves providing students with a wide variety of strategies they can use to better learn the subject matter they are expected to master.

During the last twelve years, I have held a variety of positions at my high school, as teacher leader, instructional coach, and instructional coordinator, in addition to teaching English classes. During that time, I gathered a large collection of strategies to share with teachers from different content areas and to present in instructional coaching and professional development contexts. Many of those strategies are included in this book, a resource containing a variety of excellent literacy strategies, not just for reading but also for writing and vocabulary. Many of the strategies included are also effective methods of addressing the CCSS for English language arts, which most states are now implementing. A great many of my colleagues over the years have shared with me how much they appreciate these strategies and use them regularly in their classrooms. This book is the result. It presents several different approaches and tools you can use to teach students to better read and comprehend a variety of types of text, to build academic vocabulary, and to engage in writing to learn. For the most part, the strategies are not my original inventions, but rather are commonly used strategies, many with a solid research base that supports their use in instruction. Many of these strategies have been around for many years, and I would argue they are still as effective as they have ever been. The advantage of this book is that it brings together in one easy-to-use collection a large number of excellent strategies that can help you enhance your teaching with solid literacy practices.

While part 1 provides a general introduction and overview, part 2 focuses on reading strategies. Part 3 includes numerous practical writing strategies, part 4 focuses on strategies for teaching vocabulary, and part 5 includes some multimedia and technology-related resources for building literacy skills. You will find some strategies more useful in your particular content area than others. You will also find that some fit more naturally with your own personal teaching style. My advice is to experiment and find what works for you and what works for your students.

This book is, unapologetically, a book about content-area literacy strategies, a common approach that uses numerous generic literacy strategies to help students effectively engage in reading and writing in their course work. However, it is important to acknowledge some recent debate among researchers and literacy scholars. In the last few years, some literacy scholars have argued that we need to move away from generic, content-area teaching strategies to what has been commonly called "disciplinary literacy," an approach that focuses on the discipline-based thinking strategies and language skills used in different fields of study or "disciplines" (Moje, 2008; Shanahan & Shanahan, 2008). Moje (2008) states that "part of learning in the subject area, then, is coming to understand the norms of practice for producing and communicating knowledge in the disciplines" (p. 100). Disciplinary literacy thus means teaching students how subject areas or disciplines are different and how "acts of inquiry produce knowledge and multiple representational forms . . . as well as how those disciplinary differences are socially constructed" (Moje, 2008, p. 103). The content-area literacy/disciplinary literacy divide has become a heated debate among scholars in the last few years. Some have argued that subject area teachers in middle and high schools are not well equipped to teach disciplinary literacy, and that disciplinary literacy should be left to the college level, where students focus more on becoming disciplinary experts (Heller, 2010). Fang and Coatoam (2013) also argue that it is premature to make claims about the effectiveness of a disciplinary approach to literacy.

Even more recently, Brozo, Moorman, Meyer, and Stewart (2013) suggest that a false dichotomy between the two approaches has been created, that a single theoretical perspective is not what is important to classroom teachers, and that a blend of content-area and disciplinary practices might be best for students. They suggest that it is possible to "overlay adaptable generic content and discipline-independent literacy practices to meet the learning needs of all students" (p. 356). I tend to agree with this middle-ground approach, and I also suspect that a disciplinary literacy approach, probably more appropriate for advanced and college-level students, may be detrimental for struggling readers. A more generic approach to content literacy allows teachers to pick and choose what works best with particular content areas and groups of students. While this debate may continue among literacy scholars, what matters to those of us teaching middle and high school students is how we can best help our students engage in reading, writing, and thinking in our classrooms.

So, whether we call it content-area literacy, literacy across the curriculum, academic literacy, or disciplinary literacy, what we all want to do is help students become successful and proficient readers, writers, and thinkers in our classrooms. Presented in this book are good, solid literacy strategies that help engage students in reading, writing, and speaking within the context of particular disciplines. They are the techniques we use to teach students to engage in active, strategic reading and writing.

The number one reason content-area teachers tend to shy away from using literacy strategies is their belief that using them takes too much time away from the content. Using these strategies does not have to take time away from your content;

they simply provide different ways in which to teach the material you want students to master. Remember that you are teaching *content* by way of the particular strategy. Your students' learning will also improve in both comprehension and retention. Having a wide repertoire of strategies to use and draw from as needed is important; it makes learning more interesting for students, provides variety in our instructional approaches, and helps to break the monotony of classroom routine. Many of the strategies are also interactive and collaborative, helping students become more actively engaged in their learning. Educational reform movements will come and go, and whether we are teaching to state standards, national standards, or CCSS, the strategies presented here are simply good teaching. They are equally useful for mainstream students as for English language learners, struggling readers, and special-needs students. My intention with this book was to provide clear, concise, easy-to-follow instructions for the large number of effective literacy strategies to help adolescent learners with the complex cognitive processes of reading, writing, and learning in all subject areas. The next section gives a brief overview of some of the research on content-area literacy and provides a rationale for literacy across the curriculum.

## The Importance of Content-Area Literacy

Elizabeth Sturtevant (2003) notes that the overall reading achievement of adolescents is not keeping pace with the increasing demands of today's highly technological society, and many students remain several grade levels behind in reading ability. Secondary students often have difficulty making meaning from text, and secondary teachers often have little or no training in how to give students the skills they need for reading comprehension. Even many English teachers, who may be excellent literature and writing teachers, do not know basic elements of reading comprehension (Symonds, 2002). These problems are compounded by the fact that all students today also need a more comprehensive education, including a strong base of knowledge across content areas as well as advanced reading and communicating skills in a variety of types of texts and technologies (Sturtevant, 2003). According to Vogt and Shearer (2003), today's students need instruction in literacy strategies, need to develop critical media literacy skills to understand increasingly complex information, and need to read and comprehend a number of symbol systems associated with technology and other genres of communication. In addition, of course, students need to develop strategies for independent learning.

Inadequate literacy skills result in frustration and poor academic performance for many secondary students (Biancarosa & Snow, 2006). Rose (2000) reports that survey data from students reveal many to be frustrated and underprepared readers who own few books, do not use libraries, cannot name a favorite book, possibly have never finished reading a book, and, in general, strongly dislike reading. These students are also struggling in most of their classes, both core courses and electives. While this is certainly not true of all students, as many of them love reading and engage in reading a variety of types of recreational and informational reading materials, it is nevertheless true of many of the students we see in our classes every day.

Rose (2000) argues that all content-area teachers must incorporate the teaching of reading comprehension strategies into their curriculum. Because of the increasing diversity and broad range of reading and writing skills we find in our classrooms today, many secondary teachers tend to reduce the literacy and cognitive demands in their courses (*Confronting the Crisis*, 2012). Many content teachers avoid engaging students in drawing meaning from textual material and instead try to teach the content by other means. However, students need explicit instruction in reading comprehension to understand reasoning processes and strategies in addition to the disciplinary discourses that readers use to comprehend (Donahue, 2003). One time, a teacher I was coaching said to me, "I'm just not going to use the textbooks anymore. The students can't read them. We'll just watch films and do other things instead." While this is an understandable reaction from a frustrated teacher, teachers who avoid the problem of low reading skills by retreating from print further reduce literacy demands made on students, which is not helping to solve the problem. All teachers *can* learn to use effective strategies to help students comprehend textual material, rather than reducing students' engagement with the text (Lewis & Wray, 1999).

Wray (2001) argues that content-area teachers need to understand their responsibility for the development of literacy in their subject areas, and they need training and support in effectively using content-area teaching strategies. The English language arts CCSS also insist that all teachers should share the responsibility for instruction in reading, writing, speaking, and listening (*Confronting the Crisis*, 2012). As students move into secondary levels of schooling, they encounter greater separation of knowledge into different subject areas, each one with its own literacy demands. Teaching in these subject areas needs to be planned and implemented with a clear understanding of the particular types of literacy skills needed, including forms of text and specialized language (Wray, 2001). Teachers don't have to become reading and writing teachers, but content-area teachers need to provide instruction in skills and strategies that are especially effective in the particular subject area (Biancarosa & Snow, 2006).

Secondary content teachers are also sometimes unaware of their own strategies as discipline-expert readers and feel unprepared to help students comprehend texts. These teachers are most likely to think that reading instruction or use of reading strategies take time away from teaching the content, which is the most common argument against content-area reading (Donahue, 2003). Teachers need to reconceptualize their notions of teaching in their subject areas, to recognize that they are teaching reading and writing specific to a particular subject area (Biancarosa & Snow, 2006). Thinking about and helping students understand the discipline-specific practices and strategies anchors literacy in the particular content area (Fang & Coatoam, 2013). Regardless of the discipline, however, students still need to be able to effectively read, comprehend, and process textual material they are encountering. They will also need to be able to write and synthesize information from different sources, both print and multimedia.

Many of the strategies in this book incorporate elements of cooperative learning. Cooperative learning strategies and contextualized learning experiences are ways to build upon the sociocultural nature of learning in the classroom and increase student motivation (Donahue, 2003). Struggling middle and high school students often need more contextualized learning experiences. Biancarosa and Snow (2006) also recommend text-based, collaborative learning for students in secondary schools.

Lenski and Nierstheimer (2002) point out that reading and writing strategies are sometimes developed intuitively by students or learned through direct instruction, but comprehension strategy instruction for struggling students should make use of best practices, grounded in sociocognitive theory, which also capitalizes upon the social context to promote learning. Sociocognitive strategies are the tools that readers and writers use to process and produce text. Good instructional strategies include whole-group, small group, and individual instruction that provides supportive scaffolding. Shared reading and whole-group mini-lessons in a workshop setting are examples, in addition to cueing systems, strategies for self-monitoring reading, and before-, during-, and after-reading strategies (Lenski & Nierstheimer, 2002). Social interactions influence students' thinking as they develop skills in their zone of proximal development (Vygotsky, 1978). Teachers' use of strategy instruction, in the role of the more knowledgeable adult, and consideration of the sociocultural context and social interaction in the classroom can help students develop strategy usage and improve their learning (Lenski & Nierstheimer, 2002).

Just as students need scaffolding and support in learning literacy, teachers need to engage with their colleagues in a sociocultural context to learn new skills themselves. A sociocultural group can provide scaffolding for their new content-area literacy teaching skills, until they are capable of demonstrating independence and helping others become independent (Biancarosa & Snow, 2006; Sanacore, 2000). Professional learning communities, or collaborative teacher groups, now exist in most secondary schools and can help to provide this scaffolding and support for improving student literacy. I recommend that part of the work of these groups be focused on literacy instruction in the respective disciplines.

Many teachers and scholars have also wisely observed that literacy in the modern world means much more than learning how to read and write. Content-area literacy has often been defined too narrowly. Students today must be able to effectively use oral language, cell phones, computers, e-mail, and the Internet (including Facebook, Twitter, blogs, wikis, and a variety of other online media) and also develop literacy in art, music, drama, film, video games, and digital media. Bean, Bean, and Bean (1999) argue that content-area teachers, through careful lesson design, can bridge students' school, peer, and home cultures. For example, one science teacher engages students by connecting science topics to student interests outside of school. Content teachers must "move away from a dependence on didactic, text-bound models of teaching that place adolescents in passive roles" (Bean, Bean, & Bean, p. 447) and bridge the gap between students' lives outside school and inside school. A sociocultural perspective can help us to view literacy as a social and not merely a cognitive process. Teachers who broaden their notions of literacy will recognize that all students have and use "multiliteracies." This can, in turn, help content teachers tap into students' ways of learning by widening the range of instructional methods.

Taylor and Collins (2003) note that literacy behaviors are processes students use in reading, writing, speaking, listening, viewing, and thinking: "High performing teachers regularly incorporate each of these literacy processes in their instructional plans to help students develop both the vocabulary related to a particular unit of study and an overall comprehension of that curriculum" (p. 42). What strategies and methods can teachers learn to help improve student literacy? Direct instruction in comprehension strategies can improve literacy and help students make significant improvement. Most students with poor reading skills need in-class learning strategies and accommodations to improve their academic performance (Denti & Guerin, 2004), and there are a number of proven-effective comprehension strategies teachers can use appropriate to their content area. Ideally, content-area teachers and reading/literacy specialists should collaborate to identify which tools and techniques will be most helpful for students in their particular subject areas and classrooms (Brozo, Moorman, Meyer, & Stewart, 2013).

## Benefits of Using Good Literacy Strategies

Teachers need a repertoire of usable and practical strategies, opportunities to experience the strategies in use, and ongoing support and encouragement in actually putting them into practice (Rose, 2000). A good place for teachers to start is by building on their own metacognitive awareness of their reading. Think about the strategies you use automatically when you are engaging with a difficult piece of reading material. Next, teachers need to explicitly model for students the strategies they use in reading content material. According to Brozo and Simpson (1998), teachers must demonstrate comprehension processes to all students, but doing so is especially helpful for minority and second-language students. However, teachers must first become aware of and be able to describe their own thinking and understanding so that students can understand and imitate. Metacognitive awareness, or the ability to think about our thinking, is necessary in comprehension and must be modeled for students. Teachers can make explicit to themselves and their students the strategies they use to make meaning from text in their particular disciplines (Donahue, 2003). Using the think-aloud strategy (see part 2) is a good place to start.

One of the most important comprehension strategies teachers can use is tapping into and building upon students' prior knowledge about the subject matter (Braunger & Lewis, 2006). If students do have prior knowledge, they often don't know how to access it. Reciprocal strategies help students learn to question, predict, summarize, and clarify their understanding (Rose, 2000). But content teachers often need training and support to develop the necessary expertise to use this strategy. Research clearly demonstrates the effectiveness of strategy instruction in reading. Alfassi (2004) conducted two sequential and interrelated studies to examine the usefulness of combining two different models of reading strategy instruction: reciprocal teaching and direct explanation. Her findings suggest that use of multiple or combined strategy instruction is beneficial to students by providing them with tools that help them engage in higher-order thinking processes while they are learning from textual material, even for heterogeneous groups of students.

Ridgeway (2004) reports on her unique experience as a high school science teacher who, through a staff development program in content-area reading, learned to use content-area strategies with her students, thus improving both her own teaching and her students' learning. She notes the gradual nature of change for teachers, remarking that it took her several months to abandon the lecture and note-taking methods she previously used in favor of more interactive strategies. In addition, it took her several years to develop the knowledge necessary to choose appropriate strategies for specific courses and material. Her conclusion is that it takes time and requires ongoing support to change one's teaching strategies. Like many teachers, she came to realize that semantic mapping, semantic feature analysis, graphic organizers, and think-writes, among other strategies, are "powerful tools for engaging students in learning" (Ridgeway, 2004, p. 368). Although some have argued in favor of moving away from content-area strategies to a more discipline-based approach, I believe that doing so would be a mistake. In a recent article, Brozo, Moorman, Meyer, and Stewart (2013) observe that they have "witnessed firsthand the benefits and transformative power of an approach that encourages teachers to explore feasible and relevant contextual applications of generic content area literacy strategies" (p. 355). I have seen evidence of this in my own classroom and in the classrooms of other teachers as well.

In summary, there is a great deal of evidence pointing to the need for secondary content-area teachers to include a focus on literacy in their teaching. This book will provide you with the necessary repertoire of easy and effective strategies you can use to help students achieve academic success in your classroom. Part 2 focuses on pre-, during-, and postreading strategies; part 3 includes a number of powerful writing strategies; part 4 includes a variety of strategies for teaching vocabulary; and part 5 includes online resources, tools for research, digital media, and technology to build student literacy skills.

For the strategies included in the reading, writing and vocabulary sections, a purpose statement is included, which specifies particular skills the strategy can help students build (learning targets or students objectives). Next, a CCSS connection is included, whenever the strategy could serve to meet a CCSS goal. The anchor standards are identified as follows:

RL: Reading Standard for Literature
RI: Reading Standard for Informational Text
W: Writing Standard
SL: Speaking and Listening Standard
L: Language Standard

Next is a general overview of the strategy and finally a procedure to follow for implementing the strategy.

The original source of all of the strategies is included except for those where the original source is unknown. As you are reading and thinking about this book, I would like to challenge you to set a goal for yourself: Try to choose two of the strategies each week, from any section of the book, and incorporate them into your lesson plans for that week. Also make it a goal to use each one more than once and preferably several times. This will help you, and your students as well, master the use of each strategy and make it a natural part of your approach to content-area material. Good luck, and enjoy watching your students' levels of engagement and understanding increase!

# PART TWO

# READING STRATEGIES

This section begins by discussing some of the key principles of reading comprehension and the variety of different types of reading material students encounter in different content areas. It also presents numerous useful prereading, during-reading, and postreading strategies that will help students successfully comprehend all kinds of texts and reading materials they may encounter in their classes. We know that as students progress through the grades, the level of difficulty of the textbooks and materials they encounter increases. This creates a challenge for many students, especially those who tend to struggle with reading or may even be one or more grades behind in reading ability, and their frustration often leads to discouragement and lowers their motivation.

The new Common Core State Standards (CCSS), which most districts are now transitioning into, require us to make several shifts in thinking about reading, one of which is a greater focus on careful examination of pieces of text. Students are expected to be able to read complex text closely and analytically and draw evidence from it. The same principle applies to all reading regardless of the discipline: students must be able to draw evidence and knowledge from textual material. Strategies such as the ones presented here will help build student skill in close reading of complex texts, helping them to comprehend and gain insight from reading material.

Perhaps first and foremost, teachers must *not* just assign students to read material and expect that they will know how to do it. We need to first engage their prior knowledge, teach them valuable prereading strategies, preview and pre-teach key vocabulary, and provide materials that will help them proceed through the reading, asking questions and monitoring their own comprehension. Ness (2007) notes that secondary teachers can help students become proficient readers by providing them with a variety of comprehension strategies. Tragenza and Lewis (2008) also note that research clearly shows that providing direct and explicit comprehension strategy instruction can improve students' comprehension. Even more important for students, "repeated use of a strategy over time and different texts can lead to the strategy becoming part of the child's own learning repertoire" (Tragenza & Lewis, 2008).

## Variation in Types of Text across Disciplines

At the secondary level, students may encounter a wide variety of different types of texts. The job of content-area teachers is to teach students the skills and knowledge they need to master the required reading in the particular discipline. Various types of texts we expect students to read and comprehend may include:

- In English: pieces of literature (fiction, poetry, essays, drama) and criticism, nonfiction works, biography and memoir

- In history: historical documents, timelines, research, and information-rich textbooks

- In science: lab reports and scientific research information rich in vocabulary

- In math: story problems and mathematical formulas with specialized language and symbols

- In the arts: fiction and nonfiction pieces in a second language, cultural documents and artifacts, informational or biographical material, multimedia documents, visual material

- In elective areas: instructional materials and technical pieces, instructions, online articles

Whatever material students are faced with, teachers can help students by doing three things prior to having them read:

- Pre-teach key vocabulary words: Students must understand critical vocabulary in order to comprehend well. Choose only a few key vocabulary words and concepts to focus on (no more than ten) rather than trying to identify every word students may not know.

- Access or build prior knowledge: This involves finding out what students already know about the topic and engaging their schema on the subject. This creates a framework upon which the brain can process information gained during the reading.

- Set a purpose for reading: This can be done by telling students what they need to know or be able to do after finishing the reading material. You might provide comprehension questions or tell students what you will ask them to do when they are finished.

**Table 2.1.  What Good and Struggling Readers Do**

|  | Good Readers | Struggling Readers |
|---|---|---|
| Before Reading | Think about what they already know about a subject | Read without thinking about what they already know |
|  | Know why they are reading the particular text (set a purpose) | Don't know why they are reading |
|  |  | Don't have any idea of how major ideas fit together |
|  | Have a general sense of how major ideas may fit together |  |
| During Reading | Pay attention to meaning and identify key information | Pay too much attention to individual words, missing meaning |
|  | Stop and use "fix-up" strategies | Easily defeated by difficult words |
|  | Ask questions of text and seek clarification | Unable to monitor comprehension |
|  |  | Don't know how to use "fix-up" strategies |
| After Reading | Understand how ideas fit together (can summarize) | Focus on peripheral details rather than main ideas |
|  | Can answer explicit, implicit, and application questions | Are unable to answer various levels of comprehension questions |

Source: Ciborowski (1992). Reprinted with permission from Brookline Books, Northampton, Massachusetts.

Educational consultant Larry Lewin (2009) adds a fourth item critical to preparing students to read: have students make predictions about what they are going to encounter in the reading material or what they will learn from reading.

Analyze the above chart (table 2.1) to better understand what good readers do versus what struggling readers do before, during, and after reading.

To summarize, strong readers choose appropriate strategies for reading, focus their attention, make predictions, use text structures, organize the information, reflect on what was read, and feel successful as a result of their efforts. In contrast, struggling or developing readers read without knowing why, are easily distracted, often do not recognize that they do not understand, read to get finished as quickly as possible, are unable to visualize, do not recognize key vocabulary or organizational patterns, and, in general, fail to comprehend. Teaching students to use effective pre-, during-, and postreading strategies can be invaluable to students, helping them to do well not only in the specific course but also in all of their future academic efforts. The strategies in this section all stress the importance of "active reading," as opposed to "passive reading," which students often resort to out of boredom, frustration, or lack of knowledge about how to read actively.

## Responding to Reading

When you are actively reading a piece of text, your brain is engaged in many different ways. You are asking yourself questions to make sure that you comprehend the material. You are extending your understanding by making connections between the text and your own personal experiences and prior knowledge. You are also engaging in textual and contextual analysis by recognizing literary devices and techniques authors use and the social/cultural influences upon the text. We need to help students learn to do these things also.

The best thing to do in the classroom is ask students to do something while they are completing a reading assignment. Ask them to show what's going on inside their heads (there are many strategies presented later that provide good ways of doing this). Students can ask questions, take notes, highlight text, use sticky notes, draw pictures, or answer comprehension questions while reading. One of the strategies that I highly recommend teaching students to use is text marking in the form of highlighting and annotating text (included later in this section).

This section will first include a number of effective prereading strategies, those things that you can have students do prior to reading a piece of text or textbook chapter to help activate their prior knowledge and ensure that they are ready to read. Next, there will be during-reading strategies, those things that students do while they are reading to help them monitor and enhance their understanding. Finally, the section presents several postreading strategies, activities to be used following the reading that engage students in using, reflecting upon, analyzing, and making use of the new ideas and concepts they have learned.

## Prereading Strategies

### Strategy 1: Textbook Features

*Purpose*
    To help students identify text features and parts to more effectively use the text as a resource.

*CCSS Connection*
    Standard RI.5: Analyze the structure of texts.

*Overview*
    We often assume that students know and are familiar with the various parts of informational texts such as their textbooks. However, this is often not the case. I'm always surprised when I realize some students have no idea what an index or an appendix is. It's important for us to teach students about the parts of books and how to use the book efficiently. They need to be familiar with the index, glossaries, and table of contents. Tierney and Readence (1999) present a variation of this strategy to help students understand how to use text features.

*Procedure*

When first introducing students to their textbook, take some time to teach them about the following parts of books:

- The title page: the first page of the book, which gives the book's full title, the author's name, the publisher's name, and the place of publication.

- The copyright page gives the year of copyright. Discuss with students why the copyright date might be important when very current or updated information is needed.

- The preface, foreword, or introduction usually follows the copyright page and tells something about the book and why it was written. It may also include acknowledgments or thank-yous to those who made the book possible.

- The table of contents gives the names and page numbers of chapters and sections of the book. Skim the contents to get an overall sense of the topics covered.

- The body of the book is usually divided into parts or chapters, each focusing on a different topic or aspect of the subject.

- An appendix may follow the body. It may contain information that supplements the text itself, for example, maps, charts, tables, visuals, artifacts, official documents, or other special information.

- A glossary contains a list of special terms used in the book. Teach students to refer to the glossary to determine the meaning of words and terms from the text.

- Many books will contain a bibliography or reference list or a list of other books and articles about the same subject that may be used to find additional information.

- The index is an alphabetical listing of all the important topics covered in the book. This is often the most useful part of the book because it tells the reader whether the book contains the information they may need and on which pages they will find it.

- Other textbook features and specialized elements textbook authors typically use to enhance comprehension of the material for readers include charts, graphs, tables, photos, illustrations, maps, cartoons, italic print, bold print, typographical features, titles, headings and subheadings, guide questions, purpose statements, pullouts, review questions, and icons.

There are several ways to teach students about these features:

- Teach the various features in context, as they are needed in the reading of a particular chapter or section. Preview the book or particular chapters and ask questions to help direct students' attention to these particular features. This may happen before, during, or after reading.

- Model how you use these features to improve your understanding of the material.

- Ask students questions such as the following: What is the author's purpose for using bold print? What are the main ideas represented in this visual or chart? Why did the author choose to use these features?

- Provide students with examples of text features found in other sources such as bus schedules, maps, manuals, newspapers, television guides, websites, and so on.

Here is a mini-lesson you can use to help students explore various text features found in informational text:

1. Gather samples of informational text including newspapers, brochures, maps, menus, newsletters, manuals, directions, websites, and so on.

2. Place one of each sample in a plastic bag, one for each group of four to five students.

3. Have each group of students examine the samples one at a time to determine the text features it includes. (Examples: bold words, underlining, table of contents, headings, graphs, charts, photos, captions.) Provide students with the following list of text features they can use.

   - Print Features: font, bold print, colored print, punctuation, full caps, bullets, titles, headings, subheadings, italics, labels, captions, underlining

   - Visual Graphics: diagrams, sketches, graphs, maps, tables, cross sections, timelines, photos, flowcharts, organizational charts

   - Organizational Aids: table of contents, index, glossary, preface, foreword, introduction, pronunciation guide, appendixes

   - Illustrations: colored photographs, colored drawings, black and white photographs, paintings, black and white drawings, labeled drawings or photos, enlarged photographs, other artwork

4. Have each group fill out the text chart (table 2.2) indicating their findings.

5. Finally, have each group discuss and present their findings about how text features help them understand text.

**Table 2.2.   Text Feature Chart**

| Text Read | Text Features |
|---|---|
| 1. | |
| 2. | |
| 3. | |
| 4. | |
| 5. | |

## Strategy 2: Textbook Preview Activity

*Purpose*
   To help students identify text features and parts in order to more effectively use the text as a resource.

*CCSS Connection*
   Standard RI.5: Analyze the structure of texts.

*Overview*
   One of the best prereading strategies you can use with students is previewing. Teach students to do a quick survey or preview of reading material before they actually begin the reading. This gives them a general sense of the subject and helps them form questions about the material they are about to read. It also helps them understand the conventions of the particular textbook section or piece. For informational and technical reading students are assigned to do, they must learn to decode the conventions of the particular piece. This includes decoding symbols used, punctuation, and identifying the organizational patterns of the text, which may be cause/effect, compare/contrast, concept/definition, description, problem/solution, sequential/ chronological, and so on. Students must also recognize and learn to use the organizational frameworks of the text, including titles, graphs, maps, headings, subheadings, and so on. When students learn how to understand these conventions, they will have greater success comprehending the ideas and concepts in the reading material.
   Although good textbooks are organized in a way that facilitates learning, students still need guidance to ascertain the purpose behind the textbook's organization. This activity forces students to analyze how the textbook is organized and thus enhances their learning.

PART TWO

*Procedure*

During a preview activity, have students make a list of the different parts of the textbook such as the title page, copyright page, preface, table of contents, index, glossary, and bibliography. Also have them look at the typography, illustrations, graphs, and charts (these features of reading material often get skipped). Go over the lists with students and make sure they can correctly identify all the parts of the book. Next, you might have them ask some preview questions related to the content of the book. This can be done by having them look at chapter titles and headings and turn them into questions (for example, with the heading "The Major Causes of the Civil War," students might write the question "What were the major causes of the Civil War?"). Hand out one of the following textbook preview worksheets (figures 2.1 and 2.2). Students can complete this activity individually, or with a partner or group.

---

**TEXTBOOK PREVIEW**

Complete this exercise to help you become familiar with your textbook:

Title of textbook: _____

Date published: _____

Why is the date published important to you? _____

List all of the sections you find at the front of the book (before Chapter One):




List all of the sections you find at the end of the book (after the last chapter):




Skim through the Table of Contents and read the titles of all the chapters. Choose at least five of

the chapter titles and turn them into questions:

1. _____

2. _____

3. _____

4. _____

5. _____

Examine the visuals, such as graphs and charts used in the book. What are some of the different

types?

---

**Figure 2.1. Textbook Preview Worksheet.**

**KNOW YOUR TEXT**

Title Page:

1. Title of the book: _____

2. Author or authors: _____

3. Publisher: _____

4. Copyright Date: _____

Table of Contents:

5. On what page does the Table of Contents start?

6. Identify the main divisions of the book:

      Units        Chapters     Sections     Lessons     Parts

7. How many of the following are there? Units _____ Chapters _____

8. What is the title of the second unit? _____

9. What is the title of Chapter 5? _____

10. On what page does Part 3 Start? _____

11. Name two ways the Table of Contents can help you as a reader:



Text Features:

12. How does the author make specific vocabulary stand out? (Circle)

      bold print     italics       color        separate list of terms

13. Does the author use titles and and subtitles within the divisions of text? How are they

highlighted? _____

14. What other text features are used (captions, visuals, organizational aids, illustrations)?

_____

**Figure 2.2.   Know Your Text Worksheet.**

---

Appendix/References:

15. Name two things you will find in the back sections of the text:

_____

Index:

16. If there is an index, how is it organized? _____

17. On what page does the index start? _____

18. Explain what you might use the index for:

---

**Figure 2.2—*Continued***

## Strategy 3: Give One, Get One

*Purpose*
    To access students' prior knowledge of the subject during the prereading phase.

*Overview*
    Give One, Get One is a good prereading brainstorming strategy to use with students prior to beginning the reading of a piece of text. The strategy comes from Schoenbach, Greenleaf, Cziko, and Hurwitz (1999).

*Procedure*
1. Have each student fold a piece of paper lengthwise to form two columns and write "Give One" at the top of the left-hand column and "Get One" at the top of the right-hand column.

2. Have students independently brainstorm a list of all the things they already know about the topic they will be studying, writing the items down in the left-hand column.

3. Next, have students circulate around the room and talk with other students about what is on their lists. Each student should "get" new pieces of information from others and write them down in the right-hand column

of their paper, along with the name of the person who gave him or her the information.

4. Once everyone has given and gotten some information, have the whole class discuss the information or compile a combined list.

5. Have students continue to add new information to their lists during the activity or reading. Be sure to use this activity to help students make sure their information is accurate and to correct any misconceptions about the topic. You can ask students to draw a line through any incorrect facts.

### Strategy 4: Ticket Exchange

*Purpose*
To help students identify details, facts, and ideas in reading material; to encourage interaction and discussion.

*CCSS Connection*
Standard RI.1: Read closely to determine what the text says explicitly; cite specific textual evidence; Standard RI.2: Determine central ideas or themes of a text and analyze their development; Standard SL.1: Prepare for and participate effectively in a range of conversations and collaborations with diverse partners.

*Overview*
This strategy can actually be used as a pre-, during-, or postreading strategy, at any stage in the reading process. It is engaging for students, encourages movement and discussion, and provides a needed change of pace in class.

*Procedure*
1. Write down a number of statements, questions, prompts, ideas, or facts related to the reading material on note cards or small strips of paper. These will become the "tickets" used during the strategy.

2. Give each student a "ticket" with the written side facedown.

3. Instruct students to stand up, holding their ticket facedown in the hand, and tell them not to look at the ticket.

4. Give a signal to have students begin moving about the room exchanging tickets with each other. Students should not stop moving until told to do so and they should not look at the tickets. This portion is designed simply to get students moving around and to redistribute the tickets.

5. Give a signal for students to stop the ticket exchange and pair up with the person closest to them.

6. Have student pairs reveal their tickets and discuss them.

7. Give another signal to resume the ticket exchange process and again re-distribute the tickets.

8. After a couple of minutes, have students randomly pair again and discuss. The process continues for as long as you desire.

9. Follow up the activity with a whole-group discussion and ask students to explain what they learned or reviewed.

A variation on Ticket Exchange is similar to the Save the Last Word for Me strategy, in which students get involved in small group discussions on the topic:

1. Partner one turns over his ticket and reads out loud what is written to partner two.

2. Partner one then has forty-five seconds to react and talk about his ticket while partner two listens but does not talk.

3. At the signal, partner two has forty-five seconds to talk about partner one's ticket while partner one listens and does not talk.

4. At the signal, partner one has forty-five seconds to share any final thoughts and speak the "last" word about his ticket.

5. The process repeats for partner two and her ticket.

## Strategy 5: Story Impressions

*Purpose*
   To help students access and build background knowledge to prepare for reading.

*Overview*
   Story Impressions is a way to help students access and build background knowledge before reading, make predictions about what they will be reading, and focus on key vocabulary terms all at once. This strategy comes from McGinley and Denner (1987) and is featured in the ASCD video *Reading in the Content Areas* (Association for Supervision and Curriculum Development, 2002). It can be used with informational or fictional text.

PART TWO

*Procedure*

1. Create a list of key words or terms from the reading assignment and write them down in order.

2. Present students with the list of words and ask them to write a paragraph using all the words in the order given.

3. Have students complete the reading assignment.

4. Ask students to compare their paragraphs to the information from the text.

5. Have some students read their paragraphs out loud.

Here is an example of a list of words from a science textbook chapter on indoor air pollution:

| | |
|---|---|
| pollutants | formaldehyde |
| ventilation | urban |
| respiratory | insulation |
| particulates | humidity |
| radon | carcinogen |
| organic | |

Here is the paragraph that a student might write:

Many pollutants are caused by poor ventilation in homes and buildings that cause respiratory problems for people. Dangerous particulates can float in the air. Radon can also pollute people's homes. Organic cleaning products are safer to use than those with dangerous chemicals, including formaldehyde. In urban areas where pollution is worse, homes need to have good insulation and low levels of humidity in order to keep carcinogens out of the air.

## Strategy 6: Wordsplash

*Purpose*

Prepare students for reading by accessing prior knowledge; introduce key vocabulary words.

*CCSS Connection*

Standard L.6: Acquire and use a range of general academic and domain-specific words and phrases.

*Overview*

This activity focuses on key terms and concepts related to the material students will be asked to read. It was developed by Dorsey Hammond of Oakland University (Hammond & Raphael, 1999). Similar to the Story Impressions activity, this process begins with several words/concepts related to the lesson.

*Procedure*

1. The teacher chooses several words from the text related to the content. Option: Write the words out on strips of paper or note cards that can be taped to the chalkboard and then moved around.

2. Students are instructed to write a complete sentence using any three of the words.

3. Students are asked to read and share the sentences they wrote, which will give the teacher an idea of how much prior knowledge of the subject students have.

4. Ask questions that encourage students to explore the relationships between the words. For example, "Can you arrange the terms so that they follow a particular pattern?"

5. Next, ask students to complete the reading assignment and to watch for the words in the text, noting how they are used. I like to have them use sticky notes to mark the location of each of the words in the text.

6. Next, have students revise their sentences and write three new sentences using more of the words selected.

7. Have students choose their best sentences to share with others or write on the overhead, chart paper, or chalkboard.

This activity helps focus on key concepts related to the lesson, builds upon students' prior knowledge of the material, motivates students to read, and helps them process what they know and have learned from the reading.

PART TWO

## Strategy 7: Problematic Situation

*Purpose*
  Activate prior knowledge; provide motivation for reading.

*CCSS Connection*
  Standard RL/RI.2: Determine central ideas or themes of a text; Standard SL.1: Prepare for an participate effectively in a range of conversations and collaborations; Standard SL.4: Present information, findings, and supporting evidence such that listeners can follow the line of reasoning.

*Overview*
  Problematic situation (Vacca & Vacca, 1993) is a strategy that helps students to activate their prior knowledge on a given topic and can help motivate them to read the text focusing on main ideas. It can be used with any textual material, fiction or nonfiction, which deals with some sort of problem/solution relationship. Another benefit of this strategy is that it helps students develop analytical and decision-making skills needed for active participation in a democratic society. Students are given the opportunity to create solutions to real-world problems.

*Procedure*
  1. Design a problematic situation based on the reading passage. Provide enough information so that students can focus on key ideas from the passage.

  2. Present the problem to students. Place them in small groups and ask each group to generate possible results or solutions, which they need to write down. When they have generated all their possible solutions, have each group discuss and identify their best solution and the reasons why it is a good one.

  3. Have students "test" their solutions as they read the assigned article or chapter. Each group can then refine their solution based on the new information from the text.

  4. As a final activity, have each group present their recommended solution and have the class discuss which ones are the best.

Here are two examples of the Problematic Situation from Doty, Cameron, and Barton (2003), reprinted with permission of McREL:

Topic: *Illegal Immigration*

Problem: The United States is a nation of immigrants. People from all parts of the world have been moving to our shores since colonial times. People have moved to the United States for many different reasons. Throughout our history, our government has passed a variety of laws regulating immigration. Those people entering our country who follow procedures defined by the law are called legal immigrants. Many people enter the nation each year without following legal procedures defined by law. These people are called illegal immigrants. Some citizens believe illegal immigrants are taking advantage of our nation by not following the rules. Others believe that these immigrants provide important resources for our nation, even though they do not follow the current laws.

Group Discussion: What ideas would you propose to our government about how to deal with the situation of people moving to the United States illegally?

And another example:

Topic: *Protecting Wildlife*

Humans are polluting and destroying many natural places in the world and pushing wildlife into the remotest areas. Some of the rarest animals are still being hunted for their fur and tusks. As a result, creatures such as great whales, rhinoceroses, elephants, and cheetahs could face extinction.

Group Discussion: What steps do you think should be taken to solve this problem?

## Strategy 8: Anticipation Guides

*Purpose*
    Activate prior knowledge; establish a purpose for reading.

*CCSS Connection*
    Standard RL/RI.2: Determine central ideas or themes of a text; Standard RL/RI.3: Analyze how and why individuals, events, and ideas develop and interact over the course of a text.

*Overview*
    Anticipation guides are a very useful prereading strategy to help students activate prior knowledge about any type of reading material. They were developed by Harold

Herber (1978); he originally called them "prediction guides." They are useful for helping to activate students' schema on a given topic and help them to set a purpose for reading.

*Procedure*
1. Begin by choosing a chapter or reading assignment students will be asked to complete.

2. Write a series of true/false statements having to do with the major concepts of the reading material. Option: You can also write statements and ask students to mark their level of agreement on a Likert scale from 1 to 5 or 1 to 10.

3. Leave a column or space after each statement for students to mark "true" or "false."

4. Optional: To the right of the page, use a column for "Before Reading" and one for "After Reading" if you intend to have students come back to the anticipation guide after doing the reading to see which of their answers might have changed.

5. Before students do the reading, have them complete the anticipation guide, filling in their answers, true or false. Option: Have students discuss and compare their answers with a partner.

6. Students next read the text to find out whether their answers were correct or how the statements might reflect themes and ideas in the text.

7. Optional: Have students write the page number and paragraph where the correct answer can be found in the text. This activity also functions as a useful "during-reading" activity.

8. After the reading, have students come back to the guide and complete the "after reading" column, noting which answers changed, or you can have them cross out the incorrect answers and write the correct response.

You might do the first couple of items together as a class to model the process. Figure 2.3 shows an example of an anticipation guide students might do prior to reading a short story.

Figure 2.4 shows another example of an anticipation guide for Barbara Kingsolver's novel *The Bean Trees* (from Novel Units curriculum student packet), one that uses a Likert scale to indicate level of agreement with each item.

```
ANTICIPATION GUIDE

True        False        Statement

_____       _____        All people in the U.S. are entitled to a free education.

_____       _____        One person can make a difference for many people.

_____       _____        Adults will protect children from harm.

_____       _____        People can dislike you without even knowing you.

_____       _____        Children like, dislike, and believe in the same things as their

                         parents.

_____       _____        The way other people feel about us influences the way we feel

                         about ourselves.
```

**Figure 2.3.   Anticipation Guide 1.**

**ANTICIPATION GUIDE**

Directions: Rate each of the following statements before you read the novel. In a small group, discuss your ratings and compare with those of others. After you have completed the novel, rate the statements again. Have any of your opinions changed?

1--------------------2-------------------3-------------------4------------------5

Agree strongly                                        Strongly Disagree

|  | Before | After |
|---|---|---|
| 1. A family consists of a mother, a father, and their children. | _____ | _____ |
| 2. There is just no excuse for being poor if you live in America, the land of opportunity | _____ | _____ |
| 3. Illegal aliens should be sent back to their own countries, even if doing so will endanger their lives. | _____ | _____ |
| 4. Immigrants shouldn't come here in the first place. | _____ | _____ |
| 5. "If it's you against the world, bet on the world." (Kafka) | _____ | _____ |
| 6. Most of the things you worry about never happen. | _____ | _____ |
| 7. There are some people in America who are invisible. | _____ | _____ |
| 8. The adoption process should be less difficult. | _____ | _____ |
| 9. We all need one another, and we should act accordingly. | _____ | _____ |
| 10. An adult should never strike a child. | _____ | _____ |
| 11. My country is my country, right or wrong. | _____ | _____ |
| 12. A wife should always try to please her husband, even if he doesn't treat her well. | _____ | _____ |
| 13. With good friends on your side, you can get through anything | _____ | _____ |

**Figure 2.4.  Anticipation Guide 2.  (Reprinted with permission from Novel Units, Inc.)**

## Strategy 9: KWL Charts

*Purpose*
Access prior knowledge; establish a purpose for reading; read actively.

*CCSS Connection*
Standard RL/RI.1: Read closely to determine what the text says explicitly; cite specific textual evidence; Standard RL/RI.2: Determine central ideas or themes of a text.

*Overview*
The KWL chart (see figure 2.5) is a well-known prereading strategy developed by Donna Ogle (1986). It is intended to be a framework for connecting students' prior knowledge with what they are learning through actively reading the text.

*Procedure*
1. The K column stands for "know." Have students tap into their prior knowledge about the topic of study by jotting down what they already know about the topic. They can add question marks next to those items they think they know but are not sure of. Encourage students to write something down in this column even if they know very little about the topic. Some teachers tell students they must write a minimum number of items.

2. Students use the W column, which stands for "want to know," to set a purpose for their reading by jotting down questions they have about the topic to be studied. In this column they will write questions about information they would like to know more about. Some students may respond with "I don't want to know anything about it." In this case, I recommend requiring them to write down some questions that they think the teacher will expect them to learn or understand after doing the reading. Students can do a preview activity of the actual reading material to come up with some questions for the W column.

3. The third part of the KWL is the "learned" column, where students will write down what they learned after completing the reading, and try to answer their questions from the W column. The L column is essentially for taking some notes on the reading. This column may require more space than the others, and may be continued over the course of several days or periods depending on the scope of the reading material.

| **K** | **W** | **L** |
|---|---|---|
| What I Know Already | What I Want to Know | What I Learned |
|  |  |  |

**Figure 2.5.   KWL Chart.**

## Strategy 10: Collaborative Prereading Strategy

*Purpose*
    Access prior knowledge; establish a purpose for reading; share and discuss ideas collaboratively; identify key ideas in the text.

*CCSS Connection*

Standard RL/RI.1: Read closely to determine what the text says explicitly; Standard RL/RI.2: Determine the central ideas or themes of a text and analyze their development; Standard SL.1: Prepare for and participate effectively in a range of conversations and collaborations.

*Overview*

This strategy is similar to the KWL chart, although it leaves out the postreading portion. It is to be completed in the context of a reading group or collaborative group. Teachers who frequently use cooperative learning techniques may find this adaptation more appealing.

*Procedure*

Assign the groups of students to discuss what the group members know about the topic they will be studying and also set a purpose for reading. They can use the following worksheet format (figure 2.6).

## Collaborative Pre-Reading Strategy

Step 1:  Take some individual "think time" before recording your answers.

Step 2:  Discuss and share information with your partners and write down additional information from members of the group.

Step 3:  Establish a purpose for your reading. State the purpose here:

Step 4: Before doing the reading, answer these questions together with your partners. Develop the best possible answers using everyone's ideas:

1.  What do we already know about this subject/topic (prior-knowledge)?

2.  What do we think we know but are not sure of (possible prior-knowledge)?

3.  What do we need to know? What questions will we need to answer or what task will we be asked to perform? (Set a purpose for reading.)

4.  What do we want to know? What are we curious about? Is there something we want to know or learn that goes beyond the teacher's questions? (Additional purpose for reading.)

Next, begin doing the reading assignment.

**Figure 2.6.  Collaborative Prereading Strategy.**

## Strategy 11: Folded Time Line

*Purpose*
  Access prior knowledge; identify key ideas in the text; summarize main ideas.

*CCSS Connection*
  Standard RL/RI.1: Read closely to determine what the text says explicitly and to make logical inferences from it; Standard RL/RI.2: Determine central ideas of a text.

*Overview*
  This strategy was developed by Elizabeth Sahifeld and Dorothy Syfert, teachers in Albany, Oregon, and Eugene, Oregon, respectively (Lewin, 2003). It is also similar to the KWL chart and is designed to assist students with reading comprehension by asking them to tap into prior knowledge before reading, followed by taking notes during reading, and then summarizing after reading.

*Procedure*
  1. Distribute 8" × 14" or 11" × 17" paper.

  2. Have students lay the paper on their desks with the long side facing up, fold the paper from the two ends into thirds and make the middle column the widest.

  3. Students label the three columns (figure 2.7):

     • What I already know about the topic from the past.

     • What I am learning about this topic in the present.

     • What I expect to remember about this topic in the future.

  4. The back side of the page may be used for additional room. As an alternative, the back can be used to draw an illustration related to the topic, or to take a quiz on the material.

| What I already know about this topic from the past | What I am learning about this topic in the present | What I expect to remember about this topic in the future |
| --- | --- | --- |
|  |  |  |

**Figure 2.7.   The Folded Time Line. (From Larry Lewin, *Paving the Way in Reading and Writing: Strategies and Activities to Support Struggling Students in Grades 6–12*, Copyright © 2003 by John Wiley and Sons, Inc. Reproduced with permission of John Wiley and Sons, Inc.)**

## Strategy 12: ReQuest

*Purpose*

Demonstrate and model active reading; engage in higher-level thinking about textual material; generate questions while reading.

*CCSS Connection*

Standard RL/RI.2: Determine central ideas of a text and analyze their development; Standard RL/RI.3: Analyze how and why individuals, events, and ideas develop and interact; Standard RL/RI.6: Assess how point of view or purpose shapes content and style; Standard RL/RI.8: Delineate the argument and specific claims in a text.

*Overview*

Developed by Manzo, Manzo, and Estes (2001), ReQuest provides students the opportunity to ask questions of the teacher.

*Procedure*

1. Choose a reading selection that has some obvious stopping points, such as an article divided into different sections, or a textbook chapter with subheadings. Write a few higher-level questions for each section of the passage.

2. Spend some time previewing the passage with students and building background information.

3. Ask students to read the first section of the passage and come up with questions that they will ask you, the teacher.

4. After students have had time to read, have each student ask you one of their questions, or as many as you have time for. Be sure to let students know their question has to be one different from previously asked questions. Answer the questions without looking at the passage.

5. Next, reverse the process: ask students to cover up the passage or close their books, and then ask them your questions. This gives you a chance to demonstrate the use of higher-level questions.

6. Repeat this process through the other sections of the reading passage. You can choose to stop the process at a certain point, have students make predictions about the rest of the passage, and then independently read the remainder, writing more higher-level questions as they go.

## Strategy 13: Interactive Reading Guides

*Purpose*

Engage in active reading; identify key details, ideas, and themes; discuss and collaborate in textual analysis.

*CCSS Connection*

Standard RL/RI.1: Read closely to determine what the text says explicitly; Standard RL/RI.2: Determine central ideas or themes of a text; Standard RL/RI.8: Delineate and evaluate the argument and specific claims in a text; Standard SL.1: Participate in a range of conversations and collaborations.

*Overview*

The interactive reading guide (Buehl, 2001; Wood, 1988) is a type of study guide that students complete in pairs or small cooperative groups to read text carefully and identify major ideas, themes, and details.

*Procedure*

1. Preview the text selection and identify main ideas students need to understand. Look for particular spots where students may have difficulty. The guide will give students specific tasks and questions to help guide them through the passage, highlight key ideas, and make connections.

2. Write a guide such as the one in figure 2.8, which was prepared for a chapter from a US history text about the Great Depression. The example comes from Alvermann, Phelps, and Ridgeway (2007).

3. Give students a class period to work on the reading guide while reading. Take additional time to review and go through the guides as a class.

**READING GUIDE: "THE BIG CRASH"**

Directions: With your partner, follow the instructions below. You will share your results during whole-class discussion of this section.

1. Student A: Read Paragraph 1 on p. 601 aloud. Group: Listen and briefly predict some things you will be learning in the rest of the section.

2. Student B: Read the section on "Black Thursday" aloud. Group: Listen and summarize:

   What happened to the stock market on Black Thursday?

   What did the leading bankers decide to do?

3. Group: Skim the section on "The Big Crash" and read the *New York Times* page reprinted on p. 602. Together draft a two-sentence summary:

   Sentence 1: Explain what happened in the Big Crash.

   Sentence 2: Give at least one statistic that illustrates what happened.

4. Group: Read the sections on "Unequal Distribution of Wealth" and "Other Flaws in the Economy" silently. Answer the following:

   Give three reasons why factories were laying off workers and shutting down.

   Consider what you have read since the beginning of this chapter. Why do the authors call the stock market a "gambling arena"?

5. Group: Read the next two sections, "Hoover Takes Action" and "Aid for Farmers and Business" silently. Answer the following:

   List four things that the government did to try to help ease the effects of the Crash.

   Why did imports and exports drop after the Hawley-Smoot Tariff Act?

6. Student B: Read aloud the 3rd and 4th paragraphs of the section on "The Run on Banks." Group: Listen and answer the following questions:

**Figure 2.8. Interactive Reading Guide.**

> Give two reasons why banks were failing.
>
> What did bank failures mean to the people who had money deposited?
>
> 7. Group: Read the next two sections, "Beginning of the Great Depression" and "Unemployed Strike Back" silently. Write a short summary of the effects that the Great Depression had on Americans.
>
> 8. Group: Read the rest of "The Big Crash" silently. President Hoover tried to help businesses, the unemployed, farmers, and homeowners through loans and construction projects, but he was against giving money directly to people. Answer the following and be ready to support your conclusions!
>
> > Why did Hoover take this approach?
> >
> > Do you agree or disagree with this?

**Figure 2.8—*Continued* (From Donna E. Alvermann, Stephen F. Phelps, and Victoria R. Gillis, *Content Area Reading and Literacy: Succeeding in Today's Diverse Classrooms*, 5th edition, © 2007, p. 216. Reprinted by permission of Pearson Education, Inc., Upper Saddle River, New Jersey.)**

## Strategy 14: Tea Party

*Purpose*
    Activate prior knowledge; make predictions and comparisons, draw inferences.

*CCSS Connection*
    Standard SL.1: Prepare for and participate effectively in a range of conversations with diverse partners.

*Overview*
    Tea Party is a prereading strategy that gives students an opportunity to think about parts of the reading passage before they actually read it (Beers, 2003). It encourages active participation with the text and provides an opportunity to incorporate movement into the lesson. Students will predict what they think will happen in the text, make inferences, see causal relationships, compare and contrast, practice sequencing, and draw on their own experiences.

*Procedure*

1. Select key words, phrases, and sentences from the text and write them on note cards. Identify half as many of these as you have students. Duplicate enough cards so there is one card for each student.

2. Give one card to each student and tell the students to get up and move around the room, sharing their cards with as many classmates as possible. Students must actually listen to others as they read their cards.

3. Ask students to discuss how the cards might be related, and speculate on what they are about.

4. Have students form into groups of four and complete a "We think . . ." statement. For example, one student group might formulate the following statement: "We think that this passage might discuss the causes and the effects of carbon emissions on the earth's atmosphere and the possible climate changes that might result."

5. Ask each group to share their "We think . . ." statement with the entire class. Make sure that they explain how they reached their predictions.

6. Have students read the text and compare their predictions with the actual reading passage.

## Strategy 15: Prediction and Confirming Activity (PACA)

*Purpose*

Activate prior knowledge; make predictions; identify key ideas and themes in a text; build vocabulary.

*CCSS Connection*

Standard RL/RI.1: Read closely to determine what the text says explicitly; cite specific textual evidence; Standard RL/RI.2: Determine central ideas or themes of a text and analyze their development; summarize key supporting details and ideas.

*Overview*

This strategy is based on Beyer's Inquiry Model and is a prereading strategy that uses students' predictions to set a purpose for reading. PACA allows students to make predictions based on initial information given by the teacher to build some prior knowledge. Given additional information, they can revise their predictions

(Irvin, 1998). Suppose, in the following example, the teacher wants to teach students about the Auckland area of New Zealand knowing that students probably have little prior knowledge of the region or people.

*Procedure*

1. The teacher begins by giving a short introduction to Auckland, using a map to show the location in New Zealand.

2. The teacher poses a general question such as "What are the main characteristics of Auckland?"

3. The teacher gives some initial information and places students into small groups for discussion, providing them with a list of words related to the content reading material (see figure 2.9), and then asks students, "Based on these words, what assumptions can you make about the Auckland area?" For other topics, words can generally come directly from the textbook or reading passage selected:

| | | | |
|---|---|---|---|
| Isthmus | mainland | mudflats | sandbanks |
| channels | Waitakere Ranges | fruit | wine |
| industrial areas | Samoans | Tongans | English |
| architecture | kauri wood | Kinder House | veterans |
| Polynesian arts | Aotea Centre | parks | beaches |
| yachts | regatta | shipping | manufacturing |
| farmland | fishing | terraces | land route |
| canoes | whalers | Treaty of Waitangi | borough |
| trade | gold rush | military base | nuclear-free state |

**Figure 2.9. PACA Example.**

4. Students write out several predictions based on the study of the given words.

5. The teacher presents new information such as pictures, slides, a video, websites, or a story.

6. Students will revise and modify their statements.

7. Students read a selection from the textbook, article, or watch a video.

8. Students again revise and modify their predictions based on the reading.

PACA may be used with various topics when the teacher needs to build background knowledge. This strategy is also good for vocabulary and concept building.

## Strategy 16: Imagine, Elaborate, Predict, and Confirm (IEPC)

*Purpose*

Use prediction and visualization to comprehend text; clarify understanding through active reading of text.

*CCSS Connection*

Standard RL/RI.1: Read closely to determine what the text says explicitly; Standard RL/RI.2: Determine central ideas or themes of a text; Standard RL/RI.4: Interpret words and phrases as they are used in text; Standard RL/RI.5: Analyze the structure of texts.

*Overview*

IEPC is a strategy that helps students use visualization and make predictions about a reading selection (Wood & Endres, 2005). It is especially useful to help students improve their skills in making predictions, a key element in effective reading comprehension. You can use this with a reading assignment, textbook section, or multiple sources on a given topic.

*Procedure*

Follow this procedure as outlined by Harmon, Wood, and Hedrick (2006):

1. Choose a reading selection, such as a story or descriptive, scientific, or historical piece.

2. Present students with the IEPC form on an overhead projector and tell students they are going to use their imaginations to create pictures that will help them understand what they will be reading.

3. Explain to students the four phases of the IEPC.

4. Ask students to close their eyes and imagine everything they can think of related to the selection they are about to read. They can use the cover of the book, a title, a topic, or an illustration to help them imagine. Ask students to share their responses and write them down in the I column.

5. Using their visual images, have them add details, prior knowledge, and sensory information and write them in the E column.

6. Have them make at least one sample prediction based on their images and prior knowledge and write them in the P column. For example, "I predict that this passage will be about . . ."

7. Have students read the passage or section of text while keeping their predictions in mind.

8. In the postreading phase, return to the IEPC visual and make any necessary changes in the original predictions. (You might use a different-colored marker or pen for the added information.) Write down student responses in the C column, having students provide page numbers and specific quotes to support the information they can confirm. Figure 2.10 shows one possible version of the IEPC chart.

| I | E | P | C |
|---|---|---|---|
| Imagine: Imagine the topic. What do you see, feel, hear, smell? | Elaborate: Describe, give specific details of what you "see" in your mind. | Predict: Use your images and ideas to make predictions about the reading assignment. | Confirm: While reading, confirm or change your predictions about the passage. |
| | | | |

**Figure 2.10. IEPC Chart.**

## Strategy 17: CATAPULT

*Purpose*
Activate prior knowledge; make predictions.

*CCSS Connection*
Standard RL/RI.5: Analyze the structure of texts.

*Overview*

CATAPULT is a prereading strategy created by Jeff Zwiers (2010) to help students tap their prior knowledge and make predictions about what the reading assignment is about. Zwiers originally called it "CATAPULT into Literature," so it was originally intended for introducing students to a book or novel in English or history classes, but it can be adapted for other reading material as well.

*Procedure*

1. Explain each of the steps in the CATAPULT process, and have students take notes.

2. Use the following organizer (table 2.3) for students to use during the CATAPULT process as they begin reading.

3. Have students share their CATAPULT notes in pairs or with the whole class.

PART TWO

**Table 2.3.  CATAPULT Worksheet**

| | |
|---|---|
| **C**overs (front and back)<br>What does the front cover show us about what we might visualize in the story? What does the back cover tell us about the story/reading (words, pictures, or both)? | |
| **A**uthor<br>What is the author's background? Has he or she written any other stories that might be like this? What were they about? | |
| **T**itle<br>What does the title lead us to predict about the story? Write down some possible predictions. | |
| **A**udience<br>For whom was this story written? Adults, kids, males, females, city-dwelling, country-dwelling, past, present, and future readers? | |
| **P**age 1<br>Read page 1 and write down what you can tell about the story and what it is about. | |
| **U**nderlying message or purpose<br>With what we have thought about so far, what message or purpose might the author have for readers? | |
| **L**ook at visuals, maps, or sketches in the text<br>What do the pictures, sketches, diagrams, or maps tell us? How will they add to our ability to visualize events and characters? | |
| **T**ime, place, characters<br>From clues so far, what can you say about when the story takes place, where it takes place, and the characters? What do you think might happen to the characters? | |

*Source*: Republished with permission of the International Reading Association, from Jeff Zwiers, *Building Reading Comprehension Habits in Grades 6–12: A Toolkit of Classroom Activities*, 2nd edition, 2010; permission conveyed through Copyright Clearance Center, Inc.

## Strategy 18: THIEVES

*Purpose*

Activate prior knowledge; identify key ideas and themes; draw inferences from text; analyze and interpret text features.

*CCSS Connection*

Standard RL/RI.1: Read closely to determine what the text says explicitly; Standard RL/RI.5: Analyze the structure of texts, including how sentences, paragraphs, and larger portions of the text relate to each other; Standard RL/RI.10: Read and comprehend complex literary and informational texts.

*Overview*

Another Jeff Zwiers (2010) prereading strategy is THIEVES. It asks students to engage in prereading and make predictions about the text as well as to identify and interpret text structures and features to access the key ideas and themes.

*Procedure*

Introduce this activity to students and have them use the following THIEVES practice sheet (see figure 2.11). Tell them to see how much information they can "steal" from the chapter or reading assignment before actually reading it.

| |
|---|
| **T**    **Title:** What does the title tell us? Let's think of all the possibilities |
| **H**    **Headings**: What do the headings tell us? They are the mini-titles of each section. What questions can we make from them that we think the section will answer? Let's also look at the table of contents, ask some questions, and make some predictions. |
| **I**    **Introduction:** Read the chapter introduction if there is one and think about it. Read the first paragraph of normal chapter text as well. Why do we think the author wrote the text? |
| **E**    **Everything I know**: Jot down all the facts and ideas about the topic that you think will be helpful for understanding. Create some questions about your own knowledge that you think the text might answer. Use the back of your paper, if needed. |
| **V**    **Visuals:** Let's look at all the diagrams, charts, and pictures. Let's read the captions. Why did the author include them? Can we think of any questions about them? |

**Figure 2.11.  THIEVES Practice Sheet.**

E  **End-of-chapter Material**: Let's look at the end of the chapter to read any summaries (Don't ever forget to read the summary! It will save a lot of time.) and to see which questions the author thought were important. This can help us focus on what the author's purpose is. Let's try to guess the answers to a few questions using the information we have gathered so far. Write down a couple questions that look important. Also, we should notice every boldface or italicized word, especially if it is a new word or has a new meaning in the subject area. Look at any other text clue that might strengthen your initial idea (i.e. make you a richer thief).

S  **So what**?  Now, let's ask why we are reading this text. Why might I be interested in it? How might it connect to my life? Why does the teacher or our state want me to know this? Why did the author take the time to write this? For money? To teach us about the topic? For artistic expression? To improve my life somehow? For future classes?

**Figure 2.11—*Continued* (Republished with permission of the International Reading Association, from Jeff Zwiers, *Building Reading Comprehension Habits in Grades 6–12: A Toolkit of Classroom Activities*, 2nd edition, 2010; permission conveyed through Copyright Clearance Center, Inc.)**

## Strategy 19: Guess and Check

*Purpose*
    Make predictions based on textual information; demonstrate comprehension of text by checking predictions against evidence; cite textual evidence.

*CCSS Connection*
    Standard RL/RI.1: Read closely to determine what the text says explicitly and make logical inferences from it.

*Overview*
    "Guess and check" is a phrase that may be familiar to many students from their math class. It is a simple way to remind students to check their predictions against the evidence.

PART TWO

*Procedure*

1. At the beginning of each reading section, ask students to make a prediction, an educated guess, or a hypothesis about what will follow in the text.

2. At the end of the reading or before the next section of reading, ask students to check to see if their predictions were accurate. The logs shown in figures 2.12 and 2.13 can be used for narrative or expository text in any content area and they can also be adapted for your own specific purposes. The guess and check worksheet in figure 2.13 is designed specifically for math problem solving. Students should repeat the guess and check process until they are satisfied with their solutions.

---

**Guess and Check**

Name _____ Date _____

Text _____ Pages _____

1. Re-read your prediction from the last entry. Was your prediction correct?

2. If yes, what clues helped you guess? If no, are there any clues you missed? Why did you

    make the prediction you made?

3. What prediction do you have for the next section of text?

---

**Figure 2.12.   Guess and Check.**

Directions: Read the problem you are about to solve and make a prediction before you begin to solve the problem. Choose from the following prompts:

I think I can solve this problem by _____

Estimate a range of possible answers (I think the answer will be less than _____

and greater than _____).

Two ways of solving this that might lead to the correct answer are _____

If I tried the same problem with different numbers _____, the answer would

be _____ (greater, lesser, impossible, etc.)

Problem:


Prediction:


Solution:


Check your prediction:


**Figure 2.13. Guess and Check for Math.**

# During-Reading Strategies

To review, before asking students to do any type of reading assignment, do four things:

- Access or build prior knowledge to activate students' schema prior to reading.

- Set a purpose for reading, or ask students to set a purpose for their reading.

- Ask students do a quick preview of the text and to make some predictions about what they are going to be reading. If possible, along with this step, have students identify the text structure that they think is used (narrative, cause-effect, comparison-contrast, etc.).

- Pre-teach the a few critical vocabulary terms students must know to successfully read the material.

Having the class read the material together is often a very good alternative to independent reading. In her book *Yellow Brick Roads*, Janet Allen (2000) suggests four good ways to do in-class reading, all of which help to build student fluency. Rather than using only one method repeatedly in your class, try to use all of these approaches at different times:

- Read-alouds: The teacher reads to students who do not have the text in front of them. This can be done with novel excerpts, short passages, or articles.

- Shared Reading: The teacher reads while students follow along in the text. Stop occasionally for questions and discussion.

- Guided Reading: The teacher leads the class through reading different sections of the text, one at a time. Students read silently. Between sections use discussion and review questions on the previous section.

- Independent Reading: Students read the assigned text independently and, in some cases, select their own material to read. This may be done for a specified period of time.

I like to include a couple of additional strategies for in-class reading that you may want to try. I find that pairs-read and triangle reading work well with most groups of students. Echo reading can be particularly useful for a group of struggling readers:

- Pairs-Read: Students work with a partner. Together they will decide how much each one will read, usually only one or two paragraphs, before switching to the other person, who then reads the next one or two paragraphs. After each partner has read one section, the pair should stop to review and summarize what they just read.

- Triangle Reading: This method follows the same process as pairs-read except that it is done with three students. Each person reads one paragraph or short section. When all three have read one section, the group stops to review, discuss, summarize, and ask questions. I find it works very well to place a struggling reader in a triangle with two stronger readers. Ideally, each triangle would have one student slightly below grade level, one at or near grade level, and one above-grade-level reader.

- Echo Reading: This method is useful but can be tedious and students will grow tired of it quickly, so it is best to do it only for short periods of time. Leading the whole class or a small group, the teacher reads one sentence at a time. Following the teacher's reading of the sentence, all students together repeat the teacher's reading of the sentence. This is a good way to build fluency because students are able to listen to the teacher (a strong reader) read a sentence fluently and then essentially imitate the teacher's reading.

Try some of these methods of doing in-class reading and see which ones you find work best for you and your students.

### Strategy 1: Cornell Notes

*Purpose*

Read and comprehend complex text; identify main ideas and supporting details; analyze the development of themes and ideas in a text or lecture; analyze text structure; write a summary.

*CCSS Connection*

Standard RL/RI.1: Read closely to determine what the text says explicitly; Standard RL/RI.2: Determine central ideas or themes of a text; Standard RL/RI.5: Analyze the structure of texts; Standard RL/RI.10: Read and comprehend complex literary and informational texts.

*Overview*

The Cornell note-taking strategy, originally developed by Walter Pauk (1993) at Cornell University, is sometimes called "two-column notes." There are a variety of forms of Cornell notes, and it is the note-taking system recommended in the AVID program, an excellent program in many schools that aims to prepare students for attending a four-year college. It is an excellent strategy for taking notes not only during a lecture but also while students are reading. Students are asked to review important points in the selection, find support for each point, and take notes in two columns. This strategy helps students to focus on main ideas, identifying and summarizing them in their own words.

*Procedure*

1. Have students preview the material they are about to read, looking at the title and subheadings and reading the first and last paragraphs. Ask students to generate some questions they think of as they are previewing. For example, after previewing an article on the role of women during the gold rush era, students generated the following questions: What was the gold rush? How did women survive the harsh weather in the Yukon? Why did they go? Use a premade Cornell notes handout (figure 2.14),

or have students use a piece of paper divided into two columns. In the Questions/Summary column on the left-hand side, they list key words ideas, main points, and questions they generated during prereading. The right-hand column is for note taking and listing of details and evidence that support the main ideas.

2. Have students look again at the questions they generated in part one. If they did not find the answers in the article, have them look again and add information to the notes.

3. After the reading and note taking, at the bottom of the page or on the back, students will write a summary of the article that includes all the important points in the article and some information that backs them up.

4. Have students use Cornell notes to review and prepare for tests.

## CORNELL NOTES

Class Notes
Topic: _____

Questions/Main Ideas

Name: _____
Class: _____
Period: _____
Date: _____

**Notes**

Summary:_____
_____
_____
_____
_____
_____

**Figure 2.14.   Cornell Notes.**

PART TWO

## Strategy 2: Question-Answer Relationship (QAR)

*Purpose*

Generate text-based and knowledge-based questions; use background knowledge to help comprehend text; identify main ideas and supporting detail in text.

*CCSS Connection*

Standard RL/RI.1: Read closely to determine what the text says explicitly and make logical inferences from it; Standard RL/RI.10: Read and comprehend complex literary and informational text.

*Overview*

QAR (Raphael, 1986) is a strategy that uses four levels of questions. It is designed to clarify the questioning process, providing teachers and students with common vocabulary to discuss different types of questions and sources of information for answering these questions. Two of the four types of questions are text-based, focusing students on retrieving information that can be found directly in the reading material. Two additional questions are knowledge-based questions because students must use their own prior knowledge to answer the question. The strategy helps students learn to consider information both from the text and from their own background knowledge in order to comprehend.

The text-based questions are of two types:

- "Right there" questions ask students to respond to the literal level; the words used to formulate and answer the questions can be found right in the sentences of the text.

- "Think and search" questions require students to think about how the information or ideas in the text relate to one another and search through the entire passage to find information that applies. In other words, they must find the answer from more than one part of the text.

The knowledge-based questions are of two types:

- "Author and you" questions require students to combine their prior knowledge with information gleaned from the text to answer the question.

- "On my own" questions can be answered with information from the students' background knowledge and do not require students to read the text.

This strategy teaches students that addressing different kinds of questions requires different thought processes.

*Procedure*

1. Begin by teaching students each QAR. Give examples of types of questions that might fit each category.

2. Assign passages to be read from the textbook or reading material. As students finish reading each section, ask them one question from each QAR category. Point out the differences between each question and the kind of answer it requires.

3. After students demonstrate that they understand the differences among the four levels, give them the opportunity to practice identifying QARs.

4. For independent reading, students should generate various QARs on their own and share them with partners, in groups, or with the whole class. Have students identify the type of question and state the answer. As an alternative, have students write some of each type of question along with an answer.

5. Students should use their own QARs to ask each other questions and discuss answers.

Here are some examples from math:

---

• Right There

  ○ What is additive identity?

  ○ What is the distinguishing feature of a pentagon?

• Think and Search

  ○ Explain the relationship between a rhombus and a parallelogram.

  ○ What are three examples of numbers that are both square numbers and triangular numbers?

• Author and You

  ○ Based on the author's description of a stem-and-leaf graph, identify some types of data that would be well represented in such a graph.

  ○ For what data might it be useful to determine mean, mode, median, and angle?

• On My Own

  ○ What might the number −5 represent in football?

  ○ What types of graphs would you suggest the newspaper use to display information on sports scores?

---

PART TWO

Figure 2.15 shows some examples from social studies (Doty, Cameron, & Barton, 2003).

| |
|---|
| • Right There |
| 1. Who wrote the Constitution of the United States?<br><br>2. What are the three factors of production?<br><br>3. What was the Underground Railroad? |
| • Think and Search |
| 1. Describe the roles of the three branches of government in the United States.<br><br>2. Compare and contrast a command economy and a market economy.<br><br>3. Summarize how military strategies used by Grant and Sherman hastened the end of the Civil War. |
| • Author and You |
| 1. Based on the author's description of local governments, identify what services local government provides in your community.<br><br>2. What evidence have you seen that confirms or refutes the information about supply and demand?<br><br>3. Based on the information about inventions of the late 1800s which invention from this period do you think had the biggest impact on American culture? |
| • On My Own |
| 1. Describe a way you can become involved in a project to help your community.<br><br>2. What type of business would you start that you believe would be profitable where you live?<br><br>3. Identify historical sites that are within fifty miles of your school. |

**Figure 2.15. QAR Examples. (Reprinted by permission of McREL.)**

## Strategy 3: Stump the Teacher

*Purpose*

Generate text-based and knowledge- based questions; use background knowledge to help comprehend text; identify main ideas and supporting detail in text.

*CCSS Connection*

Standard RL/RI.1: Read closely to determine what the text says explicitly and make logical inferences from it; Standard RL/RI.10: Read and comprehend complex literary and informational text.

*Overview*

This strategy is a fun technique based on reciprocal questioning and the QAR strategy. It can be used to review and practice QAR. The teacher and students take turns posing, answering, and identifying the four types of questions while listening and responding. This gives you the chance to model good questioning for students.

*Procedure*

1. Arrange students into teams of no more than four each.

2. Have everyone read the text together.

3. Have each group work together to create at least one of each type of questions based on the passage. They should use their copy of the textbook or reading assignment during the game. The teacher, however, cannot.

4. Create your own questions ahead of time.

5. The first team asks a question of the teacher and identifies the type of question that was asked.

6. The teacher answers the question. If the answer is incorrect, the group posing the question calls on another team to answer. If the teacher's answer is correct, the teacher poses a question to another team and identifies the type of question.

7. The new group answers the question and then poses a new question to the teacher, identifying the type of question.

8. Continue rounds of questioning with teacher and students taking turns until all questions have been asked. Another option for later on in the game is for the teacher to withdraw and allow teams to do the questioning process themselves.

9. Assign a student to keep record of points for each correct answer by the teacher and each team. Have them give one point for correctly identifying the question and one point for each correct answer.

10. If disputes arise over the answer to the question, they should be resolved by having the students refer to the reading assignment or a particular passage and identifying evidence to support the answer.

## Strategy 4: Thick and Thin Questions

*Purpose*

Use questioning as a comprehension strategy; identify and respond to questions at the literal, inferential, and evaluative levels.

*CCSS Connection*

Standard RL/RI.1: Read closely to determine what the text says explicitly and to make logical inferences from it; Standard RL/RI.2: Determine central ideas or themes of a text.

*Overview*

Another good questioning method to use are what Lewin (2009) calls "Thick and Thin Questions." They are a variation on Spencer Kagan's "Fat and Skinny" questions. Lewin (2009) notes that questioning is a key comprehension strategy and can help to guide a reader through the text by keeping the reader engaged and active. Thin questions are what students would call an easy question, one that you can easily answer having just read the selection. A thick question is a "hard question" that you don't know the answer to immediately because the author did not state it directly in the text. In other words, thick questions require inferential or evaluative thinking.

*Procedure*

1. Divide the reading passage or textbook chapter into sections, or use the existing sections in the text.

2. During and after students have read each section, have them stop and write one thick question and one thin question. Along with their thin and thick questions, you can ask students to write a "main point" statement for each section. This is a brief summary statement that describes the main idea of the section.

3. Following the activity, have students share their questions with partners or in small groups. They can also be turned in to the teacher who can use them to question the whole class.

Figure 2.16 shows some sample thick and thin questions written by a student after reading a chapter from a social studies textbook (Lewin, 2009).

| Section: George III Lays Down the Law: |
| --- |
| • Thin: When was George III crowned king? |
| • Thick: Why didn't he understand compromises could serve his purposes? |

| Section: Proclamation of 1763: |
| --- |
| • Thin: What did George III want immediately after the French and Indian War? |
| • Thick: Why did the colonial merchants and officials resent the faraway king's interference in colonial affairs? |

| Section: The Sugar Act: |
| --- |
| • Thin: What did Britain send to battlefields? |
| • Thick: Why did Britain send soldiers and supplies to colonial battlefields? |

| Section: The Quartering Act: |
| --- |
| • Thin: What made the colonists feel like enemies of the British? |
| • Thick: Why did King George continue to station British soldiers in the colonies? |

| Section: The Stamp Act: |
| --- |
| • Thin: Why did Parliament pass the Stamp Act? |
| • Thick: Why did licenses need stamps? |

**Figure 2.16. Thick and Thin Questions. (Reprinted with permission from Scholastic, Inc. and Larry Lewin from *Teaching Comprehension with Questioning Strategies That Motivate Middle School Readers.*)**

## Strategy 5: Margin Notes

*Purpose*
Use note taking and text marking as comprehension strategies; engage in active reading; identify main ideas and supporting details; analyze themes and ideas as well as text structure; ask questions, make predictions and connections, and evaluate text while reading.

*CCSS Connection*
Standard RL/RI.1: Read closely to determine what the text says explicitly; Standard RL/RI.2: Determine central ideas or themes of a text; Standard RL/RI.4: Interpret words and phrases as they are used in a text; Standard RL/RI.5: Analyze the structure of texts; Standard RL/RI.8: Delineate and evaluate the argument and specific claims in a text; Standard RL/RI.10: Read and comprehend complex literary and informational text.

*Overview*
As discussed previously, getting students actively engaged with the material during the reading process is very important. One way to do this is to teach students to use margin notes or text marking during reading. This is a technique that college students use routinely to engage in thinking about the texts they are reading, and secondary students can definitely benefit from learning how to use this method of active reading during their middle and high school years.

*Procedure*
Text marking is difficult to do in textbooks because students generally cannot write in their textbooks, but the method is ideal for reading material reproduced on paper handouts students can write on. It can be used with any type of reading material. Ideally, leave a wide right margin on the page to allow generous space for students' margin notes. You can also ask students to use highlighting or underlining in the text along with making margin notes. For example, you might want them to highlight main ideas in one color, supporting details in another. Or they might be asked to highlight key terminology or important words. One option is to tailor the use of margin notes to your specific purposes. If you want students' margin notes to be mostly identifying main ideas, or tracing conflicts or themes, or focusing on confusing parts, that's fine. Otherwise, ask students to do five different things in their margin notes:

- Questioning: Ask and write down questions about what is happening in the reading. Include questions about words or statements that are confusing.

- Connecting: Think of similarities between what is being described in the reading material and what you have experienced, heard about, or read about somewhere else.

- Predicting: Try to figure out what will happen next and how the selection might end.

- Reviewing: Stop occasionally to review what you have understood so far and record an occasional summary statement.

- Evaluating: Form opinions as you are reading and afterward. Develop your own ideas about the text and write them down in margin notes.

Here are some examples from a student margin notes made while reading "The Seeing See Little" from the book *Three Days to See*, by Helen Keller:

"She points out something that seems very true."

"These statements make you stop and think that we are very blessed to have our senses."

"Is she angry at us for not appreciating our senses or trying to make us humble?"

"Her friend sounds like most of us. I can see where Helen gets her points."

"Again, she seems to be angry at us, but I do know what she means."

"The author describes everything wonderfully! She also shows how much she wants to see. It's amazing how well and accurate her touch is."

And here are some examples of a student's margin notes written while reading the William Stafford poem "Traveling through the Dark," a poem about a driver who comes upon a dead deer while driving along a road at night:

"How sad! I see this sort of thing all the time because of where I live."

"Must be a semi-busy road. He must be nervous to stand there."

"Pregnant?"

"'Never to be born?' Can't he do something?"

"Symbolism"

"Interesting personification."

"I guess he couldn't do anything."

PART TWO

## Strategy 6: Sticky Note Reading

*Purpose*
　　Use note taking and text marking as comprehension strategies; engage in active reading; identify main ideas and supporting details; analyze themes and ideas as well as text structure; ask questions, make predictions and connections, and evaluate text while reading.

*CCSS Connection*
　　Standard RL/RI.1: Read closely to determine what the text says explicitly; Standard RL/RI.2: Determine central ideas or themes of a text; Standard RL/RI.4: Interpret words and phrases as they are used in a text; Standard RL/RI.5: Analyze the structure of texts; Standard RL/RI.8: Delineate and evaluate the argument and specific claims in a text; Standard RL/RI.10: Read and comprehend complex literary and informational text.

*Overview*
　　A good supply of sticky notes is one of the most important things you can have in your classroom. I use sticky notes all the time in my classes for a variety of purposes and one of the best uses is getting students to do active reading while completing a reading assignment. You can follow the procedure for the previous strategy, using margin notes, but have students use sticky notes to make their comments and then attach them to the page in the appropriate spot. Sticky notes, unlike margin notes, can be used with school textbooks and other materials that you would generally not want students marking up. Use sticky notes with fiction or nonfiction. Beth Bedard (2003) notes that using sticky notes helped her students "get actively involved and prepared them for small group discussions" (p. 36). In addition, they were better able to self-monitor their understanding and showed increased confidence in their reading ability (Bedard, 2003). Sticky notes come not only in different sizes but also in different colors and shapes. You can use different colors of sticky notes for different purposes (i.e., pink sticky notes for main ideas, green sticky notes for questions, yellow sticky notes for personal connections).

*Procedure*
　　Provide students with a supply of sticky notes. Have students mark the text with sticky notes coded to particular categories. Here are possible uses of sticky notes to engage students in active reading:

- For fictional or literary materials, have students identify elements of the author's style or use of literary techniques (foreshadowing, irony, metaphor, conflict, diction, etc.).

- Have students identify and make notes about the text features of the reading material.

- Ask students to use sticky notes to mark main ideas and supporting details.

- Ask students to use the five elements described in the section on margin notes: questioning, connecting, predicting, reviewing, evaluating.

- Ask students to write one-sentence summaries on every page.

- Ask students to write down key terminology and important words with definitions.

- Ask students to make notes about personal connections and how the text compares to other texts, to the student herself, or to the world.

- Have students make notes to trace the organizational pattern of the text.

- Have students make predictions about what will come next.

- Have students write down words or concepts they don't understand.

- Have students make comparisons, disagree with ideas, mark examples, mark analogies and comparisons, and mark interesting or unusual facts.

- Have students mark good choice of words, images, or descriptive details.

Obviously, the kind of directions you give students for using sticky notes will be dictated by the particular reading assignment. They will probably be very different for informational text than for a short story or novel.

## Strategy 7: Reciprocal Teaching

*Purpose*
   Comprehend written text; summarize, generate questions, make predictions, and reread to clarify understanding; participate in a collaborative group.

*CCSS Connection*
   Standard RL/RI.1: Read closely to determine what the text says explicitly; Standard RL/RI.2: Determine central ideas or themes of a text; Standard RL/RI.8: Delineate and evaluate the argument and specific claims in a text; Standard SL.1: Prepare for and participate effectively in a range of conversations and collaborations.

PART TWO

*Overview*

Reciprocal teaching (Palinscar & Brown, 1984) is a strategy that involves students in cooperative learning groups to help them make meaning from reading material, which they read in small segments. There are four key strategies involved: summarizing (self-review), question-generating (self-testing), predicting (preparing for further reading), and demanding clarity (noting when breakdown in comprehension occurs). Initially, the teacher must provide some modeling for students, and then follow with structured practice to help students use and refine the strategies. Once students have mastered this process, the teacher can step aside from the process and allow students in groups to teach each other.

*Procedure*

1. After selecting an informational or fiction reading selection, distribute a set of note cards to each group of students (I recommend 4" × 6" note cards). Each student receives one or more cards, depending on the number in the group. Each student is then responsible for one question/card or more:

    a. Card One: Skimming and scanning before reading. After looking over the reading material, the student asks the group, "Does anyone have a prediction about this reading?"

    b. Card Two: After reading. "What questions do we need to clarify? Write down a question you have about the reading."

    c. Card Three: Vocabulary. "Share an interesting or puzzling word you found and tell why it interests you."

    d. Card Four: Make connections. "How does this reading relate to a film, story, or real-life experience you have had?"

    e. Card Five: Summary. "This reading was about . . . "

    f. Card Six: Prediction. "What do you think is going to happen next?"

2. Each group should select a leader to facilitate the discussion. The teacher should rotate from group to group to assist students with the process.

3. Have students divide the reading up into sections, by page, paragraphs, or sections.

4. After students have read the first section, have each student respond to the prompt on his or her card. This is done out loud for the whole group.

5. Have students rotate the cards around the circle.

6. Read the second section, and have each student respond to the prompt on the card.

7. Continue throughout all the sections of the text.

Here is an adaptation of reciprocal teaching in a math class, when students are trying to solve a particular math problem:

- Card One: Does anyone have a prediction about this problem?

- Card Two: What are we trying to find or solve?

- Card Three: Share a concept word you found and will have to use in order to solve the problem.

- Card Four: What steps or strategies are needed to solve this problem?

- Card Five: What clarifications do you need to solve this problem?

One additional suggestion is the first time the students use the strategy have the groups take cards, read the first section of the text, and then ask one group to model the process for the whole class. This allows everyone to see how the reciprocal teaching process works.

## Strategy 8: Question-Predict-Clarify

*Purpose*
    Comprehend written text; make predictions, use clarifying and use questioning to clarify meaning; cite specific evidence from text and take notes; monitor one's own level of comprehension.

*CCSS Connection*
    Standard RL/RI.1: Read closely to determine what the text says explicitly; Standard RL/RI.2: Determine central ideas or themes of a text; Standard RL/RI.5: Analyze the structure of texts; Standard RL/RI.8: Delineate and evaluate the argument and specific claims in a text.

*Overview*
    This strategy helps students respond to text during reading using three of the reciprocal teaching strategies. Students can use the note-taking sheet (figure 2.17)

while they read. It is a great strategy for helping students interact with the text as they are reading, and for supporting metacognition and improving comprehension. Be sure to model this strategy aloud before asking students to use it independently.

*Procedure*

1. Use the assigned text and have students follow along as you begin reading aloud.

2. Use a document camera or an overhead projector with a copy of the Q-P-C handout (figure 2.17). Record responses in the Question-Predict-Clarify column and write down the quote that suggested that response in the "Quote" column as well as the page number in the "page number" column.

3. Ask students to help you figure out whether the response was a question, a prediction, or a clarification. Label each one on an overhead. Use the modeling portion to demonstrate that there are no right or wrong answers, but instead individual responses to the text.

4. Once students are familiar with the process, have them finish reading the rest of the text and finish the note taking on their own.

5. Have students share some of their responses with others.

6. Continue using the Q-P-C note-taking sheet for independent reading assignments.

## Question-Prediction-Clarification Notetaking Sheet

Name: _____     Date: _____

Title: _____     Time: _____to _____

Author: _____     Pages read _____ to _____

Q = Question: Ask questions about what may or may not actually be in the text using your own thoughts and experiences.

P = Predict: Make guesses based on evidence from the text about what you can expect to be presented next.

C = Clarify: Make the meaning of the text clear, explain, or restate in your own words.

| Page Number | Quote from the Text | Question/Prediction/Clarification |
|---|---|---|
|  |  |  |

**Figure 2.17.  Question-Prediction-Clarification Notetaking Sheet.**

PART TWO

## Strategy 9: Predict, Locate, Add, Note (PLAN)

*Purpose*
 Use strategic approaches to reading; read with a purpose; make predictions; cite specific textual evidence; identify and summarize main ideas and supporting details; make connections between previous learning and new content material.

*CCSS Connection*
 Standard RL/RI.1: Read closely to determine what the text says explicitly; Standard RL/RI.2: Determine central ideas or themes of a text; Standard RL/RI.5: Analyze the structure of texts; Standard RL/RI.8: Delineate and evaluate the argument and specific claims in a text.

*Overview*
 PLAN is a reading and study strategy for informational text that helps students read with a purpose (Caverly, Mandeville, & Nicholson, 1995). PLAN is an acronym for four distinct steps that students are taught to use before, during, and after reading.

*Procedure*
1. The first step is to predict the content and text structure. Students create a graphic organizer based on the chapter title, subtitles, highlighted words, and information from visuals or graphics (see figure 2.18).

2. The second step is to locate information that is familiar and unfamiliar on the map by placing checkmarks next to familiar concepts and question marks next to unfamiliar concepts. This helps students to activate and assess their prior knowledge about the topic (see figure 2.19).

3. The third step, *add*, is completed as students read; they add words or phrases to their map to explain concepts marked with question marks or to confirm and build upon known concepts, which are marked with checks. Have students draw additional boxes, and use lines and arrows (see figure 2.20).

4. The fourth step is *note*. After reading, students take notes on their new understandings by using the new knowledge to complete an activity, such as reproducing the map from memory, writing in a learning log, holding a discussion about what they have learned, or writing a summary or response. This helps to reinforce their learning.

Many subject areas have text that continually introduces new concepts and ideas that are related to previous content. PLAN provides students with a method of illustrating the relationships between ideas in the text and also provides a visual format to use to take notes during reading. Students create their own graphic organizer (see figures 2.18, 2.19, and 2.20) to help them see the connections as they construct an understanding of the concepts. It also allows students to self-monitor, organize, and summarize what they know and have learned from their reading. I recommend that you model this PLAN process for students with sample textual material when you first introduce the strategy. Then give students opportunity to practice with various pieces of text. The example in figures 2.18, 2.19, and 2.20 comes from Doty, Cameron, and Barton (2003).

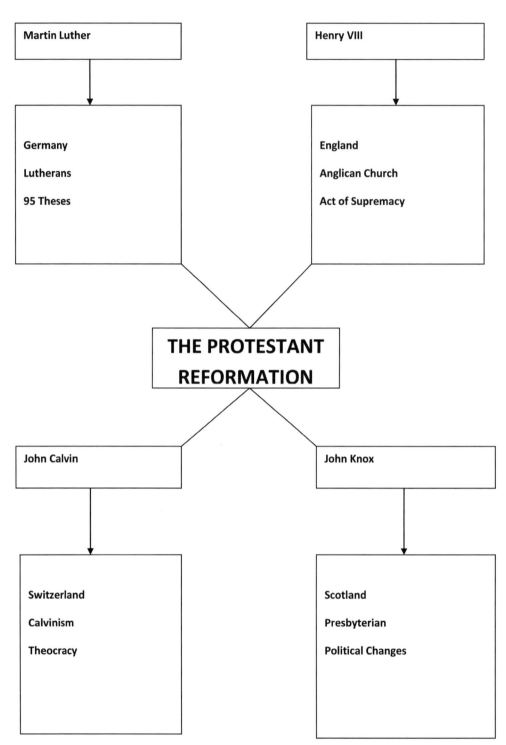

**Figure 2.18.   Step I: Predict. (Reprinted by permission of McREL.)**

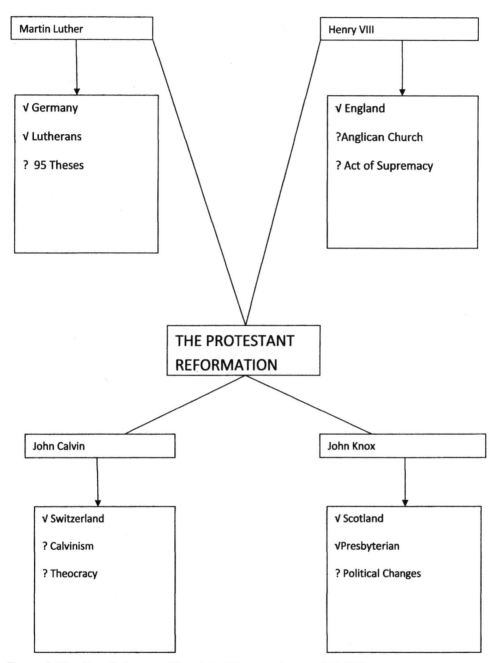

**Figure 2.19. Step 2: Locate. (Reprinted by permission of McREL.)**

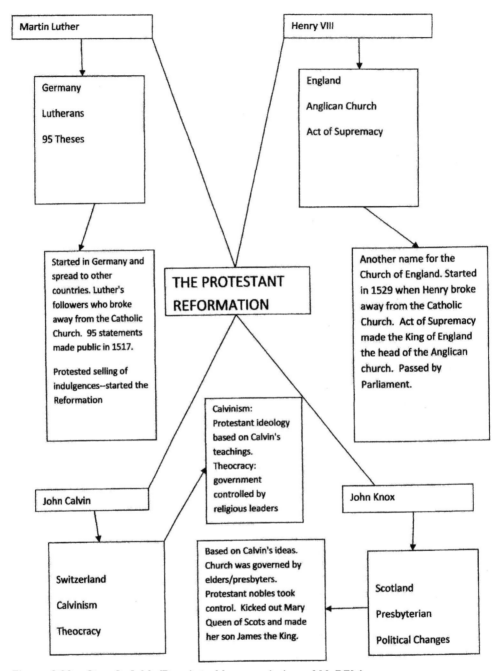

**Figure 2.20. Step 3: Add. (Reprinted by permission of McREL.)**

## Strategy 10: Think-Pair-Share

*Purpose*

Discuss and review content material; share ideas with others in the pre-reading, during-reading, or postreading phase; engage in higher-level thinking; engage in collaborative discussions.

*CCSS Connection*

Standard RL/RI.1: Read closely to determine what the text says explicitly; Standard RL/RI.2: Determine central ideas or themes of a text; Standard RL/RI.8: Delineate and evaluate the argument and specific claims in a text; Standard SL.1: Prepare for and participate in a range of conversations and collaborations.

*Overview*

Think-pair-share (Lyman, 1981) is a cooperative discussion strategy that gets its name from the three stages of student action. It can be used almost anytime in classrooms, during discussions, lecture, or as prereading, during reading, or postreading. Why is think-pair-share a good strategy to use with students? We know that students learn partly by being able to talk about and process the content. This strategy structures the discussion because students follow a prescribed process that limits off-task behavior. Partners are accountable to each other and eventually to the whole class. The strategy also helps solve the problem of individual students who may dominate discussion. It allows for everyone in class to participate and makes everyone feel more involved. Students who would never speak up in class are instead talking with their partners and their level of participation increases.

*Procedure*

1. Think: The teacher asks a question or prompt to provoke students' thinking. The students should take a few moments to silently think about the question and their answer. As an alternative, you can have students jot down their thoughts on paper or a note card.

2. Pair: Using designated partners, or the person seated next to them, students will talk about the answer each came up with for a couple of minutes. They can compare their mental or written notes and identify the answers they think are best, most convincing, or most unique.

3. Share: After students talk in pairs for a few moments, the teacher calls for pairs to share their thinking with the rest of the class. This can be done in round-robin fashion or by asking for student volunteers. Some teachers

like to add an additional step to the process: think-pair-share-square (or think-pair-square-share, if you prefer).

4. Square: After students have completed part two, have each pair form a "square" with another pair, facing or sitting next to each other. This allows each pair to gather additional thoughts and ideas from another pair.

Another variation on this strategy is a think-pair-share-write, in which students follow the think-pair-share activity with independently writing about the given topic.

### Strategy 11: The Three-Minute Pause

*Purpose*
   Discuss and review content material; share ideas with others in the pre-reading, during-reading, or postreading phase; engage in higher-level thinking; engage in collaborative discussions.

*CCSS Connection*
   Standard RL/RI.1: Read closely to determine what the text says explicitly; Standard RL/RI.2: Determine central ideas or themes of a text; Standard RL/RI.8: Delineate and evaluate the argument and specific claims in a text; Standard SL.1: Prepare for and participate in a range of conversations and collaborations.

*Overview*
   This strategy is a variation on think-pair-share and can also be used almost any time in class, during discussion or reading. The three-minute pause (McTighe & Lyman, 1988) is a pause to break up large sections of content material. It allows all students to stop, reflect on the concepts and ideas that have been introduced, make connections to prior knowledge or experience, and seek clarification. The three-minute pause allows students to do three things: summarize key ideas so far, add their own thoughts, and pose clarifying questions.

*Procedure*
   1. First, have students work in groups of three to five. Give them a total of three minutes for the whole process.

   2. Next, students focus on key points of the lesson so far. This allows them to check to make sure they understand the main ideas.

3. Then students should consider their prior knowledge and connections they can make to the new information. Use the following questions: What connections can be made? What does this remind you of? What would round out your understanding of this topic? What things can you add?

4. Finally, pose clarifying questions. Use the following prompts: Are there things that are still not clear? Are there confusing parts? Are you having trouble making connections? Can you anticipate where we are headed next? Can you find any deeper insights?

This strategy gives students a chance to process new information. It also prevents you from having to reteach information, and gives students time to organize and reflect on their learning. It provides a bridge between old information and new, helping to clarify emerging understanding before moving on to new material.

## Strategy 12: 3-2-1

*Purpose*
  Discuss and review content material; ask questions to clarify understanding; share ideas with others in the prereading, during-reading, or postreading phase; engage in higher-level thinking; engage in collaborative discussions.

*CCSS Connection*
  Standard RL/RI.1: Read closely to determine what the text says explicitly; Standard RL/RI.2: Determine central ideas or themes of a text; Standard RL/RI.8: Delineate and evaluate the argument and specific claims in a text; Standard SL.1: Prepare for and participate in a range of conversations and collaborations.

*Overview*
  The 3-2-1 strategy also gives students a chance to summarize key ideas and then pose a question to reveal where their understanding is still unclear. This activity can be used in addition to or in place of the usual worksheets or end-of-chapter questions. It can also be used midway through a lesson or reading assignment.

*Procedure*
  Give students a chart such as the one in figure 2.21, or have them use their own paper. Following a portion of reading or lecture, have students complete the 3-2-1 chart, which has three parts:

- 3 things you learned
- 2 interesting points
- 1 question you still have

The 3-2-1 can be modified in several ways. You can take frequent breaks during reading or lecture and have students complete the 3-2-1 process. You can also have students do the activity in pairs or modify the three prompts. For example, if you've been teaching the transition from feudalism to the rise of nation-states, you might have students write down three differences between feudalism and nation-states, two similarities, and one question they have.

# 3-2-1

**3 Things I Learned/Key Points**:

**2 Interesting Ideas**:

**1 Question I Have**:

**Figure 2.21.  3-2-1 Chart.**

## Strategy 13: Insert Note Taking

*Purpose*

Review and take notes on content material; identify main ideas and supporting detail; identify and interpret challenging words and phrases; analyze text structure; cite textual evidence; ask questions and clarify understanding.

*CCSS Connection*

Standard RL/RI.1: Read closely to determine what the text says explicitly; Standard RL/RI.2: Determine central ideas or themes of a text; Standard RL/RI.4: Interpret words and phrases as they are used in a text; Standard RL/RI.5: Analyze the structure of texts; Standard RL/RI.8: Delineate and evaluate the argument and specific claims in a text.

*Overview*

Insert note taking is a great strategy for students to use during the reading process to improve their comprehension. It helps students break down the text and better monitor their own comprehension as they are reading.

*Procedure*

1. Prepare a two-column graphic organizer with the left column labeled "Confusing Information or Words I Don't Understand" and the right column labeled "New Information That I Understand" (see figure 2.22). An alternative is to have students use their own paper upon which they draw the two columns.

2. Have students use sticky notes while reading the text and mark a "+" for the information they understand and a "?" for the confusing information. You can give students a list of symbols such as the following to use for text marking as they read:

   √ = I agree                ? = I wonder . . .

   X = I disagree             ?? = I don't understand

   + = New information        * = Important

   ! = Wow!

3. When they have finished reading, have students complete the graphic organizer, taking notes from the reading passage to fill in each column.

4. After students have completed their note-taking chart, have them share new information first and then the confusing information or words they don't understand. The teacher and other students can then explain new information or clarify confusing concepts while students take notes.

81

| CONFUSING INFORMATION OR WORDS I DON'T UNDERSTAND | NEW INFORMATION THAT I UNDERSTAND |
|---|---|
|  |  |

**Figure 2.22.   Insert Note-taking Chart.**

## Strategy 14: Critical Thinking Map

*Purpose*

Identify main ideas and supporting details; engage in higher-level thinking; identify and evaluate central themes and ideas; make interpretations; make connections between the text and real world.

*CCSS Connection*

Standard RL/RI.1: Read closely to determine what the text says explicitly; Standard RL/RI.2: Determine central ideas or themes of a text; Standard RL/RI.8: Delineate and evaluate the argument and specific claims in a text; Standard RL/RI.10: Read and comprehend complex literary and informational texts independently and proficiently.

*Overview*

The critical thinking map helps students evaluate text critically and learn to identify main ideas in a reading assignment. The strategy comes from Idol-Maestas (1985).

*Procedure*

1. Introduce the map (figure 2.23) and spend some time explaining each of the four parts: main idea (the most important message conveyed); viewpoints/opinions (your own response and opinion about what you have read); reader's conclusion (integrating what you have read with what you know and deciding if the author's conclusions are valid); relevance to today (draw a comparison between the reading material and real life, present and past experiences).

2. Read the assigned passage aloud or have students read it silently. Model how to use the map the first time you ask students to use this strategy.

3. Have students work in small groups to complete the critical thinking map with partners. Keep in mind that the more students use this tool, the more they will become comfortable with thinking about text in this way.

| A MAP FOR CRITICAL THINKING |
|---|

Name _____ Chapter_____ Date _____

Main Ideas/Lesson:




Other Viewpoints/opinions:




Reader's Conclusion:




Relevance to Today:




**Figure 2.23.  Critical Thinking Map.**

## Strategy 15: Folded File Folders

*Purpose*
Engage in active reading and effective comprehension strategies; access prior knowledge; make predictions and ask questions; read closely to identify main ideas and supporting detail; take notes during reading.

*CCSS Connection*
Standard RL/RI.1: Read closely to determine what the text says explicitly; Standard RL/RI.2: Determine central ideas or themes of a text; Standard RL/RI.8: Delineate and evaluate the argument and specific claims in a text; Standard RL/RI.10: Read and comprehend complex literary and informational text.

*Overview*
The folded file folder is a great during-reading activity to help students with the process of active reading (Lewin, 2003). This strategy plays off the metaphor of "file folders" for the mental categories humans create in their memories. It teaches students important comprehension strategies and can be used with any reading assignment.

*Procedure*
1. Distribute an 8½" × 11" piece of colored paper.

2. Instruct students to fold the paper in half, leaving a one-half- to one-inch tab on top, like a file folder tab.

3. Have students write the subject of the reading assignment on the "file folder tab."

4. After labeling the tab, students open the folded file folder and use the top inside section to tap their prior knowledge of the topic by jotting down anything they already know or think they might know about the topic.

5. Have students preview the reading section for a couple of minutes to gain a sense of what the author may tell them or what they may be learning. Have them record a prediction of what they expect to learn in the middle of the file folder across the center fold. As an alternative to this step, have students write a focus question they will need to answer about the topic.

6. Next, students read the assignment, individually or in pairs.

7. As students read, they use the bottom half of the file folder to write down new information they are gaining from the reading. This method of tak-

ing notes is more motivating for students than traditional note taking, and, for some, more painless because of the small amount of space to fill with notes.

8. As an optional step, for visual learners, have students draw a picture on the back related to the reading material. Ask them to write a caption beneath it.

## Strategy 16: Directed Reading and Thinking Activity (DRTA)

*Purpose*

Access prior knowledge and make predictions; engage in effective comprehension strategies; read independently; analyze text features.

*CCSS Connection*

Standard RL/RI.1: Read closely to determine what the text says explicitly; Standard RL/RI.2: Determine central ideas or themes of a text; Standard RL/RI.5: Analyze the structure of texts; Standard RL/RI.8: Delineate and evaluate the argument and specific claims in a text; Standard RL/RI.10: Read and comprehend complex literary and informational text.

*Overview*

The DRTA method works to help students make predictions about what they are going to be reading (Stauffer, 1969). It also models how good readers operate and provides students with some insights on how to read independently.

*Procedure*

Introduce the activity to students by telling them that this strategy will help them to focus on what the author is telling them by previewing the topic sentences, subheadings, illustrations, and charts. They will make predictions about what the reading passage is about, read to see if their ideas are correct, and change the predictions made if necessary. Thus, it helps them become active readers. Have students make a chart with three columns or boxes, or use the one in figure 2.24.

1. Students begin by previewing what they will read. They should look at the title, subheadings, and illustrations and make some predictions. For example, "This article is about the history of the railroad system and how important it is in America today." Next, they should make a couple of predictions and write them in the preview column.

| Preview | Take Notes | Review |
|---------|-----------|--------|
|         |           |        |

**Figure 2.24. DRTA.**

2. Have students read the passage and take notes in the "Take Notes" column. They should look for evidence to support their predictions. Tell students that if they realize their predictions were wrong, they should cross them off. They should focus on writing down facts and evidence from the passage.

3. After students have finished reading, ask them to look at the predictions they made again. Have them find evidence that supports the predictions and list it in the "Take Notes" column also.

4. Ask students to focus on remembering the important information from the reading selection: "Can you close your eyes and think of the main points? Write down the main points and important details in the Review column." For example, a student might write, "I think I understand the main points. The article discusses the history of the Transcontinental Railroad and how it came to be what it is today. It has become a vital part of American culture as well as a major method of transportation."

## Strategy 17: Discussion Web

*Purpose*

Engage in active reading of text; participate in collaborative discussions about reading of text; identify and discuss themes and ideas from the text; cite textual evidence.

*CCSS Connection*

Standard RL/RI.1: Read closely to determine what the text says explicitly; Standard RL/RI.2: Determine central ideas or themes of a text and analyze their development; Standard RL/RI.8: Delineate and evaluate the argument and specific claims in a text; Standard RL/RI.9: Analyze how two or more texts address similar themes or topics; Standard SL.1: Prepare for and participate effectively in a range of conversations and collaborations.

*Overview*

The discussion web is a during-reading activity that helps students organize their thoughts, focus on the material, and check their understanding (Alvermann, 1991). This strategy is based on McTighe and Lyman's (1988) think-pair-share discussion process.

*Procedure*

1. Present an essential question or controversial statement about the reading selection; for example, "Should scientists clone human beings?" Or, "Should the United States have bombed Hiroshima and Nagasaki?" Or, "Should the US government repeal the Patriot Act?" Give students a copy of the discussion web (figure 2.25). The chart has a "Yes" on one side and a "No" on the other.

2. Have students mark the text or use sticky notes while they are reading to find possible yes or no reasons and evidence for their answer. Tell them they should look for some of both.

3. Have students complete the discussion web individually or with partners. Their writing about the topic while creating the chart allows them to more deeply process the material.

4. Have the whole class, small groups, or pairs discuss the chart and any disagreements they may have with the information written on charts. They should attempt to develop consensus, write a conclusion in the "Conclusion" box and then report to the whole class. As an alternative, you can have students write and present their own conclusions.

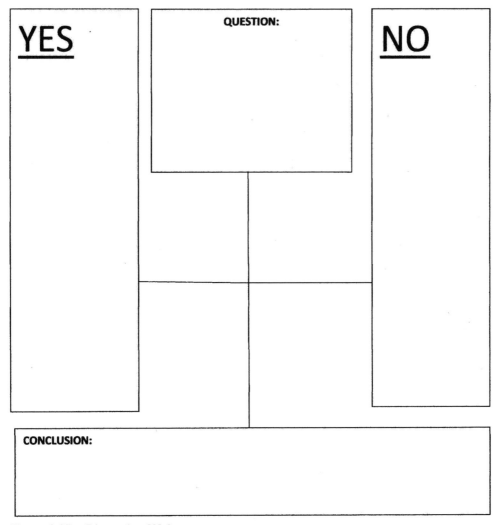

**Figure 2.25.   Discussion Web.**

PART TWO

## Strategy 18: SQ3R

*Purpose*
Read and comprehend complex text; analyze text features; read carefully and monitor comprehension; ask questions and clarify information while reading.

*CCSS Connection*
Standard RL/RI.1: Read closely to determine what the text says explicitly; Standard RL/RI.2: Determine central ideas or themes of a text; Standard RL/RI.5: Analyze the structure of texts; Standard RL/RI.8: Delineate and evaluate the argument and specific claims in a text; Standard RL/RI.10: Read and comprehend complex literary and informational text.

*Overview*
SQ3R is a well-known strategy for reading, note taking, and studying. It can help increase reading comprehension and can be used with any chapter or section from a content-area textbook (Robinson, 1961). The acronym stands for "survey, question, read, review, recite."

*Procedure*
1. Survey: Have students preview the entire passage or chapter, reading the first and last paragraphs and looking at titles, pictures, graphics, bold or italicized words, charts, and maps. They should get a general idea and sense of the content of the reading passage.

2. Question: Ask students to begin reading the text and write down a series of questions as they read. If there are titles and subtitles, turn them into answers. For example, if the title is "The Effects of Malnutrition," change it to "What are the effects of malnutrition?" If the title is "Rosa Parks, Famous American Heroine," change it to "Who was Rosa Parks and why is she famous?"

3. Read: Have students read the passage individually or in pairs. While they are reading, they should write out answers to the questions they previously wrote.

4. Review: Following reading, have students go back over their notes, looking at the questions and answers. They should also review key passages and finish answering any questions that are uncompleted.

5. Recite: Students should now use their new knowledge by discussing with others, explaining to the class, sharing the ideas, and presenting their questions and answers. They can also perform or act out something from

90

the reading and use the information to show what they have learned. Another way to review is to have students look only at the questions they wrote, and then recite the answers from memory.

## Strategy 19: Think-Alouds

*Purpose*

Monitor comprehension during reading; identify and use effective strategies while reading to improve comprehension; use strategies to identify the meaning of unfamiliar words; ask questions during reading to clarify understanding.

*CCSS Connection*

Standard RL/RI.1: Read closely to determine what the text says explicitly; Standard RL/RI.2: Determine central ideas or themes of a text and analyze their development; Standard RL/RI.4: Interpret words and phrases as they are used in a text; Standard RL/RI.5: Analyze the structure of texts.

*Overview*

One of the best strategies for teaching students to engage in active reading methods is the use of think-alouds (Davey, 1983). This strategy helps students understand the kind of thinking that is required during reading. The teacher engages in a process of modeling his thinking process by explaining thoughts as he processes information. Students observe how the teacher constructs meaning, encounters unfamiliar or challenging words, dialogues with the author, asks questions, and uses fix-up strategies to address comprehension problems encountered. Struggling readers often don't know how to monitor and adjust their thinking when they encounter new text; this method helps them understand the process that good readers use.

*Procedure*

1. Explain the complex thinking involved in reading new material and how good readers ask themselves questions to help understand what they are reading.

2. Use a passage from a textbook, article, or other material that you will read aloud. Use shorter passages to start out with. Mark your copy of the text for passages the student might have difficulty with, challenging terminology or vocabulary, and points of possible confusion. Write out questions you can ask yourself that will show students what you are thinking as you struggle to understand the text.

3. Have students follow along with you, reading the passage silently as you read it aloud. While reading, verbalize your thinking, state the questions that you have developed (plus additional ones that come into your mind), and explain the process that you are using to understand the text. For example: "Why does the passage begin with a question?" "What might this section heading mean?" "What does the author mean when he uses the phrase . . . ?" "I predict the author is going to give an example in the next paragraph." "What does the term 'kinetic energy' mean? I know that kinetic is related to 'kinesthetic' and has something to do with movement." "I didn't understand this paragraph very well, so I'm going to go back and read it again."

4. Try to model all of the following different reading strategies for students as you are reading:

    a. Making predictions and hypotheses: "I'll bet the author is going to compare this with . . ."

    b. Describing the mental pictures you get: "When the author talks about vegetables, I picture . . ."

    c. Showing your connections to prior knowledge: "I know from studying nutrition that saturated fats are the bad kinds of fat."

    d. Creating comparisons and analogies: "The description of clogged arteries reminds me of a traffic jam."

    e. Showing breakdowns in comprehension and use of fix-up strategies: "Maybe if I reread this section, I'll be able to figure out the meaning of that word."

5. Once you have demonstrated the think-aloud process a couple of times, have students work with partners to practice doing think-alouds with short passages of text. You might also ask for student volunteers to demonstrate think-alouds with short passages for the whole class. Ask students to assess themselves on how they are doing with think-alouds over time. Continue to revisit the strategy so that these methods of active reading become ones that students will use whenever they are reading.

## Strategy 20: Jigsaw

*Purpose*
    Use effective strategies for reading and comprehending text; read closely to comprehend text; collaborate with others in making meaning from text.

*CCSS Connection*

Standard RL/RI.1: Read closely to determine what the text says explicitly; Standard RL/RI.2: Determine central ideas or themes of a text and analyze their development; Standard RL/RI.4: Interpret words and phrases as they are used in a text; Standard RL/RI.5: Analyze the structure of texts; Standard SL.1: Prepare for and participate effectively in a range of conversations and collaborations.

*Overview*

The jigsaw strategy is a great cooperative learning strategy appropriate for material that can be divided into sections or subunits. It allows students to be both learner and teacher of the material. This description of the jigsaw and the example here come from Aronson (2013).

*Procedure*

1. Divide the class up into five- or six-person jigsaw groups. Mixed ability groups work well. Identify one student from each group as the leader.

2. Divide the day's lesson into five to six segments. For example, history students are learning about Eleanor Roosevelt, so you might divide a short biography of her into stand-alone segments on: her childhood, her family life with Franklin and their children, her life after Franklin contracted polio, her work in the White House as First Lady, and her life and work after Franklin's death.

3. Assign each student in each group to learn one segment, making sure students have access only to their own segment.

4. Give students time to read over their segment at least twice and review to make sure they understand it.

5. Have students form temporary "expert groups" by having one student from each jigsaw group join other students assigned to that same segment. Give students in these expert groups time to discuss the main points and summarize their segment and to prepare for the presentations they will make when they go back to their jigsaw group.

6. Have all students return to their jigsaw groups.

7. Require each student to present her or his segment to the group. Encourage others in the group to ask questions and prompt discussion about the material.

8. The teacher should move among the groups, observing the process and giving students suggestions. Watch for signs that the group is not following the jigsaw process. Group leaders should be instructed to facilitate and monitor the process in their own groups.

9. At the end of the session, quiz students on the material or use some other culminating activity that provides accountability for each group.

## Strategy 21: Bookmarks

*Purpose*

Make connections and ask questions to aid reading comprehension; create visual representations of ideas and themes in the text; identify main ideas and supporting details.

*CCSS Connection*

Standard RL/RI.1: Read closely to determine what the text says explicitly; Standard RL/RI.2: Determine central ideas and themes of a text.

*Overview*

This strategy involves students in creating a bookmark for keeping their place during the reading of a novel, textbook, or other material. Students fold a piece of paper into thirds and use the bookmark to write and illustrate their thoughts (connecting, questioning, visualizing, etc.). The strategy comes from Carol Porter and Janell Cleland (1995).

*Procedure*

1. Use an overhead transparency to model for students what the bookmark might look like.

2. Give students specific directions for what to do on each part of the bookmark. For example, one side could include a visual, diagram, or picture. Another might have personal connections the reader is making. You can have students do any of the following, or whatever is appropriate to the particular type of material students are reading: make personal responses, jot down important passages or quotes, write questions about the material, list facts or statistics, note puzzling or confusing information.

3. Begin by having students practice. Have everyone read one page of the reading assignment and complete a bookmark using the directions you provided, and have students compare and give examples of what they wrote.

4. After the reading is finished and bookmarks are complete, have students use their bookmarks to have discussion in small groups or with the whole class.

## Strategy 22: Double Entry Journal

*Purpose*

Engage in active reading strategies in order to comprehend text; identify main ideas and supporting detail; cite textual evidence; summarize information from the text; make personal connections to ideas and themes.

*CCSS Connection*

Standard RL/RI.1: Read closely to determine what the text says explicitly; Standard RL/RI.2: Determine central ideas or themes of a text.

*Overview*

This strategy is similar to many of the other reading strategies presented in this section in that it provides a way to help students engage in active reading. Similar to the Cornell notes, two-column notes, and other strategies, students take notes on their reading in two columns (see figure 2.26).

*Procedure*

1. Have students draw a line down the center of the page (or use figure 2.26).

2. Have them label the first column "Summary." This is where they will summarize main ideas and important information from the text.

3. Have them label the other column "Notes and Responses." Here they will write down their own thoughts, responses, opinions, questions, and personal reactions, and make note of any confusing information.

4. Begin by using a short selection on the overhead to model the process. Write a quick summary in column one. Write down your thoughts and responses in column two and think aloud so students can see how the process should work.

5. You might next have students practice independently with another short piece of text to monitor and make sure they understand how to do this process.

6. Finally, have students independently complete a double entry journal while completing a reading assignment on their own.

PART TWO

This strategy can be used over a period of time (i.e., throughout reading of several textbook chapters, or a class novel). In this case, have students do all the double entry journals in a spiral notebook that they can turn in to you periodically for evaluation.

| Summary | Notes and Responses |
|---------|---------------------|
|         |                     |

**Figure 2.26.  Double Entry Journal.**

## Strategy 23: Visualizing: Sketching Characters and Historical Figures

*Purpose*

Create visual images based on ideas and information in text; cite textual evidence.

*CCSS Connection*

Standard RI.1: Read closely to determine what the text says explicitly; Standard RI.2: Determine central ideas of a text.

*Overview*

We know that one of the things good readers do as they are reading is visualize, creating pictures in their heads as they are reading. We also know that struggling readers have a great deal of difficulty visualizing what they are reading. Sketching characters and historical figures is a visualization activity that can be used with informational text. It requires students to use the text to create visual images of the people or historical figures based on quotes from the text (Strategic Literacy Initiative, 2004).

*Procedure*

1. During a reading assignment, ask students to identify a historical figure, character, or type of person that they want to focus on.

2. Ask students to identify and write down quotes that help readers visualize the person and the setting they inhabit. Ask them to write down seven to ten quotes that describe the character or figure or his surroundings. You can begin this process by modeling the identification of a couple of quotes.

3. Have students work in groups of four as arranged by the character chosen. Ask students to share their quotes with the group and add quotes to their own lists. Direct students to discuss how the character or figure might look based on the selected quotes.

4. Have students individually draw a picture or illustration of their character and annotate the page with some of the quotes they have selected. These illustrations can then be displayed around the classroom.

## Strategy 24: Visualizing: Illustrated Passages

*Purpose*
   Create visual images based on ideas and information in text; cite textual evidence.

*CCSS Connection*
   Standard RI.1: Read closely to determine what the text says explicitly; Standard RI.2: Determine central ideas of a text.

*Overview*

   This strategy is another example of a visualization activity similar to sketching characters, except that illustrated passages helps students understand complex graphics or images in math, science, or technical areas. It involves students in reading the text and then working in groups to create an illustration, series of illustrations, or storyboard. The illustration will create a concrete image or visual that represents an abstract concept (for example, the laws of thermodynamics), a complex process, or powerful imagery (Strategic Literacy Initiative, 2004). For different subject areas, students might create illustrations to depict trench warfare, the concept of pi, the force of gravity, or a line drive to center field.

*Procedure*

   Follow the same procedure as the description in Strategy 23 for sketching characters and historical figures. Have students identify quotes from the reading material that help them to visualize the concept. Individual students can create their own illustration, or groups can choose sections of the text and create a series of illustrations or a storyboard that will illustrate the concept or process. Have each group assemble the final product to display in the classroom.

## Strategy 25: Who's on First?

*Purpose*
   Monitor comprehension during reading; preview and access prior knowledge; make predictions and ask questions during reading; summarize information from text.

> *CCSS Connection*
> Standard RL/RI.1: Read closely to determine what the text says explicitly; Standard RL/RI.2: Determine central ideas or themes of a text; Standard RL/RI.4: Interpret words and phrases as they are used in text; Standard RL/RI.10: Read and comprehend complex literary and informational texts.

*Overview*

A fun strategy to use with students is Who's on First? This strategy was designed by Betty Jean Shoemaker. An earlier version was included in the book *Great Performances: Creating Classroom-Based Assessment Tasks* (Lewin and Shoemaker, 1998). Who's on First? can be done in electronic format or done on paper. Obviously, the strategy plays upon a baseball metaphor. For the particular reading assignment, choose six different stopping points in the reading (in the dugout, up to bat, at first base, at second base, at third base, and home plate). At each point, students respond to specific prompts provided by the teacher. This helps them monitor their comprehension as they are reading.

*Procedure*

Copy and enlarge the Who's on First? worksheet (figure 2.27) or have students draw a large baseball diamond. Explain how students will use the baseball diamond to track their comprehension as they go. The teacher will need to write questions or prompts for each of the six stopping points:

- In the dugout: After reading the title and previewing the reading selection write down what you think you know about the author or topic of the reading (prior knowledge).

- Up to bat: After reading the first paragraph, make a prediction about what the rest of the reading is about or what you think will happen or be discussed.

- On first base: About one-quarter of the way through, respond to a question about the characters or the content.

- On second base: About halfway through, respond to a question about the setting, characters, or organization.

- On third base: About three-quarters of the way through, respond to a prompt about the plot, conflict, comparisons used, or some aspect of the content.

PART TWO

- Home plate: At the end of the reading, wrap up your understanding in the middle of the diamond by writing a summary of the reading selection.

As an option, have students label the border of the page as "The Stands" and use this space to record vocabulary they are unfamiliar with or terminology that is confusing. Students can complete this process independently or in small groups.

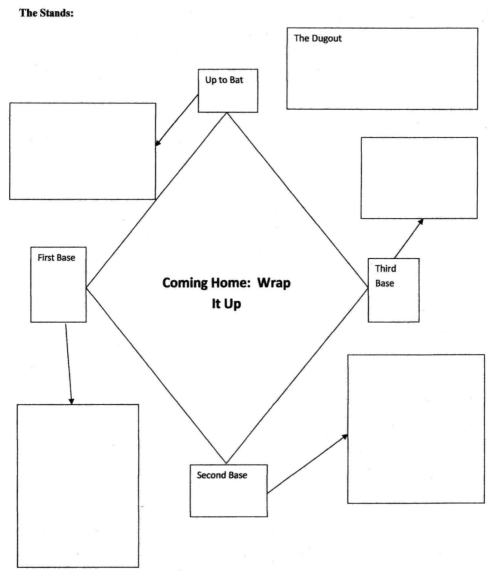

**The Stands:**

The Dugout

Up to Bat

First Base

**Coming Home: Wrap It Up**

Third Base

Second Base

**Figure 2.27. Who's on First? (Reprinted with the permission of Betty Jean Shoemaker.)**

## Strategy 26: Open Mind

*Purpose*

Read and comprehend textual material; engage in critical thinking; make interpretations and inferences; cite textual evidence; create visual representations of text.

*CCSS Connection*

Standard RL/RI.1: Read closely to determine what the text says explicitly; Standard RL/RI.2: Determine central ideas or themes of a text; Standard RL/RI.3: Analyze how and why individuals, events, and ideas develop and interact.

*Overview*

Open mind is an activity that allows students to think critically about a character in a story or work of literature or history. (It can also be completed for a concept or principle rather than a person.) It can be done during or immediately after the reading of a story or reading selection. The open mind handout is an outline form of a human head. Lewin (2003) attributes the open mind to teacher Grace Herr. (It was also used for many years by the state of Oregon in their reading assessment materials.)

*Procedure*

Use the open mind handout (figure 2.28) and have students draw symbols and write words and phrases from the text that represent what a character or figure is thinking or feeling. They can also draw pictures and symbols. When using the open mind with informational text, you can ask students to write more objective biographical or factual information outside the outline of the character's mind. Students can also accessorize their character with hair and facial features, write a title at the top of the page, and include lines from the text as well as symbols to show what the character's values are and how the character perceives himself. Encourage students to use shapes, color, and words symbolically. As another option, you can also include speech bubbles and thought bubbles attached to the open mind outline.

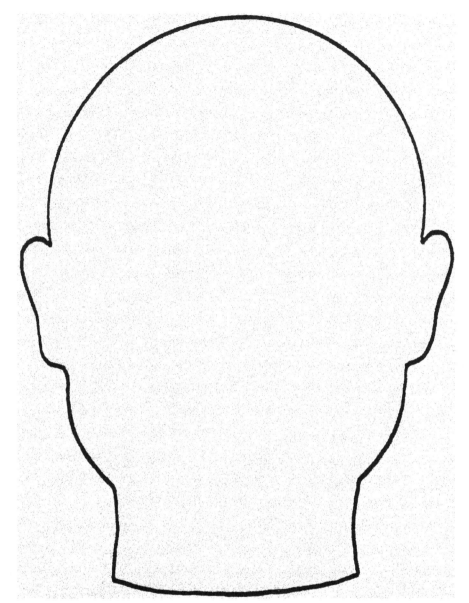

**Figure 2.28.   The Open Mind.**

## Strategy 27: Say Something

*Purpose*

Engage in active reading to promote comprehension; make predictions, ask questions, monitor comprehension, make connections, and clarify understanding of ideas in text; use rereading and clarifying ideas as an effective reading strategy; clarify comprehension through collaborative discussions with others.

*CCSS Connection*

Standard RL/RI.1: Read closely to determine what the text says explicitly; Standard RL/RI.2: Determine central ideas or themes of a text; Standard SL.1: Prepare for and participate effectively in a range of conversations.

*Overview*

Readers who struggle often don't view reading as an active process and as a result, they can't construct meaning from the text. Say Something is a during-reading strategy that helps students make predictions, ask questions, monitor their comprehension, use fix-up strategies, clarify parts that are confusing, comment on their understanding, and make connections. The strategy interrupts a student's reading, giving her a chance to think about what she is reading and encourages conversation (Beers, 2003). Students work in groups of two or three and take turns reading a portion of the text out loud, occasionally pausing to "say something" about what has been read. The other members of the group offer a response to what was said.

*Procedure*

1. Use a short piece of text to model the strategy for students.

2. Explain the strategy and procedure and assign a certain number of paragraphs to read before they stop to say something. Tell them they should make a prediction, ask a question, clarify something they misunderstood, or make a comment or a connection. Two or three paragraphs are recommended.

3. Have each partner or member of the group offer a response to what was said and help answer any questions that may come up.

4. Give students stem starters such as the ones below that they can use to "say something."

Here are some sample stem starters to use for say something comments:

- Make a prediction:
  - I predict that . . .
  - I bet that . . .
  - I think that . . .
  - Since this happened, I bet the next thing that will happen is . . .
  - Reading this part makes me think that _____ is about to happen.
  - I wonder if . . .
- Clarify something:
  - Oh, I get it . . .
  - Now I understand . . .
  - This makes sense now . . .
  - No, I think it means . . .
  - I agree with you. This means . . .
  - At first I thought _____ but now I think . . .
  - This part is really saying . . .
- Make a connection:
  - This reminds me of . . .
  - This part is like . . .
  - This is similar to . . .
  - The differences are . . .
  - I have also experienced this . . .
  - I never have experienced this . . .
- Ask a question:
  - Why did . . . ?
  - What's this part about?
  - How is this _____ like this _____?
  - What would happen if . . . ?
  - Why . . . ?

- ◦ Who is . . . ?

- ◦ What does this section mean?

- ◦ Do you think that . . . ?

- ◦ I don't get this part here . . .

- Make a comment:

  - ◦ This is good because . . .

  - ◦ This is hard because . . .

  - ◦ This is confusing because . . .

  - ◦ I like the part where . . .

  - ◦ I don't like this part because . . .

  - ◦ My favorite part so far is . . .

  - ◦ I think that . . .

## Strategy 28: Graphic Organizers

*Purpose*

Use a visual format to explain, review, and clarify information from text; identify relationships among ideas; recognize main ideas and supporting details; cite textual evidence.

*CCSS Connection*

Standard RL/RI.1: Read closely to determine what the text says explicitly; Standard RL/RI.2: Determine central ideas or themes of a text; Standard RL/RI.10: Read and comprehend complex literary and informational texts.

*Overview*

Graphic organizers are one of the most powerful literacy and comprehension tools that teachers can use. In my files I keep a whole collection of graphic organizer templates. I have included graphic organizers here among the during-reading strategies, although they can also be used when students are in the postreading stage. They provide a visual and holistic representation of facts and concepts and their relationships by providing a visual frame. Students can use them to display abstract information in concrete form, show the relationship among facts and concepts, organize ideas, and relate new information to prior knowledge. Graphic organizers are especially useful for those students who tend to be more visual learners. Here are some ways in which graphic organizers can be used:

- Have students prepare a graphic organizer to present to the class to demonstrate their understanding of concepts.

- Have students use a graphic organizer to explain information learned from a reading selection, film, book, or speech.

- Have students work in cooperative groups to complete graphic organizers.

- Have students make their own graphic organizers to demonstrate their understanding.

- Use a graphic organizer in place of test questions.

- Have students use a graphic organizer to take notes.

*Procedure*

1. Present or display the particular graphic organizer you want students to complete and discuss how it can be used to organize information. Describe its purpose and form. Some common forms include Venn diagrams used for comparison, overlapping circles, flowcharts, concept charts, and classification charts.

2. Give students an example of how the graphic organizer might be used with material students already know.

3. Assign students to use the graphic organizer to outline or visually present information from a reading passage or lecture.

4. Have students read the material individually or in pairs and complete the graphic organizer as they read.

Figure 2.29 shows an example of a graphic organizer.

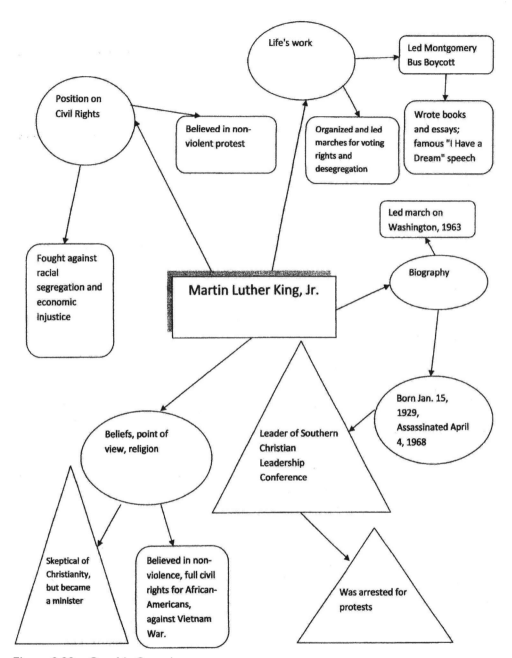

**Figure 2.29. Graphic Organizer.**

# Postreading Strategies

Many teachers typically rely on some form of questioning of students as their only postreading strategy. Some limit their students to the end-of-chapter review questions or some other form of discussion questions or assessment following the reading. Often, the questions used do not extend much beyond the literal level of comprehension. However, there are many highly effective postreading strategies that we can use to engage students with the material they have read. Many of them push students toward higher levels of thinking as well: to extend their understanding, synthesize ideas, apply the material learned to other situations, or make comparisons. Several of these strategies also are engaging because they stimulate students' thinking and imagination or involve students in cooperative learning groups. These strategies will help your students to better learn and retain the important content knowledge and skills you want them to have.

## Strategy 1: Save the Last Word for Me

*Purpose*

Cite textual evidence; make interpretations; identify themes and ideas in text; use collaborative discussions with others as a comprehension strategy.

*CCSS Connection*

Standard RL/RI.1: Read closely to determine what the text says explicitly; Standard RL/RI.2: Determine central ideas or themes of a text; Standard RL/RI.8: Delineate and evaluate the argument and specific claims in a text; Standard SL.1: Prepare for and participate effectively in a range of conversations.

*Overview*

This postreading strategy, which comes from Rasinski and Padak (1996), gives students an opportunity to practice with new material they have learned and enhance their understanding through group interaction and collaborative problem solving.

*Procedure*

During their reading of the text, ask students to search for important statements or quotes. Give students five note cards each and have them write one statement on each card. The statements should be ones that cause some reaction or have some significance rather than just random excerpts. On the back of each card, the student writes down either a question or a reaction to the statement on the front. These comments might be interesting points, questions, or things they do not understand. The writing students do here helps increase comprehension of the reading material. Next, arrange students into groups of four and follow this process:

- Each student will read one statement or question from one of the cards.

- Taking turns, every other student in the group will respond with an answer or comment.

- After each student has spoken and commented, the student who wrote the question or comment has the "last word," explaining its significance or drawing a conclusion.

I strongly recommend having one group model the process for the class before all the groups begin the process. Monitor the groups to make sure that they are following the process; otherwise, you end up with general small group discussion. Make sure that the student presenting the statement from her card understands that she cannot speak again until all the other group members have made their comments and given their answers. This strategy allows students to find key ideas and information from the reading material and process it rather than simply reading or being told what is important. As a possible follow-up or closure activity, have each group choose the two most significant statements and share them with the whole class.

**Strategy 2: Dialectic Notebook**

*Purpose*
   Read and comprehend written text; evaluate and interpret themes and ideas; elaborate and expand on ideas and reactions; summarize information from text; write to share ideas with others.

*CCSS Connection*
   Standard RL/RI.1: Read closely to determine what the text says explicitly; Standard RL/RI.2: Determine central ideas or themes of a text; Standard RL/RI.8: Delineate and evaluate the argument and specific claims in a text; Standard SL.1: Prepare for and participate effectively in a range of conversations; Standard W.9: Draw evidence from literary or informational text to support analysis and reflection.

*Overview*
   This strategy is often called by many other names, including the written conversation and dialogue journal. The dialectic notebook process should be used after students have read the particular work or reading material or studied the particular class content. It is a conversation in writing between two people. Dialectic notebook is an excellent writing-to-learn activity as well as a good postreading strategy that

helps students to process and think about the subject matter in any lesson or reading assignment. Using the text, document, or subject of analysis, each person reads a passage, and then writes down her thoughts and ideas (or have students write down a quote from the text, followed by their comment about it). Next, students exchange papers with partners and read what their partners wrote. This is followed by writing a response to their partners, passing the papers back, reading again, and so on. During the exchange, ideally partners will attempt to challenge each other to do some more elaborate thinking, the goal being to increase the depth of reading comprehension and improve thinking skills.

The dialectic notebook is useful for examining and exploring a literary work, prose, poetry, speeches, political cartoons, editorials, articles, song lyrics, websites, problem-solving procedures, pieces of art, photographs, foreign language dialogues, math problems, and so on. Basically, it can be used for any material you ask students to read and think about.

*Procedure*

1. Ask students to reread and select a passage that has significance, meaning, or some impact on them, one that caused them to think or react.

2. Each student copies down the passage at the top of the paper.

3. Next, the students will write a response below the passage, including their thoughts, feelings, ideas, reactions, questions, and points of confusion.

4. Students then exchange papers with their partners, read what their partner has written, and respond to their partner's thoughts on the paper, below the student's own writing.

5. Students will then pass back the papers and again write in response to their partner. Students are essentially having a conversation in writing. They can pass the papers back and forth several times but it is best to stop it before the conversation runs out or degenerates into unproductive comments.

I would recommend establishing clear guidelines for students. Tell them ahead of time how long they have to write; generally a five-minute time limit before passing the paper is adequate. Also, let students know that your expectation is that all writing will remain on topic and not drift into idle conversation or extraneous comments on another subject (such as "Are you going to the game on Friday?"). Follow up by asking some pairs of students to share their dialectic notebooks by reading their conversation aloud for the class. Showing students a model of a good dialectic notebook ahead of time is also recommended.

## Strategy 3: Word Sorts or Concept Formation Activity

*Purpose*
Use deductive thinking to analyze concepts; classify ideas and concepts; identify key relationships among concepts; participate effectively in collaborative discussion.

*CCSS Connection*
Standard SL.1: Prepare for and participate effectively in a range of conversations and collaborations.

*Overview*

The word sort (Gillet & Kita, 1979; Gillet & Temple, 1983) is a classification or categorization activity, also called concept formation activity, which engages students in higher-order thinking skills and requires the use of deductive thinking. Students must recognize the semantic and conceptual relationships among key concepts. Word sorts can be either "open sort" or "closed sort." In an open sort, students group the words and create labels for the categories. In a closed sort, the teacher provides the categories. I prefer the open sort activity because it requires students to use more higher-level reasoning and deduction skills. This activity works particularly well at the end of a unit or the conclusion of a reading activity.

*Procedure*

1. Identify a number of different terms, concepts, and related words. Make a random list of these words for students on a handout or the chalkboard. They can also be written on strips of construction paper or note cards, but you will need several sets of the words.

2. Place students in groups of four to complete the activity.

3. Instruct the groups to categorize the terms into at least three and not more than six groups. They must follow these rules:

   a. Each category must have a name or label that is descriptive of all the items in that group.

   b. All the categories must have more than one term or concept in them (no single-word categories).

  c. No group may be labeled "miscellaneous" or "other."

  d. All the concepts must be included—no words may be left out.

4. After the groups have had time to classify the terms, have each one explain to the class their rationale and thinking for the categories and identify similarities and differences between the different groups. If you have the terms on strips of paper or note cards, each group can glue or tape them to poster board and then hang them up for display and review.

This strategy is an excellent way for students to review all the major concepts in a unit or reading assignment prior to a test or quiz. Figure 2.30 shows some examples of concept groups that could be used for the activity, some of which have the categories included.

**Boston Tea Party**:

Stamp Act

"No taxation without representation"

Boston

Tea tax

Loyalists

King

Colonists

Sons of Liberty

British Parliament

India

British patriots

Samuel Adams

Ship

(Possible groupings: Colonists, Boston Tea Party, British, Groups of People)

**Food Groups**:

| | | |
|---|---|---|
| Oil | Celery | Fats |
| Cheese | Liver | Cucumber |
| Watermelon | Beans | Fruit Juice |
| Corn | Protein | Honey |
| Fish | Carbohydrates | Bread |
| Rice | Minerals | Nuts |
| Peas | Salt | Oranges |
| Carrots | Eggs | Water Fried Foods |
| Tomatoes | Cereals | Vitamins |
| Soup | Peas | Cabbage |
| Apples | Broccoli | Meat |
| Milk | Poultry | Butter |

(Possible Categories: Carbohydrates, Fats, Proteins, Vitamins, Minerals, Water-Based Foods)

**Geometric Shapes**:

| | | |
|---|---|---|
| Diagonals | Circle | Radius |
| Triangle | Prism | Symmetry |
| Sphere | Volume | Intersecting |
| Length | Adjacent | Congruent |
| Parallel | Lines | Area |
| Perpendicular | Hexagon | Pyramid |
| Perimeter | Cone | Rhombus |
| Cube | Circumference | Rays |
| Square | Opposite points | Bisector |
| Vertices | Parallelogram | Angles |
| Edges | Cylinder | Similar |

(Possible categories: Parts of shapes, plane figures, solid figures, measures, relations)

**Biomes**:

| | | |
|---|---|---|
| Permafrost | Aloe Plants | Phytoplankton |
| Savannas | Lichen | Deciduous |
| Sahara | Giraffes | Freshwater |
| North Pole | Camels | Canopy |
| Grasses | Conifers | Estuary |
| Cactus | Taiga | Tropical |
| Zebras | Marine | |

**Figure 2.30. Possible Word Sorts.**

PART TWO

## Strategy 4: Fishbowl

*Purpose*
   Participate effectively in collaborative discussion; identify main ideas and supporting details from visual or written text; identify and discuss themes and ideas from visual or written text; engage in higher-level thinking; make interpretations and inferences about events and ideas; use effective listening skills.

*CCSS Connection*
   Standard RL/RI.2: Determine central ideas or themes of a text; Standard RL/RI.3: Analyze how and why individuals, events, and ideas develop and interact; Standard SL.1: Prepare for and participate effectively in a range of conversations and collaborations; Standard SL.2: Integrate and evaluate information presented in diverse media and formats; Standard SL.4: Present information, findings, and supporting evidence such that listeners can follow the line of reasoning.

*Overview*
   The fishbowl is an effective postreading and group discussion strategy that allows for full participation from every student. Although it is highly structured and is facilitated by the teacher, the teacher does not participate in the discussion. The responsibility for speaking rests entirely with students.

*Procedure*
   1. After students have read the particular assignment, which may be a magazine article, editorial, book, or even a movie, choose a focal point, either a statement or a discussion about the reading assignment that students have completed. It should be a controversial statement or a higher-level question that will encourage students to discuss and share ideas. (For example: "Is the portrayal of President Abraham Lincoln in Spielberg's movie historically accurate to the real Lincoln based on our study of history?")

   2. Place chairs or student desks into two circles, an inner circle facing inward and an outer circle also facing inward. Ask for volunteers or assign students to take seats in the inner circle. Have the remaining students take seats in the outer circle. Limit the inner group to six or eight students to allow everyone adequate chance to participate.

   3. Once the teacher has presented the focal point, it is the responsibility of the inner group to sustain the dialogue for a given time period. I recommend using a shorter time period, such as five minutes, for groups using

the strategy for the first time. With more practice, the amount of time may be increased.

4. The outer circle should listen carefully or take notes on the discussion but they may not interrupt the discussion taking place. When the first discussion finishes, a second group of students takes the inner seats and continues the discussion. Continue the process until all students have had the opportunity to participate in the inner circle.

5. As a follow-up activity, have the whole class debrief on the fishbowl discussions. Give each student a chance to comment on what he or she heard or allow for some general discussion. Students can also be asked individually to write a summary on the discussion or an explanation of what they learned during the activity.

## Strategy 5: Socratic Seminar

*Purpose*
   Participate effectively in collaborative discussion; identify main ideas and supporting details from visual or written text; identify and discuss themes and ideas from visual or written text; engage in higher-level thinking; make interpretations and inferences about events and ideas; summarize information; use effective listening skills.

*CCSS Connection*
   Standard RL/RI.2: Determine central ideas or themes of a text; Standard RL/RI.3: Analyze how and why individuals, events, and ideas develop and interact; Standard SL.1: Prepare for and participate effectively in a range of conversations and collaborations; Standard SL.2: Integrate and evaluate information presented in diverse media and formats; Standard SL.4: Present information, findings, and supporting evidence such that listeners can follow the line of reasoning.

*Overview*
   Socratic seminar, similar to fishbowl, is a discussion format done in whole or small group through collaborative, open-ended dialogue about a topic of text. It is based on the pedagogy of Socrates, who believed in the power of questioning and inquiry as being more valuable than debate. Israel (2002) sums up the process and value of Socratic seminar as "a formal discussion, based on a text, in which the leader asks open-ended questions. Within the context of the discussion, students listen closely to the comments of others, thinking critically for themselves, and articulate

their own thoughts and their responses to the thoughts of others. They learn to work cooperatively and to question intelligently and civilly" (p. 89). The students who participate in the seminar raise questions and discuss issues related to the topic, analyzing, interpreting, and listening to others' ideas.

The thing I most like about Socratic seminar is that it is the responsibility of students to bring good questions and comments to the discussion and keep it going, rather than the teacher playing the role of facilitator. While the teacher *can* function as a facilitator if necessary, once students have learned how to use this process, the teacher is able to step away and observe from the sidelines. Good discussion depends upon starting with good questions, studying the topic or text carefully, and sharing ideas and responses. The process can also include searching a text for evidence to support the ideas. Perhaps most important, the Socratic seminar is a discussion and not a debate. Follow the steps carefully to successfully conduct a Socratic seminar.

*Procedure*

1. Arrange the classroom in a large circle so that students can look at each other. If the group is too large for one circle, create an inner circle and an outer circle. The students in the inner circle can carry on discussion for a period of time, while the outer circle observes and takes notes. Then have students switch from one circle to the other. I strongly recommend having students in the outer circle take Cornell notes or use some other form of note taking during the inner circle's discussion.

2. Prepare discussion norms for the group to follow such as speaking one at a time, listening carefully, not interrupting or shouting, not conducting side conversations, basing ideas only upon the text or topic, allowing everyone a chance to speak, and so forth.

3. If you are using a specific text students have read as a starting point, prepare several higher-level discussion questions. Questions should lead participants to think in an open-ended way and be at the interpretive or evaluative level rather than literal. An alternative to teacher-written questions is to have each student prepare two questions of his own to bring to the discussion. This requires teaching students the difference between literal, interpretive, and evaluative questions. Students often need practice at first in writing higher-level discussion questions.

4. Introduce the seminar process and purpose to students if they have not used this method before. Review discussion norms and procedures. Remind students that during the seminar their comments should be directed at each other, not at you, the teacher.

5. When the seminar begins, use one of the teacher or student questions to begin the discussion. Groups can often spend quite a bit of time discuss-

ing one question. The teacher may reserve the right to stop the discussion and move the group on to the next question. Use as many questions as you find possible during the allotted time period.

6. If using an inner and outer circle, have the groups switch positions half-way through the allotted time. The inner group carrying on the discussion then steps out to the outer circle while the outer circle group moves in to participate in their own discussion. Students in the outer circle should take notes on the discussion.

7. If the conversation gets off track, refocus students on the question or move on to another question. Some teachers like to use talking chips (students are given a certain number of chips to use) to prevent certain students from dominating the discussion. Encourage those who have not spoken to contribute to the conversation. Some teachers keep a diagram during the seminar that shows names of participants as they are arranged in the circle and then draw lines from one name to another to track which students are contributing to the conversation and how many times.

8. After the seminar, spend some time debriefing the process. Share your observations and ask students to share theirs as well. Finally, have students write a summary of the Socratic seminar to help solidify the discussion in their minds. They can use their notes taken to help them write the summaries. Ask them to include in their summary some evaluation of their own level of participation in the seminar.

## Strategy 6: RAFT

*Purpose*
   Interpret information and make inferences, apply learning from content material to generate an original creation; draw upon content information and textual evidence to compose a new piece of text; use the writing process; consider audience and topic in using an appropriate format for the text.

*CCSS Connection*
   Standard RL/RI.2: Determine central ideas or themes of a text and analyze their development; Standard RL/RI.7: Integrate and evaluate content presented in diverse formats and media; Standard W.3: Write narratives to develop real or imagined experiences or events; Standard W.4: Produce clear and coherent writing; Standard W.5: Develop and strengthen writing as needed; Standard W.9: Draw evidence from literary or informational texts.

PART TWO

*Overview*

RAFT is an excellent postreading strategy as well as a writing activity. It stands for role/audience/format/topic (Santa, 1988). The RAFT strategy provides many options and choices for students, allowing them to extend their learning following a particular unit or reading assignment. The teacher must provide some options for each part of the RAFT. Each student then designs his own personal assignment by choosing from the four lists or options:

- Role: The role or persona the writer takes on; the voice he chooses to write in.

- Audience: The person or group to whom the writer is speaking/writing.

- Format: The form or genre of the writing, which may be a letter, poem, news article, speech, and so forth.

- Topic: The subject of the piece of writing that comes directly from the reading material or reflects the central ideas in the reading.

One of the biggest advantages this strategy provides is that it gives students choices. It allows students to interact with the content in an unusual and creative way. Thus the task becomes differentiated appropriately for each student. This will better motivate students and allow them to use their creativity.

*Procedure*

1. Generate a list of choices for each part of the RAFT. In some cases, students might be able to create their own options. Create several roles, which might be literary characters, historical figures, scientists, or even objects or elements. Choose some possible audiences for the figure to write to. Generate a list of a variety of genres for the "format": for example, letter, brochure, pamphlet, speech, story, set of instructions, telegram, blog, news story, newspaper article, review, Facebook update, diary entry, and so on. Also generate a list of possible topics related to the class content that could serve as the subject of the RAFTs.

2. Provide the class with time to work on the assignments once they have finished the unit or the reading assignment. Check to make sure all students have made their RAFT choices.

3. Once students have written and revised their RAFTs, give them some opportunities to share their pieces with partners, in small groups, or with the whole class. You might want to have students post their RAFTs around the room and have the class do a gallery walk. Figure 2.31 presents an example of a RAFT chart on the topic of radioactivity, which comes from Daniels and Zemelman (2004). Direct students to choose one from each of the four parts.

ROLE:

Antonine Henri Becquerel
Marie Curie
Albert Einstein
mother of a U.S. soldier in 1945
nuclear medicine doctor
home repair company owner
head of Atomic Energy Commission
head of an environmental protection organization

AUDIENCE

Pierre and Marie Curie
Director of Paris Industrial Physics School
President Truman
newspaper readers
medical patients
home owners, potential customers
members of environmental organization
U.S. Senators

FORMAT

personal letter
written request
invitation
formal letter
editorial
brochure
advertisement
speech at a national conference
testimony for senate hearing

TOPIC

The mysteriously ruined film in his desk drawer, and what caused it
Explaining why it's important to use a lab in the school for experiments on radioactivity
How a new, more powerful bomb could be built
Why an A-bomb should or should not have been used on Japan
How lung and heart problems can be diagnosed using radioactive chemicals
Why home owners should use the company to have their basements radon-proofed
Why it's a good idea to build new nuclear-powered electric generators
Why it's not a good idea to build new nuclear-powered electric generators

**Figure 2.31. RAFT Example. (From Harvey Daniels and Steven Zemelman, *Subjects Matter: Every Teacher's Guide to Content-Area Reading*, Copyright © 2004 by Harvey Daniels, Steven Zemelman, and Nancy Steineke. Published by Heinemann, Portsmouth, NH. Reprinted by permission of the publisher. All rights reserved.)**

PART TWO

## Strategy 7: Philosophical Chairs

*Purpose*

Participate effectively in collaborative discussion; identify main ideas and supporting details from visual or written text; identify and discuss themes and ideas from visual or written text; engage in higher-level thinking; make interpretations and inferences about events and ideas; summarize information; use effective listening skills.

*CCSS Connection*

Standard RL/RI.1: Read closely to determine what the text says explicitly; Standard RL/RI.2: Determine central ideas or themes of a text; Standard RL/RI.3: Analyze how and why individuals, events, and ideas develop and interact; Standard SL.1: Prepare for and participate effectively in a range of conversations and collaborations; Standard SL.2: Integrate and evaluate information presented in diverse media and formats; Standard SL.4: Present information, findings, and supporting evidence such that listeners can follow the line of reasoning.

*Overview*

Philosophical chairs is an activity that is designed to encourage students to think critically, discuss, and in some cases write about open-ended or controversial topics. Desks should be arranged in a horseshoe pattern, and students are asked to sit on a side of the room that reflects their position. For example, students who strongly agree with a statement sit on the right side and students who strongly disagree sit on the left. Those undecided or leaning toward one side or the other sit in the chairs between the two sides. As students discuss the topic and express arguments for or against the statement, all students have the option of moving to an undecided position or to the other side to reflect their changing views.

*Procedure*

1. Students read a newspaper article, short story, essay, editorial, or literary selection, taking notes as they read.

2. The teacher will present students with a statement that will elicit thought and discussion and that asks them to respond with their own opinion. For example: use of plastic bags in grocery stores should be banned; nuclear energy is a safe source of energy that should be encouraged; offshore oil drilling should be prohibited in order to protect the ocean's ecosystem; censorship of pieces of music or art is wrong; legalization of drugs would result in less crime; every student has an equal opportunity to succeed in school.

3. Have students place themselves on one side of the room or the other, or in the undecided section.

4. The teacher should function as facilitator or appoint a student facilitator to call upon participants during the discussion. Students must argue the merits of a statement and why they have chosen the position they have. Make sure they understand that they can move to a different side if their position changes.

5. Set some ground rules and time limits for the discussion before it starts (students must listen to others, move quietly, make respectful comments, not interrupt, speak only when called on by the facilitator, etc.). Also, make it clear that you expect that all students will participate in the discussion and share their ideas.

6. Optional approaches: Use a "talking stick" or other object to indicate whose turn it is to speak. Some teachers like to require students to briefly summarize the statement of the previous speaker before they present their own argument. Remind students to criticize the ideas, not the other students. You might also want to model appropriate discussion stems, such as "I disagree with Dustin's position because . . ."

7. After the discussion, ask students to write a short reflection response in which they summarize their position on the topic, including their rationale. They should also write about whether their position changed during the discussion and how their thinking was influenced during the discussion.

## Strategy 8: Asked and Answered

*Purpose*

Engage students in discussion about text; generate questions during reading; check understanding; engage in close reading of text; establish a purpose for reading.

*CCSS Connection*

Standard RL/RI.1: Read closely to determine what the text says explicitly; Standard RL/RI.2: Determine central ideas or themes of a text; Standard RL/RI.3: Analyze how and why individuals, events, and ideas develop and interact over the course of a text; Standard RL/RI.8: Delineate and evaluate the argument and specific claims in a text; Standard RL/RI.10: Read and comprehend complex literary and informational texts; Standard SL.1: Prepare for and participate effectively in a range of conversations and collaborations.

PART TWO

*Overview*

Asked and answered is a strategy that comes from Brunner (2011). It is designed to help students generate questions and to engage in close reading of text. In this strategy students both formulate and provide answers for comprehension questions. They also have the chance to collaborate and discuss the text with each other.

*Procedure*

1. Give students three to five note cards.

2. Assign students to read the text and write three to five questions, one on each card. If you have already taught students about levels of questions, encourage them to ask questions that require comparison, application, analysis, or evaluation. Otherwise, just instruct students to write challenging questions, ones that cannot be answered easily by simply referring to one spot in the text.

3. After students have written their questions, have them form pairs and trade cards.

4. Students then write their answer to the questions on the back of their partner's cards.

5. Next, have students discuss the questions and answers.

6. Next, have students collaborate to generate additional questions and write them on new cards. This encourages a deeper level of reading and thinking about the text.

7. Next, have each pair of students join with another pair to form groups of four. As a group, they should discuss the questions that have been generated.

## Strategy 9: Pinwheels

*Purpose*

Participate effectively in collaborative discussion; identify main ideas and supporting details from visual or written text; identify and discuss themes and ideas from visual or written text; engage in higher-level thinking; make interpretations and inferences about events and ideas; summarize information; use effective listening skills.

*CCSS Connection*

Standard RL/RI.1: Read closely to determine what the text says explicitly; Standard RL/RI.2: Determine central ideas or themes of a text; Standard RL/RI.3: Analyze how and why individuals, events, and ideas develop and interact; Standard SL.1: Prepare for and participate effectively in a range of conversations and collaborations; Standard SL.2: Integrate and evaluate information presented in diverse media and formats; Standard SL.4: Present information, findings, and supporting evidence such that listeners can follow the line of reasoning.

*Overview*

Pinwheels is a strategy that is useful for encouraging full student participation. It helps students form educated opinions and develop their ability to consider other points of view and what others have to contribute to a discussion (Tama & McClain, 2007).

*Procedure*

1. Have students individually or as a class read the assigned story or article.

2. Have students form pinwheels in groups of six. This can be adapted for odd-numbered groups.

3. Three students sit in the middle of the circular group with their backs to the center. Each of the other students sits facing one of the students in the middle, so there will be three pairs of students facing each other in a circular group.

4. Each of the three students in the middle is assigned a different discussion question, which can come from the teacher or be student generated.

5. Students on the outside will move clockwise to each member of the center to discuss that member's question. A recorder will summarize on butcher paper the various solutions for each question.

6. Summaries are posted and the different groups will circulate to read what other groups have suggested.

Here are some sample pinwheel questions based on a reading assignment about the environment:

- Why is it important to save the environment?

- What can students do immediately to help save the environment?

- What is the government doing to support these efforts?

## Strategy 10: Music to My Ears

*Purpose*

Establish a purpose for reading; review content and concepts learned during a lesson or unit; read closely and identify main ideas in text; engage in collaborative discussion about content and concepts learned.

*CCSS Connection*

Standard RL/RI.1: Read closely to determine what the text says explicitly; Standard RL/RI.2: Determine central ideas or themes of a text; Standard RL/RI.8: Delineate and evaluate the argument and specific claims in a text; Standard RL/RI.10: Read and comprehend complex literary and informational texts; Standard SL.1: Prepare for and participate effectively in a range of conversations and collaborations.

*Overview*

Music to My Ears is a fun and engaging activity that incorporates both movement and music. It comes from Brunner (2011). The strategy requires students to read closely and summarize assigned text. It has the added benefit of allowing students to move around the room while listening to some upbeat music. The strategy is a great culminating activity that helps students to review material they have learned during a unit.

*Procedure*

1. Assign students to read the text (unless you are using the strategy as a culminating activity at the end of a unit).

2. Have students identify the essential ideas and information, which they will be expected to summarize for their fellow students.

3. Have students write down five to seven sentences that express ideas or concepts learned during the reading or unit.

4. Tell students that they will be moving around the room as the music plays. Turn on the music and allow it to play for a minute or so as students circulate around the room.

5. When the music stops, students are to pair up with the person closest to them, and explain one of their concepts or ideas that they have learned and want to remember. Their partner then explains one of his ideas.

6. As students discuss and learn or remember new ideas and concepts, have them add additional ideas to their own lists.

7. Turn the music back on and have students again move around the room until the music stops, at which point they will again pair with the person closest to them to share another idea.

8. Continue the activity for as long as desired or until students have had a chance to share most of their ideas.

## Strategy 11: Hot Seat

*Purpose*

Use effective questioning techniques to generate and clarify ideas and information; work collaboratively to ask questions from text.

*CCSS Connection*

Standard RL/RI.1: Read closely to determine what the text says explicitly; Standard RL/RI.2: Determine central ideas or themes of a text; Standard RL/RI.3: Analyze how and why individuals, events, and ideas develop and interact; Standard SL.1: Prepare for and participate effectively in a range of conversations and collaborations.

*Overview*

Hot Seat is a strategy that can be used after students have mastered the use of QAR and the four types of questions (right there, think and search, author and you, and on my own). Hot Seat offers another opportunity for students to practice with these types of questions. Use it when students are reviewing a reading assignment, or preparing for a writing assignment or test. This strategy requires students to work collaboratively to develop four types of questions, which they will then direct to students playing the role of a character in the text. Thus, this process should be used with reading material that involves characters, historical figures, or topics or ideas that can be personified (i.e., chemical elements) (Strategic Literacy Initiative, 2004).

PART TWO

*Procedure*

1. Students silently read the required text.

2. Introduce the hot seat activity as one that uses questioning to review the reading assignment and better understand it.

3. Choose a character, concept, or historical figure to be the focus of the hot seat. Have a student volunteer to sit in the hot seat. This student will play the role of the character and answer questions about the reading. You can also choose several different characters or concepts to personify and have different students volunteer for each one.

4. Place students in groups to develop questions while the hot seat student is reviewing the reading. Each group should write two of each of the four types of questions from QAR. These are questions that will be asked directly of the hot seat character. They must be questions that are related to the text but also extend beyond the text.

5. Each group will take turns asking the student in the hot seat questions until every group has had a chance to ask at least two of their questions. The person in the hot seat should play the role of the character, figure, or concept, speaking in the voice of the persona and answering the questions.

6. During the process the teacher should observe, take notes, facilitate the process, and provide minimal feedback.

7. End with a brief reflection and whole-class discussion about the process and what it contributed to students' understanding of the reading. Have each group turn in their written questions, which can be used as test questions for the reading assignment.

## Strategy 12: Gallery Tour

*Purpose*

Create a visual representation of concepts or content of a text; collaborate with others to diagram or map information from text; review and respond to others' ideas.

*CCSS Connection*

Standard RL/RI.1: Read closely to determine what the text says explicitly; Standard RL/RI.2: Determine central ideas or themes of a text; Standard RL/RI.5: Analyze the structure of text; Standard RL/RI.7: Integrate and evaluate content presented in diverse formats and media; Standard RL/RI.8: Delineate and evaluate the argument and specific claims in a text; Standard SL.1: Prepare for and participate effectively in a range of conversations and collaborations; Standard SL.2: Integrate and evaluate information presented in diverse media and formats.

*Overview*

The gallery tour is an interactive and collaborative strategy that involves students in producing a visual display of the content and ideas in a text. It comes from Rasinski and Padak (1996). Gallery tour can also be used as a review activity at the end of a unit of instruction, and can be used for any type of content or textual material.

*Procedure*

1. Assign students to read the textbook chapter, article, or other material (unless you are using the strategy as a culminating activity at the end of a unit).

2. Explain to students that they will be working with their group to create a visual representation of the content they have learned. It could include a map, a diagram, a drawing, a chart, collage, or some other type of visual that summarizes the important ideas and concepts they have learned. Their creation can include symbols, words, pictures, or some combination of them. Provide each group with a piece of poster board or chart paper to draw the visual.

3. Have each group work together to create the visual representation.

4. When the visuals are completed, have each group tape or attach their finished product to the wall, one in each corner, or in various places around the room.

5. Next, give each student some sticky notes to attach to the products around the room. These notes will provide feedback, comments, and critique on the finished products.

6. Either individually or in their groups, have students go on a "gallery tour" around the room, moving from one visual display to another. Ask each student to provide at least one comment for each of the visuals on display, attaching his or her sticky notes to the visual.

7. After the tour is finished, have each group return to their original product to review the notes and discuss them. During this part of the activity, they should also compare their product with the others that they viewed on the gallery tour.

PART TWO

## Strategy 13: The Twenty-Five-Word Préci or Abstract

*Purpose*
   Use active reading strategies to comprehend text; identify and summarize main ideas; write concise summaries.

*CCSS Connection*
   Standard RL/RI.2: Determine central ideas or themes of a text; Standard W.4: Produce clear and coherent writing.

*Overview*

The twenty-five-word abstract was created by Tim Tindol, a science teacher who was interested in helping students proficiently summarize classroom texts in addition to understanding the concept of the abstract, a formal summary used in academic research papers (Strategic Literacy Initiative, 2004). This strategy is also sometimes called the préci, or short summary. I have used it for many years, especially in writing classes, to help students identify main ideas in a text or essay by writing a twenty-five-word summary. However, the activity can be used with many different types of texts. It is also important to have students practice this strategy several times with different reading selections. When I use this strategy, I require that students' summaries be *exactly* twenty-five words—no more and no less. This is a challenge for students, and a great writing activity because it generally requires students to write and rewrite several times to get exactly twenty-five words. I also make it clear that their sentence or sentences must be complete, grammatically correct sentences.

*Procedure*

1. Choose a piece of informational text such as an magazine article, newspaper article or report, editorial, or some other piece of informational text. (The strategy works best with expository text rather than fictional.) Have students read the article independently.

2. Ask students to highlight the text using one color pen to highlight the main ideas and a second color to highlight unknown words or terms.

3. Assign students to work in groups. Each person should share what he or she has highlighted in the article. This process will also help to clarify vocabulary and any unfamiliar terminology used. Have groups compare their choices of main ideas by using their highlighting. Ask each group to come to a consensus about which items are main ideas.

4. Next, each student individually will write a twenty-five-word abstract that includes the main ideas chosen by members of the group. You have

the option of telling students to get as close to twenty-five words as possible or to write the abstract in exactly twenty-five words.

5. Have each group member share their completed abstract with the group. They should discuss the similarities and differences. Another option is to have the group create a collective abstract with no more than twenty-five words. Then have them copy the final abstract onto poster board to display in the classroom.

6. Have students do a gallery tour to read through all the abstracts posted and rate them on the basis of clarity, conciseness, and completeness.

## Strategy 14: Group Summarizing

*Purpose*
Identify main ideas and supporting details from text; summarize information concisely and accurately; work effectively in a collaborative group.

*CCSS Connection*
Standard RL/RI.2: Determine central ideas or themes of a text; Standard W.4: Produce clear and coherent writing; Standard SL.1: Prepare for and participate effectively in a range of conversations and collaborations.

*Overview*
Group summaries are a good strategy for helping students review information from reading material. They encourage students to identify main ideas and details and also practice condensing information (Brown, Day, & Jones, 1983).

*Procedure*
1. Have students survey a textbook chapter or reading selection and identify major topics contained in the reading.

2. On a piece of poster board or overhead transparency, either as a whole class, independently, or in pairs or groups, have students make four sections based on the major topics. This part of the strategy helps students establish a purpose for reading.

3. Have students read the text. Then individuals or groups will provide information for the different categories, which should be recorded on the poster board or transparency. Doing this process as a whole class has many benefits because it allows for discussion and review as students complete the summary.

4. Have students individually, as a class, or in pairs write a summary for each separate section. The example in table 2.4 comes from Olsen and Gee (1991) and is adapted by Doty, Cameron, and Barton (2003).

**Table 2.4.  Group Summarizing**

| Description | Childhood |
|---|---|
| Alexander was the king of Macedonia from 366 to 323 BC. He was well educated. He was a military leader who wanted to rule the known world. | Alexander was the son of King Phillip. He learned science, geography, and literature from Aristotle. He learned how to ride a horse, use weapons, and command troops at an early age. |
| Accomplishments | Interesting Facts |
| Alexander defeated the Persians in three major battles. He ended up conquering the entire Persian Empire. He founded many towns and cities, including Alexandria, Egypt. In eleven years, he led his army over 11,000 miles. | Alexander became king when he was only twenty years old. He died when he was thirty-two. He was crowned pharaoh of Egypt. |

Source: Reprinted by permission of McREL

# WRITING STRATEGIES

## The Power of Writing

Astrong focus on writing across the curriculum is one of the most important elements in improving student achievement. Students are too often graduating from high school lacking the writing skills necessary for success in college and in the workplace. A 2004 report noted that 14 percent of entering four-year college students and 23 percent of two-year college students must take remedial writing courses (National Center for Education Statistics, 2004). A national survey of high school writing instruction noted that students were seldom assigned to do writing involving analysis or interpretation, and writing assignments of more than one paragraph were assigned less than once a month in half of all high school classes (Kiuhara, Graham, & Hawken, 2009).

Writing across the curriculum first gained prominence back in the 1980s, and more recent research still shows the benefits of a strong writing curriculum and focus on writing to learn as a key element in literacy reform in secondary schools. In 2007, an Alliance for Excellent Education report to the Carnegie Corporation of New York called *Writing Next* warned that US students were failing to meet even basic writing standards. It also included meta-analysis of research in writing instruction that identified eleven key elements of effective adolescent writing instruction. Those elements are writing strategies, summarizing, collaborative writing, specific product goals, word processing, sentence combining, prewriting, inquiry activities, process writing approach, study of models, and writing to learn (writing for content learning) (Graham & Perin, 2007). The report also notes that students are too often taught the rigid structure of the five-paragraph essay and that teachers tend to place too much emphasis on grammar and spelling and not enough on content and process (Graham & Perin, 2007).

Writing is integrally linked to reading and communication skills in general, and research shows that writing instruction also improves reading comprehension.

Whereas grammar instruction lacks a positive effect in improving writing and may, in fact, have a negative effect, elements such as sentence combining, summarizing, and use of writing strategies positively improve writing. Writing process instruction is important as is practice with real-world writing tasks (Biancarosa & Snow, 2006).

Students who graduate from high school with strong writing skills are much more likely to be academically successful as college students. In his book *Teaching Adolescent Writers*, Gallagher (2006) notes that "we have a long way to go overall to bring many of our students up to the levels of writing proficiency they will need to walk through those key gateways awaiting them: the gateway to academia; the gateway to an emerging workplace; the gateway to the global economy" (p. 6). Gallagher identifies ten "writing wrongs" typical of secondary schools:

- Students are not writing enough.

- Writing is assigned rather than taught.

- Below-grade-level writers are asked to write less than others.

- English language learners are shortchanged in writing.

- Grammar instruction is ineffective or ignored.

- Students are not given enough timed writing instruction or practice.

- Some teachers have no knowledge of district and state writing standards.

- Writing topics are mandated "with little thought about the prior knowledge and interests of the students" (p. 11).

- Teachers are doing too much of the work and students not enough.

- Teachers need help assessing student writing.

To right these "wrongs," Gallagher (2006) proposes a model for promoting more writing success. The model consists of six principles: students need more writing practice; students need teachers to model good writing; students need to read and study other writers; students need choice of topics; students need to write "for authentic purposes and for authentic audiences" (p. 13); and students need feedback from teachers and peers. Gallagher's model, if implemented in all secondary schools across the curriculum and not just in English classes, would indeed have a profound impact on student writing ability.

This section of the book presents strategies that can be used by teachers in all content areas to help counter the "wrongs" identified and promote many of the principles in Gallagher's model. It is important to distinguish between learning to write and writing to learn. Because content-area teachers are focused on helping students lcarn concepts in their subject matter, they are naturally going to focus more on disciplinary literacy. Disciplinary literacy refers to the forms of discourse and genres that are used in the particular subject area. A science teacher, for example, may gather several model texts, or pieces of writing that might typically be written within the discipline of science. These might include a lab report, research articles, an article in a science-related magazine, or some other forms of informational text. Content-area teachers want to help students learn to do the particular kinds of writing that are involved in that discipline. Thus, writing to learn differs from learning to write in that rather than focusing on teaching students the process and conventions of writing, teachers are using writing to help students further their own learning and meaning-making within the particular subject area. Writing to learn "engages students, extends thinking, deepens understanding, and energizes the meaning-making process" (Knipper & Duggan, 2006, p. 462). This can be done through even short, informal pieces of writing. This section of the book will help you learn to use a variety of simple but effective writing-to-learn strategies.

Writing can maximize student learning of content, but content-area teachers are often reluctant to assign students to write. Ask yourself how many times recently you have considering assigning students to write something in class—a list, a paragraph, directions, a short essay, or whatever—but decided not to do it because you knew it would mean 150-plus papers that you would have to somehow evaluate, assign points to, grade, enter, and return. Teachers are understandably reluctant to use writing because they are afraid of being buried under stacks of papers to grade. However, there are ways to provide feedback to students on their writing that are not time consuming. Remember, the most important thing is the writing practice that students get and the increased understanding of the subject matter they will gain as a result of writing to learn. This means it is not always necessary for the teacher to read everything students write. (This is addressed in more detail later in this section.) You can have students do three or four short pieces of writing but collect only one for a grade. In many cases, you can have students do quick responses and evaluations of each other's pieces of writing. You can also design a simple rubric to use to give you a sense of differences in quality of student performance on the task. To design a simple rubric, use three evaluative categories such as exemplary, satisfactory, and unsatisfactory (or developing). Identify characteristics of the particular type of writing you would expect to see at each level. For example, an "introduction that is interesting and clearly states the purpose of the paper" might be a trait you would include in the exemplary category. The rubric can help you quickly assign points or provide feedback on the quality of the particular writing project. Checklists can also help to identify a set of dimensions or characteristics that you expect to see in the finished piece of writing. Figure 3.1 is an example of a simple checklist.

| **Writing Assignment Checklist** | | | |
| --- | --- | --- | --- |
| | Very Good | Average | Needs Improvement |
| Ideas and Content: | | | |
| Clear main idea | _____ | _____ | _____ |
| Topic matches assignment requirements | _____ | _____ | _____ |
| Ideas and details are strong and support the topic | _____ | _____ | _____ |
| Clear and fully developed ideas | _____ | _____ | _____ |
| Sufficient detail | _____ | _____ | _____ |
| Good use of language and word choice | _____ | _____ | _____ |
| | | | |
| Organization: | | | |
| Includes an introduction, body, and conclusion | _____ | _____ | _____ |
| Details arranged logically | _____ | _____ | _____ |
| Transitions between parts | _____ | _____ | _____ |
| Includes paragraphing | _____ | _____ | _____ |
| | | | |
| Conventions: | | | |
| Correct grammar and usage | _____ | _____ | _____ |
| Mostly correct spelling | _____ | _____ | _____ |
| Correct capitalization and punctuation | _____ | _____ | _____ |
| Correct sentence structure | _____ | _____ | _____ |
| | | | |
| Comments: | | | |

**Figure 3.1.  Assignment Checklist.**

It is clear that writing can be a very powerful element in improving academic performance for students in secondary schools. A review of research on high-poverty schools beginning in 1995 revealed some interesting findings. All of the high-performing, high-poverty schools (where 90 percent or more of the students met district and state standards) placed an emphasis on writing, and, more specifically, informative writing. Teachers in all areas used writing rubrics and maintained high expectations for student writing despite the content area or type of writing. In addition, the researchers found a strong association between writing and academic performance in other disciplines (Reeves, 2003). In other words, a strong focus on writing can improve student learning in *all* areas of the curriculum.

One Massachusetts high school provides an interesting case study that reveals the power of writing and the impact of reading and writing across the curriculum on student academic success in general. The *New York Times*, in 2010, reported the story of Brockton High School, a large Massachusetts school with over four thousand students, where one in three students dropped out and only a quarter of students passed state exams. A new principal and handful of teachers organized a schoolwide reading and writing initiative that incorporated reading and writing lessons into every class in every subject (Dillon, 2010). As success increased, teachers learned to use writing lessons that encouraged students to think through the process, reluctant staff members were provided with training and encouragement, the school eliminated much of its tracking program, and gradual success was acknowledged and praised. Within a few years, Brockton High was outperforming 90 percent of Massachusetts high schools and was featured in a Harvard report on exemplary high schools (Dillon, 2010).

We must never underestimate the power of writing as a part of good literacy instruction. This section of the book will focus on multiple ways that content-area writing can be used to increase the amount and frequency of student writing. Many of the strategies included are simple, not time consuming, and can be easily incorporated into all classes.

## What Is Content-Area Writing?

Content-area writing is also known as "writing across the curriculum" and "writing-to-learn." It reflects the theory that writing is a process that reinforces learning, an active process that involves not just writing about what one knows or has learned but also a process of discovery. It provides a means for students to reflect on and reinforce their learning in any subject area. Engaging with content material in written form helps students to synthesize, analyze, and also acquire information as they make sense of key ideas. Content-area writing is based on several principles:

- Different content areas have different conventions of writing. Students learn not only to read but also to write using the discourse conventions of the particular discipline.

- The best writing is produced by following a process writing approach that includes planning, drafting, revising, and proofreading.

- Students need opportunity to collaborate with others during the writing process and engage in self-reflection about their learning.

- Students need to write frequently, both formally and informally, engaging in both process writing and on-demand writing tasks.

- Students need authentic, real-world audiences and purposes for their writing whenever possible.

- Students should make use of models of different types of writing and rubrics, checklists, or other criteria by which their writing will be evaluated.

Content-area writing can be done in a variety of simple ways. It *does not* have to take time away from teaching of your content. In fact, by having students frequently engage in writing, they will learn the content material *better* as a result of writing about it. It is also important to remember that students will benefit from any type of writing practice. You do not have to assign and grade large numbers of formal essays and papers. Even simple, short writing activities are very beneficial.

Writing can be used to help students engage in higher-level thinking about the content material. They can use writing to:

- defend a position, idea, or decision

- describe something

- speculate about possible outcomes or results

- design schemes or systems

- explain procedures for solving a problem or completing a task

- make a decision about a direction or action

- justify a behavior or position

- explore feelings and values

- critique ideas, actions, or systems

- refute other points of view

- expand on an idea, attitude, or opinion

- distinguish between two things, methods, systems

- restate a problem or dilemma

- describe a person, object, event, place, or time

- state or restate an idea or problem

- imagine or imitate

- discuss an example

- evaluate a text

- make a list of events or steps

- conjecture about the meaning of words, phrases, events

- synthesize information from a variety of sources

This list is by no means exhaustive. Students can be asked to write for any number of different purposes or even audiences in the classroom.

## Writing to Learn and Handling the Paper Load

Busy classroom teachers are often reluctant to assign writing in their classes because they know it means they will have to grade students' papers. A teacher with 150 or more students may end up with many hours of grading to spend even a short amount of time on each student's paper. First of all, it is important to understand that not everything that students write has to be graded. For example, over a two-week period, you might assign students a series of quick-writes that ask them to reflect on their learning, or short papers on particular topics related to the content being studied. They may even do one of these quick-writes each day. At the end of the two-week period, you can ask students to choose two of their short pieces of writing they wish to turn in for a grade. In addition, many types of student writing can be quickly skimmed and assigned a grade without requiring a huge amount of your time. There may be still be a few more formal papers, ones students have worked on over a longer period that you want to grade more carefully, but the important thing to remember is that the benefit comes from students engaging in the writing process itself. It is not necessary that they receive detailed feedback from the teacher on everything they write.

For these next sections of this chapter, I need to acknowledge Professor Lois Barry, who was my language arts methods and writing instructor at Eastern Oregon University in the 1980s. Professor Barry was an early proponent of process writing and writing across the curriculum, and many of these ideas are hers. Over the years, I have expanded and added to them. The following are some suggestions and particular writing activities that will help you handle the paper load and still help your students improve their understanding and critical thinking about the content material you are teaching:

- Just because students write something doesn't mean you have to actually collect and read them. If you've ever asked a question in class and been frustrated when no one responds, try having students write on the topic or question for five minutes and then use it as a springboard for discussion. This increases individual engagement because each student has the chance to think through the question and compose a response on paper (or a note card). Then call on students to read their answers aloud and build the lecture and discussion from their responses.

- Group Writing: Assign group writing activities and collect only one piece of writing from each group. Groups of three or four will cut the grading load by two-thirds or three-quarters. Students will learn from each other as they exchange ideas, write, edit, and create a final piece.

- The One-Minute Essay: As a way of monitoring students' learning and stimulating class discussion and careful reading, consider the one-minute essay. It simply asks two questions: What's the most important thing you learned today (or this week)? What's the most significant question you still have? This one-minute essay can be done at the beginning or end of a week or a unit.

- Joint Response: Have students trade papers and read what others wrote. Have each pair then write a joint response and read it aloud to the rest of the class. This allows you to simply listen and jot down a grade.

- Microthemes: Longer is not always better. Have students write reviews or summaries of magazine articles, books, films, or other textual material on note cards. The shorter space helps them focus on key ideas. (A format for the microtheme is included as a separate strategy later in this section.)

- Writing Roulette: As a review activity, ask students to write about what was significant about the material they learned. After two to three minutes, have students pass their papers to the person behind them. Then have students comment, clarify, and add to what the other student wrote. Stress to students they should try to focus their comments directly on what the first writer wrote. Repeat this process four times and then return the papers to the original writers. Collect them and read some aloud to the class, using the papers to respond by clarifying and emphasizing important points.

- Believing-Doubting Game: For controversial issues, consider the claim, identify all the reasons to support the claim, and then identify all the reasons to doubt the claim. Students can do this in pairs or small groups.

- Data Sets: In some courses, data set assignments that ask students to draw conclusions from charts, graphs, tables, or even a series of factual statements are a good way to get students writing. Present a data set to a group of students and have them collaborate on a short piece of writing to draw their conclusions.

- Descriptive Outlining: For short reading assignments, consider the use of descriptive outlining (indicate main points from each paragraph). You can provide a simple outline form for the particular reading passage and have students complete it.

- Idea Maps: As a substitute for traditional outlining when students are beginning a paper, consider using an idea map that orders information visually in a diagram or web.

- The List: Sometimes it's more effective for students to practice with shorter forms of writing; in fact, that's always a good place to start with struggling students. Have students make a list of steps in a process, causes, effects, reasons, examples, items, suggestions, ideas, and conclusions. Tell students they must have a certain minimum number of items in their list.

- Journals: A whole chapter of this book could be written on the value of journal writing. Journals are a good way to have students engage in regular, preferably daily, writing practice. They are excellent for building writing fluency and increasing student comfort level with writing. Have students write in their journal daily or weekly using prompts that you have designed and that are related to course content. Journal writing can also be used to promote classroom discussion.

- Freewriting: At the beginning of a lecture, discussion, chapter, unit, or period, ask students to write nonstop for five to ten minutes on what they know about the concept to be introduced. This will help them focus on the learning, activate their prior knowledge, and share what they have written. Use the same freewriting activity at the end of the lecture, film, chapter, unit, and so forth. Ask students to write nonstop about what they have learned.

- Notebooks or Portfolios: Have students collect their freewriting in a notebook or portfolio, date the entries, and collect them at the end of the grading period. Or have students choose one out of several they want to turn in for credit.

- Note Cards: Have students write responses on note cards rather than paper. After a reading assignment, film, lecture, or activity, ask students to write down "wondering" questions about the material. Redistribute the cards to other members of the class and ask each student to respond and answer the question he receives. Return the cards and have students read the responses.

- Test Questions: Ask students individually or in groups to write test questions on note cards. You can specify the format: multiple choice, true/false, or short answer. Collect and redistribute these and have students answer the question on the cards they've been given. They can also be collected and used on the actual test that you prepare.

Here are a few other useful methods of handling the paper load:

1. If you have students write research papers, limit them to three pages. Better yet, have students turn in sections of their paper over a period of time.

2. Rather than collecting and grading all the papers students write, ask them to choose the best of their papers to be graded. Besides cutting down on your paper load, it also requires students to reread and evaluate the quality of their work, and so serves a self-reflective purpose.

3. Ask students to read each other's papers and respond in writing with their reactions, questions, praise, and suggestions for improvement. Then have students rewrite the papers.

4. Design writing assignments that can be read or presented to the class and evaluated by you at the actual time of the presentation: oral reports, reviews, character dialogues, plays, panel discussions, debates, and so forth. Collect what students prepare for their presentation to make them accountable for their work.

5. Have you ever written the same comment on ten to fifteen papers in a set of thirty? Why not present your comments to the entire class? Let them know their strengths as well as areas for improvement. I often cover up the student names, make overheads of some papers, and use them as models to show students' common strengths and weaknesses.

6. When appropriate and for longer papers, grade only one paragraph or a two-hundred-word passage. Let students know ahead of time that this is what you will do, but don't tell them which section you will read.

## Simple Ways to Improve Learning through Writing

This section includes some simple ways that you can use writing to help students learn content material. Remember that by engaging in writing about the content material, students are solidifying their thinking and new concepts in their minds, and they will also better retain what they have learned.

- Prereading or Postreading: During the last five to ten minutes of class, have students look over the next reading assignment. Ask them to write what they think the title and headings suggest. Let them write about how the new reading might relate to previous course material. As a follow-up to the reading, have students respond to prereading questions or summarize what they have learned.

- Microtheme: A microtheme is a brief, in-class essay, written on a note card, and about a topic specified by the teacher. The brevity forces students to practice summarizing and concluding concisely. They also give you quick, valuable feedback on learning and encourage students to reflect on the meaning of what they are learning.

- Mid-semester Course Evaluation: Have students do a written evaluation at midterm or semester, at a point when there is still time to make adjustments or reteach. Have students evaluate the course material and their own performance in the class.

- Counterarguments: If an argument has been raised in class, an alternative method of solving a problem has been shown, or more than one theory has been advanced to explain a phenomenon, stop for five minutes and allow students to write down all the counterarguments or counterevidence, list the benefits and drawbacks of the alternative methods, or present the case for accepting one theory or the other.

- One-minute Papers or Closure Statements: At the end of class, have students summarize a lecture or discussion, identify the key points learned, or pose a final question.

- Exit Box: Place a box by the door and ask students to drop off closure statements or brief comments, queries, concerns when they leave the class. These provide valuable feedback and keep students alert during class.

- Admit Ticket: When they enter class students must hand you a brief summary of a reading assignment or two questions about the reading.

- Student Note Takers: Assign one student each day to be the official note taker. In a large class, three or four students could be assigned. These students compare notes at the end of class and choose the best set of notes or create a polished version for distribution. This is especially helpful for students who are absent from class.

- Priming the Pump: Ask students to spend the first five minutes of class responding to a question that will be addressed in the lecture or discussion. Let them know that a few people will be called on to read their responses.

- Class Dictionary: Ask students to write brief definitions of key terms. Definitions can be displayed for discussion and debate.

- Breakthrough Metaphors: Try using metaphors to help students do some creative and exploratory thinking. Ask them to compose metaphors or analogies to help them think through a concept. For example, "The unconscious mind is like a machine" or "Erosion is a deadly plague." Ask students what properties does each metaphor include or suggest. What does each leave out?

The following are a few additional writing-to-learn activities from *Writers Inc.: A Guide to Writing, Thinking, and Learning* (Kemper, Meyer, & Sebranek, 1990).

- Unsent Letters: Have students write letters to someone or something having to do with the content material. The topic should be something the student is concerned about, questions he has, or points of critique.

- First Thoughts: Have students write a list of immediate impressions about something they are studying or reading.

- Dramatic Scenarios: Have students develop a scenario or plot in writing. If studying World War II, write a dramatic conversation President Truman has with someone else on the day before he decides to drop the bomb on Hiroshima.

- Free Association: Have students start with one word or concept, and then jot down additional words and phrases that come to mind as fast as they can and without stopping.

- Acrostics: Have students write acrostic poems for vocabulary words. The letters of each vocabulary word are used as the first letter of each line in the poem.

- Word Works: Have students use as many vocabulary words as they can in a short piece of writing. Tell students it can be as crazy as they want it to be but must use each vocabulary word correctly.

- Nutshelling: Have students write down in one sentence the importance or relevance of something they have heard, seen, read, or studied.

- Debate: Have students engage in a written debate with themselves, splitting their mind into two separate persons. Have one side debate with the other on the subject.

## Alternatives to Formal Writing

Remember that using writing in your classroom does not mean that you have to assign students to write full-length, multiple-page essays or long research papers. This section presents useful writing activities and assignments that will help students learn the content material, but they are *short* (like many of the other ideas in the previous two sections). This makes grading them quick and easy for you:

- Twenty-Five-Word Préci: Have students summarize the ideas in an article, story, or reading selection in exactly twenty-five words. (This strategy was discussed in part 2.)

- Discussion Warm-up: Students write for a few minutes in response to an open-ended discussion question or questions. They can share and discuss these responses either in small groups or with the whole class.

- Prewriting: Have students do a prewriting activity prior to any more formal writing assignment such as an essay. The purpose is to get down initial thoughts and ideas in the form of a freewrite, a list, a brief outline, or a diagram or cluster.

- Mind Mapping: This is a form of brainstorming to activate prior knowledge. Place a key word or concept in the center of a page and have students write down associated ideas around it. Ideas can then branch off from each other.

- Classification: Prepare groups of related ideas on note cards. Place students in groups, give each group a set of cards, and have students sort them into categories to help make sense of the information.

- Case Study/Role Play: Have students write in the voice of a character, historical figure, chemical element, mathematical symbol, scientific principle, or object. Specify the audience for the piece of writing.

- Drafts for Peer Response: When students are working on an essay or formal paper, have them bring their first draft or part of a draft to work in small groups and revise them. Students in the group should be able to read other students' drafts and give suggestions for revising.

- Group Paper: Ask students to produce a group paper that integrates the work of all the students in the group. The group needs to select a topic, assign a particular role to each group member, and then produce a final group paper.

- Critiques: Have students read an article from a newspaper or magazine, editorial, website, or chapter, and then critique the piece of writing for content, organization, layout, and so forth.

- Letter to an Imaginary Other: Students write about an event, person, place, story, concept, or idea to another person involved in some way, to an imaginary person, a historical figure, or a friend.

- Special Formats: Have students write in alternative formats or genres such as advertisements, news stories, poems, songs, flyers, blogs, raps, websites, Facebook pages, brochures, memos, magazine articles, plays, and so forth, to express their understanding of a topic of concept.

- One-Hundred-Word Papers: Assign students to write a paper no more than one hundred words on a particular topic. Give some specific guidelines for what must be included or present a discussion question or prompt.

- Journals/Conversation Books: Encourage freewriting and exploration of class ideas through journals to share with other class members. These can follow specific requirements. Use them to allow students to reflect on what they are learning. Journal writing should be read and responded by you or other students, but should not be graded.

## Writing Activities for Specific Content Areas

I've often heard teachers say things like, "I teach math. We don't do writing in math." Very similar statements I have heard from teachers of computer science, vocational and technical courses, art, music, and even science. However, writing can be effectively used in all content areas, including those just mentioned. One of the interviews I conducted for my dissertation research was with an industrial arts teacher who described to me how important reading and writing are in his content area, how important it is for students to be able to read and follow directions for handling materials and equipment. He also described several writing projects he required students to do as part of his course. I have always argued that writing can and should be used in *all* content areas, including elective areas. It is critical to include writing in areas such as language arts and social studies, also very important in science and math, but it can be effectively used in every other area of the curriculum as well. Here are some suggestions. (Note that English language arts is not included here, although there is a section on literature. The reason for this is that English teachers routinely have students write in a variety of forms, both analytically and creatively.)

*Math*
- Choose a concept such as one of the following: carbon dating, compound interest, inflation, population growth, bacterial growth, total square feet of a home, the yearly depreciation of a car's value. Form groups of two or three and discuss the subject chosen. Identify what kind of mathematical problem you are dealing with. Write a couple of paragraphs that explain the problem you are trying to solve. Use a mathematical procedure to arrive at the solution, and explain what mathematical principles are involved.

- Explain in writing the steps for solving a particular math problem. Explain your proofs in geometry, and write about which types of problems are hardest for you to solve.

- Write from the point of view of a mathematical symbol or formula. Explain your purpose and what role you play in equations and your importance in mathematics in general.

- Write story problems to help others learn mathematical functions and calculations.

*Art*

- Write a description of a visually interesting object. Use it as a guide for other students who have not seen the item and have them produce a drawing of it.

- Mold a series of beads that represent important events in your life. After you have fired the beads and painted them, write an explanation of the significance of the beads.

- From three or more works of art presented to the class, choose one that you would like to encourage the school administration to purchase for permanent display. Write a letter to the principal. Another option: Write a letter to your parents urging them to purchase the work of art for your home. The letters must be persuasive with lots of reasons and specific detail.

- Arrange three objects cut from magazines or online illustrations. Write an explanation that identifies the objects, their significance, and your reason for arranging them as you did.

- Write a self-evaluation for your artist's portfolio.

- Write about your best piece of work and explain why you think it is the best.

- Write a report on a famous artist.

- Write a critique of a painting, drawing, sculpture, piece of stained glass, or other work of art that clearly explains the criteria you are using to evaluate it.

*Social Studies*

- Write an explanation of capitalism to a pen pal in Denmark, pointing out the strengths and weaknesses of capitalism in contrast to Denmark's socialist form of government.

- Write a letter to your congressman about an issue that concerns you.

- Write a description of the location of your birthplace so that it can be located on a large map of the United States.

- Write a description of a place in the United States you would like to visit. Choose interesting information from your research to persuade your classmates to share your enthusiasm for this place. Share the descriptions in groups and vote on the top five places to visit.

- Write a letter from one historical figure to another historical figure explaining why you disagree with his actions or decisions. For example, at the time of the Civil War, write a letter from Jefferson Davis to President Lincoln.

- Write a conversation or dialogue between two historical figures—for example, President Franklin D. Roosevelt and Winston Churchill.

- Create a hierarchy of important historical figures or events in a period of time. List them in order from one to ten and then write a rationale for the class to explain your reasoning.

- Write short essay responses for test questions.

- Write research papers on particular historical issues or topics, geographical places, economics concepts, or forms of government.

- Adopt the persona of a historical figure and keep a journal that records the attitudes and concerns of the figure during the events occurring.

- Write a newspaper article about an important historical event as it would appear in a front-page news story. Compare student versions with actual newspaper articles.

- Write a critique and response to a particular historical document.

- Write an essay comparing and contrasting two presidents, periods of times, wars, or other events.

- Create a timeline with detailed explanation of each part.

- Create a Facebook page or personal website for a historical figure.

*Vocational/Technical Education*
- Write a book of directions for next year's students, outlining basic safety rules, location of equipment, and other dos and don'ts for success and safety in the classroom shop.

- Write a paragraph or essay clearly explaining one important process you have learned that will help other students who have not yet mastered this process.

- Write directions for operating or cleaning a particular piece of equipment.

- Write instructions for completing a particular task.

- Write a proposal to the instructor for your choice of a term project. What have you decided to make or do for the project? What materials will you need? What difficulties do you anticipate in completing the project? What skills will you gain?

- Write a set of instructions or process used for building or making something.

- Write a self-evaluation or critique of your completed final project.

*Computer Science*

- Write computer software using a common computer language.

- Write online instructions for a computer program, software installation, or computer game.

- Design and write content for a website.

- Research a computer science topic and write an article for a popular computer magazine such as *PC World*.

- Write a troubleshooting manual for computer care, operation, and maintenance.

*Science*

- Write a lab report that is so clear and complete that it can be used by another student to duplicate the experiment. You might include warnings of specific problems that may be encountered in the experiment.

- Decide how to divide the equipment for your lab work into two or three drawers. Write an explanation of this method of organization for students in other periods to justify your system of organization.

- As you complete a problem or experiment, keep a record of your thinking. Draw a vertical line about a third of the way in from the right-hand edge of your page. Use the left-hand column to report the facts and steps in the experiment. Use the right-hand column as a journal to record your thoughts as you proceed through the experiment.

- Write a report on a famous scientist or scientific discovery.

- Write a paper that evaluates the work of a well-known scientist.

- Write summaries of magazine articles about current scientific issues and topics.

- Write directions for setting up a lab or preparing for an experiment.

- Write a paper that argues for the importance of understanding a particular scientific concept or theory.

- Write a comparison of a subject discussed in your textbook and the same subject in an online article or webpage.

*Physical Education*
- Keep a daily or weekly journal recording your progress on the skills you are practicing. Record areas of improvement and evaluate your progress.

- Write a simple "getting started" basic skill and rule book for a sport played in the United States. (The act of writing about a specific technique in a particular sport may help students understand what they are not doing successfully.)

- Write a set of instructions for handling, maintaining, and organizing gym equipment/supplies.

- Write a letter as a varsity team member to give encouragement and helpful tips to a junior varsity team member.

- Write an evaluation of your performance in physical education during a particular unit or grading period.

- Write a report on a well-known athlete.

- Write a set of instructions for how to do a particular activity.

- Write a letter to your parents about your goals and progress in physical education.

*Health*
- Write a letter to a friend or family member who needs to change his eating habits, exercise more, quit smoking, or make other lifestyle changes. Explain tactfully and convincingly the importance of making this change.

- Keep a daily or weekly journal of references to specific health issues that you have studied in class. Clip articles from newspapers and record conversations you have heard about health issues.

- Write a newspaper article that reports on a new medical or health discovery or a new disease or health issue and how to prevent it.

- Create an informational poster on some aspect of public health, such as preventing the spread of the flu.

- Write a report on a common disease or health problem, or a report on a person who has made a lasting contribution to health science.

- Write a report analyzing the benefits of exercise and healthy diet.

- Make a brochure to inform the public about various health problems and what to do about them.

*Music*
- Write a paper evaluating your contribution to the musical group. Outline your strengths and be honest about your challenges.

- Write a press release prior to the concert or performance. Send it to local newspapers and media outlets.

- Write a descriptive paragraph about a piece of music to be included in the concert program.

- Write a paragraph to describe the mood created by a piece of music.

- Research a piece you are performing and write notes to be included in the concert program.

- Write a report on a famous composer or musical artist.

- Write a letter to school administration encouraging them to support and fund music activities.

*Literature*
- Write a letter from one character in the story to another character explaining why you agree or disagree with his actions or decisions.

- Write a ballad or poem that retells a story.

- Write a "wanted poster" for the villain of a story or play you have read. Illustrate it with artwork or pictures and details about the story.

- Rewrite the conclusion of a story or novel to present an alternative ending.

- Write a continuation of a story of novel to show what will ultimately happen to the characters.

- Write a newspaper article about the events in the story.

- Write a biopoem (see part 3) about an important character in the story or novel.

- Create a Facebook page for an important character from the story or novel.

- Write a critique or book review of a class novel or a book read independently.

- Write a research paper about the life and work of a famous artist.

*Family and Consumer Studies*
- Write a process paper explaining to a student who has not mastered the procedure for performing a skill learned in class, such as sizing a pattern, kneading bread, or doubling ingredients.

- Write a formal invitation to parents for an annual spring breakfast or tea, an awards ceremony, a curriculum fair, or some other special occasion.

- Write a letter to a company whose product has been less than satisfactory or whose advertising is misleading.

- Write a complimentary letter to a company to share your satisfaction with a particular product.

- Create your own recipe and write it out clearly.

- Write an evaluation of your performance in completing a class project.

- Write directions for safety, maintenance, and cleaning of the school kitchen.

- Write a menu for a special dinner or catered event.

# More Writing Strategies

## Strategy 1: Admit Slips

*Purpose*
Write to reflect on learning; summarize content concepts and ideas; use explanatory/expository writing to reflect and summarize.

*CCSS Connection*
Standard W.2: Write informative/explanatory texts to examine and convey complex ideas; Standard W.3: Produce clear, coherent writing.

*Overview*

Admit slips are a type of writing that many teachers use regularly. Students are expected to bring a short piece of writing to class with them for the start of the next day's class. This piece of writing is their "ticket to get in the door" or what they must complete to be admitted to class. The teacher has the option of collecting these admit slips as students enter the room. They can be written on a note card, a regular piece of paper, or a handout. Some teachers will print a piece of paper that looks like an admission ticket. For example, I printed a form that states, "Admit One to Dr. Berry's First Period Class." Usually, admit slips require students to write a reflection on their learning from the previous class day or a review of a reading or homework assignment students are to complete.

*Procedure*

1. Write a prompt or topic based on the current day's lesson, which students will be given for their admit slips. Here are some example questions for different content areas that come from Daniels, Zemelman, and Steineke (2007):

   a. Math: Find some examples of math or numerical evidence being used in the media and explain it.

   b. Social Studies: How would the United States have been different if FDR lost the election in 1932?

   c. Social Studies: Of the three main causes of the Civil War, which one do you think is most important and why?

   d. English: After reading the poem aloud a few times, comment on the poem's rhythm and rhyme patterns.

    e. Science: Explain the advantages and disadvantages of indicators versus meters.

    f. Science: On page x, the textbook says that global warming may be caused by human activity or may be part of a natural, random cycle of variations. Which theory do you believe and why?

2. As students enter the classroom, collect an admit slip from each student.

3. Use the admit slips as an introduction to the lesson or current day's activity.

4. You have many choices and options in terms of how admit slips can be used. Here are some suggestions from Daniels, Zemelman, and Steineke (2007):

    a. Collect them at the door, quickly skim as you gather them, and read a few out loud to prompt discussion.

    b. Find two opposing sides or opinions on a particular topic and read each one to spark discussion.

    c. Don't collect them, but ask for volunteers or call on students to read theirs aloud.

    d. Shuffle the admit slips, pass them out to students randomly (you should have the same number of admit slips as you have students) and have students read them aloud without identifying the author.

    e. Have students keep their own admit slips and pass them to the person behind them. Write a response to the other student's comments and them pass them back again for another round of comments. Have volunteers read all three sets of comments on their papers.

Here are some of my additional suggestions for using admit slips:

- Have students pass their admit slip to a partner, read each other's comments, and then discuss briefly. Call upon random pairs to share their comments and discussion.

- Have each student post the admit slips around the room; then have the class do a gallery walk to read other students' comments and ideas.

- Place students in groups of four and have each student read his admit slip aloud to the group. Group members should compare ideas and have some discussion.

### Strategy 2: Learning Logs

*Purpose*
    Use writing to reflect on learning; use writing as a tool for learning, remembering, and reflecting on content learning; summarize and clarify information.

*CCSS Connection*
    Standard W.4: Produce clear, coherent writing; Standard W.10: Write routinely over extended time frames.

*Overview*
    Learning logs are an excellent writing-to-learn activity that can be used in any content area, core course, or elective. Learning logs encourage students to reflect on their learning in the particular subject area. Learning logs are not the same as personal journals in that they focus on content material being studied in class. They can be used as a part of any lesson and in any part of the lesson. Students can complete a brief journal entry at the beginning of class, in the middle of an activity, experiment, film, or reading assignment, or at the end of class as a review activity. They are simply an excellent way to make writing an active part of your teaching of the content material. Students will learn more and experience a higher level of retention. The journals can also be used as way to help students organize and collect information and to assess their own learning.

*Procedure*
    If you decide to use learning logs for a particular class, unit, or grading period, build in regular time, frequently or even daily, for students to write learning log entries and reflect on their learning. They can be easily graded by simply skimming through the journals every few weeks or at the end of the grading period. Figure 3.2 includes some sample learning log prompts for social studies that come from Doty, Cameron, and Barton (2003).

- Which of the textbook chapters we have read so far this year has been the most difficult for you to understand? Analyze what it was about that particular chapter that made it hard to comprehend.

- Which historical character from this unit did you find the most interesting? Explain your answer.

- Art has been a major topic during this unit on Italy. Why do you think this topic has been the focus of so much of our text?

- The idea of mental maps is often confusing to students when they first hear it. Do you find this concept difficult to understand? What could you do to gain a better understanding of this idea? How could you teach this concept to others?

- Summarize the text material we read in class today. How does it connect and build on what we studied earlier this week?

- Write a letter to the editor of the school paper, or to another local paper, in which you argue for or against a controversial issue we have studied in class.

- Write about an upcoming test. List the questions you might be asked and develop answers for each.

- Consider how your perspective has changed as a result of what we have studied during this unit. How has learning about how others perceive things influenced the way you think about this topic?

- Summarize what you have  learned about how industrialization impacts cities.

- Explain in your own words how a bill becomes a law.

**Figure 3.2.   Learning Log Prompts. (Reprinted by permission of McREL.)**

## Strategy 3: Carousel Brainstorming

*Purpose*

Engage in collaborative writing; use writing to summarize, clarify and review content information; brainstorm to generate ideas; engage in collaborative discussion.

*CCSS Connection*

Standard W.4: Produce clear and coherent writing; Standard W.8: Gather relevant information from multiple print and digital sources; Standard SL.1: Prepare for and participate effectively in a range of conversations and collaborations.

*Overview*

Carousel brainstorming involves students in a process of brainstorming and writing about several different topics at once. This strategy comes from Daniels, Zemelman, and Steineke (2007). It can be used for introducing a new topic, or as a review activity for a unit, topic of study, or reading assignment.

*Procedure*

Begin with three or more different prompts for a particular unit, topic, or reading assignment. Place each of the prompts on a separate sheet of poster board or chart paper. Place students in groups of three to five students, and have each group use a different-colored marker. It works best to have the same number of prompts as you have groups of students. Each group should also appoint a recorder who will do the writing for the group. (Groups can switch to a different recorder at each new station.) Place each prompt in a given station, assign each group to a station, and then have groups rotate from one station to another. When they reach a new station, they read the prompt, discuss it, and add their own contribution, which will be identified by the color of their markers. Remind students that it is a brainstorming activity and encourage them to write down everything they can think of quickly. Give students a few minutes at each station before rotating. Tell students that when they get to a new group, they should first read through what all the other groups have written and add whatever new information and ideas they can. This makes the task increasingly harder as students proceed through it. If students think and talk about the responses already written on the paper, it will help them to come up with new things to add. Daniels, Zemelman, and Steineke (2007) suggest the following ways to use this strategy:

- Have each group present the items on their chart to the class and emphasize those they think are most important.

- Have each group do a second gallery walk to read all the responses. Then use whole-group discussion to focus on the highlights.

- Have each student do a quick-write or nonstop write about what he or she has read following the gallery walk. Ask students to share their quick-writes in small groups or with the whole class.

### Strategy 4: Cubing

*Purpose*

Engage in higher-level critical thinking; examine a topic or idea from various perspectives; use writing to demonstrate comprehension of a topic; use writing to describe, analyze, compare, and argue.

*CCSS Connection*

Standard W.4: Produce clear and coherent writing; Standard W.8: Gather relevant information from multiple print and digital sources; Standard W.9: Draw evidence from literary or informational text.

*Overview*

The use of the "cubing" technique is a great higher-order thinking strategy that asks students to look at a topic from several different sides. It helps students develop their conceptual understanding of a topic and work on writing skills.

*Procedure*

1. Choose a topic in your content area or from a particular unit of study that could be examined from multiple perspectives. Some examples might be genetics, global warming, or heredity from science; the American Revolution in US history; the concept of realism or romanticism from English or art; a piece of literature in English; the Fibonacci sequence in math; or use of nutritional supplements in physical education.

2. Use the graphic organizer in figure 3.3 to have students quickly examine and jot down notes about the subject from each different perspective, each one being a side of the "cube":

   a. describe it

   b. compare it with something else

    c. associate it with something else

    d. analyze it

    e. discuss its applications

    f. argue for or against it

3. When students have finished jotting down ideas for each perspective, ask them to write a paragraph about the topic.

4. Have students reread their paragraphs and make any necessary changes or corrections.

5. Have students share their paragraphs by reading them out loud to a partner or small group.

## CUBING: AN EXERCISE IN PERSPECTIVE

Topic: _____

| Describe It: Examine the subject closely and describe what you see. | Compare It: What is it similar to? Different from? |
|---|---|
| Associate it: What does the subject make you think of? | Analyze It: Break the subject into parts; tell how it is made. |
| Apply It: Describe the subject's uses. | Argue for Or Against It: Use any kind of reasoning to take a stand for or against the subject. |

**Figure 3.3.   Cubing Worksheet.**

## Strategy 5: Double Entry Journal

*Purpose*

Use writing to reflect on content information; use writing regularly over an extended time period; use writing to summarize and respond to content information; use writing as the basis for collaborative discussion; use writing to extend and deepen comprehension.

*CCSS Connection*

Standard W.2: Write informative/explanatory texts to examine and convey complex ideas; Standard W.4: Produce clear and coherent writing; Standard W.9: Draw evidence from literary or informational texts; Standard W.10: Write routinely over extended time frames; Standard SL.1: Prepare for and participate effectively in a range of conversations and collaborations.

*Overview*

This strategy is also sometimes called the summary-response notebook. It is a strategy that can be used in the classroom long term, throughout a unit, or for a whole semester or year. For any given reading assignments, ask students to write a page in a journal or notebook.

*Procedure*

1. Draw a line down the middle of the page.

2. In the left-hand column write a summary of the section of reading you have just completed.

3. In the right-hand column, write your personal responses and thoughts.

4. Use the journal to share ideas during class discussion and to share with a partner.

5. Review your entries in the journal to review for tests.

This strategy gives students practice in writing summaries, helps them connect their prior knowledge to what they are reading about, and increases the time students spend thinking about the reading material. You might consider giving students a guideline sheet that explains the purpose of this assignment and specifies this procedure. It should also include your specific requirements for the summary and response, length requirements, information about how it is graded, and due dates. Collect the journals periodically, more frequently during the first period of use. If you would rather not have students use a journal or notebook, but might like to use this strategy periodically, you can have them turn in each summary-response assignment separately. When grading, all you need to do is skim through the entries and holistically evaluate the summary and response. Use plus signs, minus signs, or checkmarks. Give detailed feedback only for students who have trouble responding. It is also helpful to show the class examples of good summaries and responses. The double entry journal entries can be used at the beginning of class to jumpstart the discussion.

Daniels, Zemelman, and Steineke (2007) note that the double entry journals can also be used to deepen understanding of the text, show the thinking behind solving a problem, or compare ideas. They offer a few variations (see figure 3.4) on use of the two-column structure.

| Column 1: | Column 2: |
|---|---|
| Computations | Explanation of thinking for each step |
| Problem | Solution |
| Reasons for | Reasons against |
| Opinion | Proof |
| Quote from Text | Explanation of importance |
| Quote from text | Personal connections |
| Quote from text | Relationship to previous unit |
| Quote from text | discussion questions |
| Agreements | Disagreements |
| Notes | Interpretations |
| Observations | Inferences |
| Advantages | Disadvantages |
| Words | Images |
| Facts | Feelings |

**Figure 3.4. Two-Column Variations.**

## Strategy 6: Quick Questions

*Purpose*

Use writing to summarize key information; write to analyze and apply content information; use writing to reflect on learning.

*CCSS Connection*

Standard W.4: Produce clear and coherent writing; Standard W.9: Draw evidence from literary or informational texts.

*Overview*

Quick questions is a strategy that forces students to go beyond simple note taking and summarizing and into analysis and engagement with the content.

*Procedure*

Following viewing of a film or doing a reading assignment, ask students to write responses to any or all of the following items:

- After reading, I know . . .
- After reading, I would like to know more about . . . because . . .
- The main question raised by the author is . . .
- The author assumes that everyone knows/believes that . . .
- The central idea is . . .
- People are likely to agree with the author if . . .
- People are likely to disagree with the author if . . .

You can also use quick questions as an exit activity during the last five minutes of class:

- One thing I learned today is . . .
- One question I have from class today is . . .
- One thing I hope we cover next class is . . . because . . .

An alternative activity is to assign different quick questions to each student, have him respond and then share his ideas with the class or in small groups. Student answers can be graded or ungraded. As teachers, they also can help us to understand what concepts students are struggling with and help us to identify what topics might require reteaching.

### Strategy 7: Microthemes

*Purpose*

Use prewriting to generate ideas and prepare for writing; use the planning phases of the writing process to identify thesis and support for an essay; understand and apply essay structure; use outlining to organize and review content material.

*CCSS Connection*

Standard W.5: Develop and strengthen writing as needed; Standard W.8: Gather relevant information from multiple print and digital sources.

*Overview*

The microtheme is actually a prewriting organizer or outline form used to help students prepare for writing a paper or essay (Brozo & Simpson, 2003). However, the microtheme can also be used as an assignment for students to identify key ideas in a reading assignment, demonstration, experiment, lecture, or film.

*Procedure*

The microtheme requires students to think about three different ways they might begin the paper. Then they state the thesis, main body points, and support for each point. They also identify how they will conclude the paper with a dominant feeling, impression, or message. This strategy not only helps students review content material but also helps those students who struggle with organizing a paper prior to writing it. Students find it more understandable and useful than a traditional outline.

Some teachers have students write microthemes for a quick review on index cards. They are easy to check and allow you to give quick feedback. Microthemes can be used in any content area. For example, students in English might use it to analyze the role of a particular character in a piece of literature. Students in science might use it to write a short report on a particular scientific principle. Use the worksheet format in figure 3.5.

## MICROTHEME

Introduction: I could begin my paper one of the following three ways . . .

- _____
  _____

- _____
  _____

- _____
  _____

Thesis: The claim I want to make and support in my essay is:

_____

_____

_____

Body:

Main points I want to make:                Specific references or examples to support:

- _____        _____

- _____        _____

- _____        _____

- _____        _____

- _____        _____

Conclusion: A feeling, impression, message, or idea I want to leave my reader with is:

_____
_____
_____
_____

**Figure 3.5.  Microtheme.**

## Strategy 8: Exit Slips

*Purpose*
    Write freely in response to a given prompt; summarize and clarify key learning from content material; generate questions and use writing as a tool to clarify points of confusion; evaluate and assess one's own learning.

*CCSS Connection*
    Standard W.4: Produce clear and coherent writing; Standard W.9: Draw evidence from literary or informational text; Standard W.10: Write routinely over extended time frames and shorter time frames.

*Overview*

Many teachers like to use exit slips as a way of incorporating writing into their classes. They can be done quickly and easily during the last five minutes or so of class, time that is often wasted in many classrooms as students have already mentally checked out and are packing up to leave.

*Procedure*

Exit slips are very simple. Just save the last five minutes of class and ask students to write about a particular prompt to review the lesson presented that period. It can be worded as simply as "Summarize what you have learned during this period" or "What points of confusion do you have about today's lesson?" Require students to actually keep writing for the entire five minutes. You can quickly read through these responses and get a good sense of what students know or don't know and what you might need to review.

You can tailor the exit slip prompt to cover a range of specific topics or just ask for a general summary of what the student has learned during that lesson. Most teachers will stand near the door as the bell rings and collect an exit slip from each student. (I watch for students who try to hand in a blank note card or piece of paper and make them stay until they have written a response.) In addition, you can begin the next day's class by reading some of the exit slips from the previous day aloud. They can prompt some further discussion and questions. Figure 3.6 shows possible exit slip topics from Daniels, Zemelman, and Steineke (2007).

One of the biggest benefits of exit slips is that they can show you what students are not understanding or are struggling with. You will get much more honest answers in exit slips than students will give you orally. They also do not have to be graded. You can just read them quickly to get a sense of what the class or particular students might need to review or what you would like to emphasize the next day.

- What did you learn today?

- How is this unit going for you?

- What was the most difficult or confusing idea you learned today and why?

- What were the three most important ideas you learned today and why?

- Pick one quote from today's class discussion or reading and comment on it.

- What are some questions you have about today's lesson? Where do you think you can get the answers to those questions?

- Predict what we will need to learn next in this unit and why.

- What would you like to have reviewed in class tomorrow?

- If you were going to teach this to someone else, what would be in your notes?

- If you were going to make up an essay test question based on today's class, what would it be?

- What do you need to concentrate on to finish this unit successfully? What goals can you set for yourself?

- What would be some good review questions about this material?

- What can I do to help you learn better?

- Summarize today's lesson in twenty-five carefully chosen words (or 100).

**Figure 3.6. Exit Slip Topics. (From Harvey Daniels, Steven Zemelman, and Nancy Steineke, *Content-Area Writing: Every Teacher's Guide*, Copyright © 2007 by Harvey Daniels, Steven Zemelman, and Nancy Steineke. Published by Heinemann, Portsmouth, NH. Reprinted by permission of the publisher. All rights reserved.)**

## Strategy 9: Timed and On-Demand Writing

*Purpose*

Generate writing in response to a given prompt; practice and prepare for timed and on-demand writing for high-stakes tests; build fluency by generating a coherent piece of writing in a given time frame; analyze a writing prompt; generate ideas, brainstorm, organize, write, and edit a piece of writing in a limited time frame; build and use academic vocabulary.

*CCSS Connection*

Standards W.1, W.2: Write arguments/informative texts; Standard W.4: Produce clear and coherent writing; Standard W.10: Write routinely or extended time frames and shorter time frames; Standard L.6: Acquire and use accurately a range of general academic and domain-specific words and phrases.

*Overview*

In his book *Teaching Adolescent Writers*, Kelley Gallagher (2006) argues that on-demand writing, or timed writing, is one of the most important writing skills we should be helping students to develop. In secondary school, particularly high school, and on into college, students are often asked to write to a prompt for a given time period, anywhere from thirty minutes to a couple of hours. These forms of writing are often high-stakes writing as well. Students may be required to write for state and district assessments (which in some states are graduation requirements), for Advanced Placement and International Baccalaureate exams, for college admission tests (the SAT test now requires a written section), and in other classroom testing situations in high school and college. Many employers are now requiring a writing sample as a part of application materials or an interview. Students often face these types of high-stakes writing situations, yet spend only about 15 percent of their time in school writing, most of which is note taking or copying down information. Students need to spend more time practicing writing in school settings and they need practice with on-demand and timed writing to build fluency and prepare for the situations mentioned here. Teachers in all disciplines can require students to complete occasional timed writing tests or assignments.

*Procedure*

Here are some suggestions for implementing on-demand writing in your classroom:

- Have students frequently do quick-writes, journaling, admit slips, exit slips, conversation logs, and other free-response writing in the classroom so that they become comfortable with writing and build writing fluency.

- Use Gallagher's (2006) four-step process for approaching on-demand writing prompts. He calls it the ABCD method:

  o *Attack* the prompt by circling all the words that indicate what the writer is to do, drawing arrows from the circles to what the prompt specifically tells the writer to do, and then numbering or ordering the circled words. A frequent mistake students make on these types of writing assignments or tests is misreading or misunderstanding what the prompt is asking them to do. Attacking the prompt in this manner will help prevent that.

  o *Brainstorm* possible answers and content for your response. This can be a quick list, map, web, or chart.

  o *Choose* the order of the responses. Using the numbered words from part one, outline what will be included in each part of the response. Students then write their response.

  o *Detect* errors by rereading the piece of writing during the last five minutes of time.

- Teach students the academic vocabulary they will need for various essay questions and topics found in on-demand writing, words commonly used in academic writing. We often assume that students understand what these words mean, when they may actually not. Common academic vocabulary includes words such as the following: analyze, compare, critique, assess, consider, diagram, describe, define, discuss, cause/effect, enumerate, explain, identify, evaluate, illustrate, interpret, list, justify, outline, prove, respond, relate, summarize, state, solve, support, synthesize.

- How should you score, grade, or assess the students' timed writings? Make a simple rubric or checklist, tell students ahead of time what you are specifically going to look for in their response (paragraphing, length, organization, content, etc.), score the essays holistically using a 1–5 scale, or simply give students credit for having written a sufficiently long piece in the given time period.

## Strategy 10: Freewriting/Quickwriting

*Purpose*

Write freely in response to a given prompt; summarize and clarify key learning from content material; generate questions and use writing as a tool to clarify points of confusion; evaluate and assess one's own learning; build fluency through freewriting/quickwriting practice.

*CCSS Connection*

Standard W.4: Produce clear and coherent writing; Standard W.9: Draw evidence from literary or informational text; Standard W.10: Write routinely over extended time frames and shorter time frames.

*Overview*

One of the simplest and easiest writing strategies to use is called by different names: freewriting, quickwriting, nonstop writing, or fastwriting most commonly. Like all writing assignments, it helps to improve students' learning and thinking, increases their engagement with the material, and can be used in any content area.

Consider the fact that in classrooms students do a lot of passive learning, in which teachers deliver information, students absorb it, and interaction is often minimal. Writing helps us get closer to active learning, in which students are thoughtfully engaging with the material and working collaboratively. Freewriting is also in some ways the opposite of formal writing. Whereas formal writing is planned, drafted, and revised, and usually graded or evaluated by the teacher, informal writing such as freewriting is composed quickly, not revised or edited, is not graded in any formal way, and serves only its primary purpose of stimulating thinking about the topic. The great thing about freewriting, much like most forms of writing, is that it encourages the student to explore his thoughts on a topic and becomes a process of discovery. When we engage in freewriting, we discover new ideas and connections.

*Procedure*

Freewriting sessions will typically last anywhere from five to fifteen minutes. I recommend shorter times of five minutes, and you can gradually work up to ten minutes or longer. Simply present students with a topic or prompt and then ask students to follow three rules:

- Start writing and try not to stop.

- Don't make corrections.

- Don't go back to reread or rewrite; just keep writing.

Encourage students to try not to take their pen or pencil off the paper (or hands off the keyboard). Since the goal of freewriting is to generate new ideas, students should be encouraged to keep ideas flowing and let one idea lead to another. Students are often uncomfortable with this type of writing at first, partly because the importance of correctness has been drilled into them through all their years of school. But with freewriting, no attention should be paid to spelling, punctuation, capitalization, grammar, and so on. The focus should be entirely on the ideas and content. *No correcting!*

Students can do occasional or daily freewriting on any given topic, but here is one possible application: You have reached the end of a particular unit and are expecting students to begin preparing for a test. Have them do a ten-minute freewrite to summarize or review everything they have learned during the unit or about the particular topic. As they are writing, they will remember additional information they were not consciously aware of. Another possible way in which freewriting could be used as an end-of-class activity is to ask students to complete a short freewrite to reflect on their learning during that class period. Obviously, if you have your students keep journals, freewriting can be included as part of the journal. As far as grading, simply skim through the freewrites and give students points based on completion. Some other possible uses of freewriting: as a prelude to a discussion (to activate prior knowledge), as a postdiscussion activity, as a postreading activity, as an icebreaker, as a beginning or end of class activity, as review for a test, as a way to share thoughts and personal opinions on a topic, as a way to reflect on what they have learned, as a way to extend and apply classroom learning. Also, many teachers often give students an opportunity to read or share their freewriting with the class or in small groups.

I recently asked my technical writing students, as the term was just beginning, to do some freewriting on the topic of technical writing, what it means, how it is used, and why it is important. These freewrites functioned as a useful pre-assessment for me, to help me understand how much students already knew about the subject and what some of their misconceptions were. Here are a couple of examples:

Kham's freewrite:

Technical writing is a way to communicate through various resources. Technical writing consists of things included in reports, charts, e-mails, and ways people in business communicate with each other. The way to write them depends on who you are trying to communicate with. An example could be a boss, colleague, friends, etc. Technical writing is something that is used every day and can be learned by anyone willing to learn about it. Sometimes, though, it is very difficult for those who are new to the technical side of writing. It is a very important tool to grasp because it is an essential way to communicate with various people that you may meet in your profession.

Luis's freewrite:

> Technical writing might be all about the punctuation and structure of the English language. It could also be a more advanced skill such as organization, structure, citation, and so on. Technical writing sounds a bit intimidating like something that a professional may talk about, but I'm sure that after studying it, it will not be as bad as I thought. Technical writing might not be as regular writing such as stories or poems but more about the structure of them, like the components: from heading to ending, the punctuation, and the way it is presented. For example, a letter has the date and the name of the person sent, the body and at the end the name of the person that sent it. So for me at this point, that's what technical writing is.

(Student examples reprinted with permission.)

## Strategy 11: Praise-Question-Polish (PQP) or Questioning the Author

*Purpose*

    Engage in active reading of text; evaluate and critique the writing techniques and content of a given text; generate questions about text; learn and use memo format; write clearly and coherently; write for a specific audience; revise and proofread one's own writing.

*CCSS Connection*

    Standard R.1: Read closely to determine what the text says explicitly; Standard R.2: Determine central ideas or themes of a text; Standard R.8: Delineate and evaluate argument and specific claims of a text; Standard W.4: Produce clear and coherent writing; Standard W.5: Develop and strengthen writing as needed; Standard W.9: Draw evidence from literary or informational text.

*Overview*

    Praise-question-polish is both a reading and a writing strategy that provides a way to teach students to "talk back" to the author, and also involves students in writing a memo to the author of the book or particular reading assignment. It asks students not only to read carefully and clarify understanding of text but also to critique and evaluate the author's techniques. The strategy comes from Larry Lewin (2003), who notes that it originated with Tom Cantwell, a middle school teacher from Eugene, Oregon. PQP teaches students to create a successful critique of an author's work. A similar strategy is called "questioning the author" (Beck, McKeown,

Hamilton, & Kucan, 1997), in which the teacher poses particular questions about the reading material to students, such as the following: What are the authors trying to help you understand? Why is this information important? Did the authors explain the information clearly? Did the authors explain why it is important to understand the topic discussed?

*Procedure*

1. When students begin reading the article, chapter, or passage, provide them with three different colors of sticky notes. One color is for the P comments, one for the Qs, and one for the Ps. Teach students the three parts of PQP (shown in the following section). As students read the selection, they should be thinking about what the author is doing and recording feedback on the sticky notes.

2. Teach students the three parts of the critique:

   a. P = Praise for what you like about the author's writing style and ideas.

   b. Q = Questions for the author about what aspects of the reading were confusing, not explained well, or hard to understand. Questions may also be directed to why the author chose to include (or not include) certain elements.

   c. P = Polishing ideas recommended to the author, or rather, suggestions for improvement in his or her writing, book, chapter, or article.

3. When students have completed a unit or a particular reading assignment, tell them that they are going to be writing a critique of the work. Explain that critique doesn't mean only what one doesn't like, but also what one likes as well as suggestions for improvement.

4. Provide students with the memo format (see figure 3.7). Have them use the three colors of sticky notes and write a memo to the author to provide feedback in all three areas. Some alternatives to memo format might be a formal letter, a postcard, an e-mail, or a blog.

5. Have students share their completed memos with a small group or the whole class. Have students check each other's memos for evidence of each of the three parts: PQP.

TO: _____

FROM: _____

DATE: _____

RE: _____

_____
_____
_____
_____
_____
_____
_____
_____
_____
_____
_____
_____
_____
_____
_____
_____
_____
_____

Figure 3.7. Memo to the Author. (From Larry Lewin, *Paving the Way in Reading and Writing: Strategies and Activities to Support Struggling Students in Grades 6–12*, Copyright © 2003 by John Wiley and Sons, Inc. Reproduced with permission of John Wiley and Sons, Inc.)

## Strategy 12: Genres

*Purpose*

Identify and recognize various genres of writing; write in a specific chosen genre; write in a disciplinary genre appropriate for particular content area; compose clear and coherent writing following the conventions of a specific genre; revise and proofread one's own writing; write for a particular audience.

*CCSS Connection*

Standard W.4: Produce clear and coherent writing; Standard W.5: Develop and strengthen writing as needed; Standard W.8: Gather relevant information from multiple print and digital sources; Standard W.9: Draw evidence from literary or informational text.

*Overview*

The word "genre" refers to type or form of something. Writing, painting, music, and other forms of art can be produced in many different genres when specific examples share a particular content, purpose, format, or style. One excellent writing strategy is to have students practice writing on content topics in different genres. This lends itself naturally to various content areas, because the content areas themselves focus on disciplinary forms of writing in particular genres. Genres are a key concept in academic writing because people use the particular forms to share knowledge and conduct research within the field. They are germane to artistic and cultural expression in forms such as storytelling, song, or poetry. If students are given exposure and practice with writing various genres, they can better understand content knowledge. One time, when teaching a novel to an English class, instead of having students complete a traditional study guide, I had students create their own version of CliffsNotes (e.g., Justin Notes or Olivia Notes!). This required helping them identify the features and sections typical of CliffsNotes for works of literature (list of characters, character analysis, discussion of style, discussion of themes, chapter summaries, critical response, review questions).

*Procedure*

Below are several different common genres for academic text as well as a list of possible purposes. Try choosing two or three of the following genres and having students write one of their own choosing as an alternative to a more traditional essay or report. (Another option, of course, is to assign students to learn about a particular genre that is an important form of disciplinary writing in the field.) Doing this activity does require teaching students about the features of the particular genres and providing several examples from the real world.

173

*Genres*

| | |
|---|---|
| argumentative essay | e-mail message |
| article | ethnography |
| editorial | poem |
| review | abstract/summary |
| business letter | recommendation |
| memo | reflective journal |
| case study | outline |
| lab report | research paper/essay |
| annotated bibliography | technical report/analytical report |
| essay exam | personal essay |
| multimedia essay | interview |
| webpage | Facebook page |
| multimedia presentation | blog |
| narrative | Twitter posting (tweet) |
| news article | other possibilities? |

Purposes of genres are to amuse, beguile, delight, entertain, introduce, organize, celebrate, convince, announce, cajole, demonstrate learning, gratify, persuade, lead, teach, argue, charm, discourage, guide, change policy, plan, test, assure, convert, dissuade, impress, notify, please, and request.

Provide students with lots of examples of the particular type of genre from the real world. You may also need to teach students that genres may have many different purposes and subtypes and that there are certain assumptions about particular genres. For example, a narrative essay about a personal experience suggests that sharing experiences can teach us something of value. A letter focuses on a specific issue or problem and is written for a specific audience. A scientific research report conveys knowledge that is verifiable. An analytical essay divides the subject into parts and relates each one to the whole. Some genres, such as a review, seek to evaluate or test the quality of something. In short, help students to identify the features of various genres and how different genres function in particular subject areas (e.g., a lab report in science), and try having students write in a genre that may be unusual for your subject areas (e.g., a poem or interview about or with a historical figure). After students have written initial drafts, spend some time having them revise, edit, and proofread and then create a polished final copy.

## Strategy 13: Journalist's Questions

*Purpose*

Generate questions to gather information; use brainstorming as a way to generate ideas about a given topic; review and summarize content knowledge on a given topic; use writing as a way to clarify concepts and generate new ideas.

*CCSS Connection*

Standard W.8: Gather relevant information from multiple print and digital sources; Standard W.9: Draw evidence from literary or informational text.

*Overview*

Journalists traditionally ask six questions when they are assigned to write a news story; they are sometimes referred to as the five Ws and an H: Who? What? Where? When? Why? How? Have students approach a particular concept or topic they are studying by using these six questions to explore the topic in a writing assignment. For example, if you are studying the rise and fall of the Puget Sound tides and their effects on salmon spawning, the "Who" may be not people, but rather the salmon, or perhaps the people dependent on the salmon population.

*Procedure*

Try assigning students to write about a particular topic using the following generic questions for each category:

- Who? Who are the participants? Who is affected? Who are the primary actors, characters or people? Who are the secondary actors, characters, or people?

- What? What is the topic? What is the significance of the topic? What is the basic problem? What are the issues?

- Where? Where does the activity take place? Where does the problem or issue have its source? At what place is the cause or effect of the problem most visible?

- When? When is the issue most apparent or relevant—past, present, or future? When did the issue or problem develop? What historical forces helped shape the problem or issue? At what point in time will the problem or issue culminate in a crisis? When is action needed to address the issue?

- Why? Why did the issue or problem arise? Why is it an issue or problem at all? Why did the issue develop in the way that it did?

- How? How is the issue or problem significant? How can it be addressed? How does it affect the participants? How can the issue or problem be resolved?

The journalist's questions are a great way to generate lots of information about a topic very quickly. Guide students in the process of asking appropriate and relevant questions. This strategy is also a particularly good brainstorming technique for generating ideas in preparation for writing an essay. Here are some possible applications for particular subject areas:

- English: An event in a story, novel, or play
- Social studies: Any historical event such as the dropping of the bomb on Hiroshima and Nagasaki, or a geographical region
- Science: An environmental problem or issue, a chemical reaction, an alternative to a lab report
- Math: A story problem and how to solve it
- Art: Any painting or work of art

## Strategy 14: Proposal Arguments

*Purpose*

Use techniques of argument and persuasion; conduct research as necessary to write about a real-world topic, issue or problem; identify and apply the conventions of proposal writing; write clearly and coherently; use specific detail to support one's ideas; use the writing process; generate a claim or thesis statement; create an organizational plan and outline for one's writing; write for a specific audience; revise, proofread, and edit one's own writing.

*CCSS Connection*

Standard W.1: Write arguments to support claim; Standard W.4: Produce clear and coherent writing; Standard W.5: Develop and strengthen writing as needed; Standard W.7: Conduct short as well as more sustained research projects; Standard W.8: Gather relevant information from multiple print and digital sources; Standard L.3: Apply knowledge of language to understand how language functions in different contexts.

*Overview*

This writing activity can be used in a number of different content areas with a variety of topics. It is easily adapted to various content situations and also lends itself to real-world writing and helps teach civic responsibility. It is an excellent way to show students how writing works in the real world. Any situation in the school, community, or subject area that involves a problem, issue, or dilemma in need of a solution is an appropriate topic for this activity.

*Procedure*

1. Teach students that in a proposal argument, they will be asked to identify a problem, propose a solution, and justify the solution with reasons and evidence. This may require doing some research and incorporating some source material in the writing.

2. Have students choose a topic. They might look for possible solutions to problems at school, such as problems in the neighborhood, parking, over-crowding, noise, inappropriate behavior, or student activities. The problem might also be one that applies to the neighborhood, community, town, or even on a larger scale, a national issue such as energy resources, the deficit, global warming, inequitable taxation, funding of elections, voting laws, poverty, racism, and so on. The particular content area you teach will likely determine the type of topic students can choose.

3. Begin by considering the general problem and have students do some brainstorming about the nature and extent of the problem in the particular context. Students should explore various possible alternatives to solving the problem. Assure them that most problems have more than one solution. Use some type of brainstorming such as the following to help students think through the problem:

   a. Write down the problem statement in the center of a piece of paper and draw a circle around it.

   b. Draw lines out from the center and write down several possible solutions for the problem at the end of each line.

   c. Add details to each solution by adding additional lines and circles.

4. Have students spend some time doing research into the nature of the particular problem. They should try to identify some of the solutions others have thought of and tried. If it is a school issue, they may need to interview some school officials. Have them think about why some solutions were tried and failed.

5. After doing some research, students should choose the solution they think is the best one possible. Have them freewrite a list of reasons why this solution is better than others. Then have them write out a thesis statement that states the problem, solution, and the overall reason for choosing that solution. For example: "The problem of poverty, one that is widespread today, can be solved through _____. This is the best way to solve the problem for three major reasons: first, _____; second, _____; and third _____." Providing students with a sentence frame such as this one may assist them in preparing a good thesis statement.

6. Students should next create an outline of their proposal, followed by a first draft. Scaffold this process as much as necessary, depending on the level of writing ability of the particular group. Tell students that their draft should show how the solution addresses all the different aspects of the problem, explain why the solution is better than others that have been tried or recommended, and address any strong arguments against your solution.

7. Have students think about the potential audience for the proposal, and once the project is completed, encourage them to actually send a copy of the proposal to the intended audience. Possible audiences may include, depending upon the topic, the principal or school district officials, community officials or leaders, legislators or other elected officials, local newspapers, online forums, and so on.

8. Finally have students edit and proofread carefully, check to be sure they have addressed all the possible concerns people may have and have correctly cited sources, and then prepare a final copy to go to the audience and to turn in for a grade.

## Strategy 15: Writing a Summary

*Purpose*

Identify main ideas and supporting details; write a summary; use information from text or other sources to generate a concise piece of writing on a given topic; take notes to prepare for writing; revise and edit one's own writing.

*CCSS Connection*

Standard R.1: Read closely to determine what the text says explicitly; Standard R.2: Determine central ideas or themes of a text; Standard R.7: Delineate and evaluate the argument and specific claims in a text; Standard W.4: Produce clear and coherent writing; Standard W.8: Gather relevant information from multiple print and digital sources.

*Overview*

Summary writing is a very important skill and it is a type of writing that students need to learn to do well and practice. College students are often assigned to write summaries of articles and other textual materials. It is also a common form of workplace writing. Students can gain practice writing summaries in any content area in the curriculum. They can be written for an article, book, chapter, website, or any other text. You can also have students write summaries of a discussion or film on a particular topic. The goal of a summary is to accurately provide a full sense of the original text, but in a more condensed form. It should restate the author's main points, purpose, intent, and supporting details in your own words.

*Procedure*

1. Ask students to review the original text and, if possible, skim through it again. Identify and write down the main idea or ideas and refer to any headings or graphics. Also read the conclusion of the text.

2. Ask students to go through the text and pull out all the major ideas and main supporting points. Either highlight them or jot them down on a piece of paper. You may want to make a brief outline to follow while writing the summary.

3. Have students write out the summary, making sure to state the title and author's name in the first sentence. For example: "In the essay 'Race by the Numbers,' Orlando Patterson argues that . . ." Give several suggestions: Be sure to include all the main ideas followed by all the supporting points. Avoid including too many of the author's ideas or examples. Focus on how the author supports, defines, and or illustrates the main idea. *Do not* copy the exact words from the original. Rewrite the ideas in your own words. Your summary will be approximately one paragraph to one full page in length. For an article or textbook chapter, no more than one page is recommended.

4. Remind students that a summary should summarize only; that is, it should be completely objective and not include one's own personal opinions, ideas, or reactions.

5. As students revise and edit their summaries, have them compare it to the original and ask themselves if they have rephrased the author's words without changing the meaning. Also, have they restated the main idea and supporting points accurately.

6. Have students share summaries with each other and identify similarities and differences.

For assessment, you can quickly skim through student summaries and use a holistic method such as a score from 1 to 5. It's very easy to determine with a quick reading how accurately students understood the material.

## Strategy 16: Framed Paragraphs

*Purpose*
Use a template for writing; develop and use appropriate academic language for writing; learn conventions and skills necessary for writing in various disciplinary modes.

*CCSS Connection*
Standard L.3: Apply knowledge of language to understand how language functions in different contexts; Standard L.6: Acquire and use accurately a range of general academic and domain-specific words and phrases.

*Overview*
Summary writing can be challenging and overwhelming for many students. Framed paragraphs provide students with more guidance and structure. They are excellent scaffolding to help students build more sophisticated skills in writing of various types of text. Brozo and Simpson (2003) call them "skeletal paragraphs with strategically placed transitions or cue words that signal to students a particular way to think about and write about a concept" (p. 272).

*Procedure*
Following a particular reading assignment, lecture, film, or activity, have students use the framed structure to complete their piece of writing. This helps to gradually move students into the academic language needed to write about the concepts in the particular content area. You can quickly and easily write paragraph frames for a number of different types and modes of writing, such as cause and effect or comparison contrast. Figure 3.8 shows an example of a paragraph frame I created for analyzing plot development in a piece of literature.

The AVID college readiness curriculum also includes frame templates in their critical reading materials. Figure 3.9 is the AVID template for analyzing and summarizing evidence (LeMaster, 2009, p. 140).

The plot of the story begins when _____

_____. The main conflict is _____.

The first major event is _____

followed by _____ and _____

_____. The main character,

_____, responds by _____ which results in

_____.

The climax occurs when _____.

The resolution of the story is when _____.

At the end _____.

**Figure 3.8. Paragraph Frame.**

_____ in the article _____
(author's full name)                                        (article title)

_____s that _____
(verb)                          (what is the author's claim?)

_____

_____.

In his/her article, _____     _____
                        (author's last name)

_____     _____
(verb that describes how the author collects evidence)     (discuss the type of evidence the author

uses and explain why the author uses it)

_____

in order to_____     _____     _____

_____.

For example, _____     _____(s) _____
                (author's last name)                  (verb)

_____
(list or describe the evidence)

_____
(describe specific evidentiary details)                                            .

This evidence suggests that _____

_____
(analyze the evidence and discuss its significance to the author's claim)

_____

**Figure 3.9. AVID Template for Analyzing and Summarizing Evidence. (Reprinted with permission from AVID Press.)**

## Strategy 17: Reflective Writing

*Purpose*
   Write freely in response to a given prompt; summarize and clarify key learning from content material; generate questions and use writing as a tool to clarify points of confusion; evaluate and assess one's own learning; build fluency through reflective writing practice; reflect on one's own learning.

*CCSS Connection*
   Standard W.4: Produce clear and coherent writing; Standard W.9: Draw evidence from literary or informational text; Standard W.10: Write routinely over extended time frames and shorter time frames.

*Overview*

One way to use writing in your classroom is to have students frequently engage in writing for reflective purposes. This strategy, which is similar to a freewrite or non-stop write, comes from Daniels, Zemelman, and Steineke (2007). Reflective writing involves students in thinking about their learning following the completion of an assignment or project. Students can reflect on the activity itself and on the learning they experienced from doing it. Whether it is a discussion, a test, a field trip, a group project, or a major term project, you can have students complete a reflective write afterward, either a short, informal piece of writing or a longer piece.

What is the purpose of having students reflect on their learning? First of all, students often complete projects or assignments and then quickly forget about them. But having them reflect on their learning requires them to evaluate the level of their work, the amount of effort they put into it, and their level of success. It better cements the learning in students' minds through the metacognitive process. Students can also use it to set goals for themselves in terms of what they can do to improve their future work. Another benefit of reflective writing is that it gives you, the teacher, lots of information and awareness about how much students have learned and how successful you have been as a teacher. We can see what was easy for students, what was challenging, and what the long-term impact of the learning may be.

*Procedure*

Some suggestions for using reflective writing: Model the process for students by writing a sample reflection on the computer or overhead projector. Also, save some copies of good student reflective writes in order to show students some examples. The reflective write generally works best if you have students complete it during class, where you can ensure that everyone spends some thoughtful time on their reflection. Another suggestion is to have students do reflective writes following a reading assignment; thus it helps students and you become more aware of what the general level of understanding is, where there may be areas of confusion, what you might need to focus on in discussion, or where some review and reteaching may be necessary.

Here is an example of a student's reflective write following a reading assignment on FDR and the New Deal.

> When I first started this assignment I didn't know very much about the New Deal or what it was. I knew a few things about the Great Depression like the fact that people were really poor and there were not very many jobs for people. Reading this selection made me realize how bad things were after the Stock Market Crash in 1929. People blamed the depression on President Hoover and the Republicans in Congress, so FDR won a really big victory when he was elected president. I never knew before that one of Roosevelt's first acts as President was repealing Prohibition, which led to a big boom in the alcohol making industry. There were also lots of poverty-relief programs, and the Civilian Conservation Corps for young men who could not find jobs. Some of the greatest engineering projects of the whole century came out of this time, such as the Hoover Dam and the Tennessee Valley Authority. There were also lots of rules and laws to help farmers and industries. The Social Security Act in 1935 provided older people with monthly payments. I know my grandparents and older people today still depend upon the money they get from this program. I've also heard the President and Congressmen today talking about reforming Social Security. After doing this reading, I think that it is important for our government to step in when things are really bad and try to do things to help people and families who are struggling. It seems like a lot of these programs created by FDR have been very important to the people in our country and have helped the country stay strong. I guess the people of America appreciated President Roosevelt and the New Deal programs because he was re-elected in 1936 in the greatest landslide in history.

(Student work printed with permission.)

## Strategy 18: Writing and Question Starters

> *Purpose*
>
> Learn and practice multiple ways to begin sentences; use questioning to generate ideas; develop critical-thinking skills; respond to questions at the knowledge, comprehension, application, analysis, synthesis, and evaluation levels; write clearly and coherently on a given topic; use writing to summarize learning; apply content learning to multiple situations and contexts; think and write critically and creatively.

*Overview*

One way to get students writing is to provide them with options for sentence starters. The following are question starters and potential writing topics that are arranged according to the levels of Bloom's taxonomy.

*Procedure*

These questions can obviously be used for discussion questions, for designing study guide questions or test questions, and they can be used for providing students with a way to approach writing about a particular topic. You could print these writing and question starters on a card or sheet of paper and make them available to students to use during discussion and writing. Another possible application is to have them choose one starter from each level and use it to write about a particular topic as a postreading assignment or in preparation for a test.

Level One: Knowledge

What is the definition for . . . ?

What happened after . . . ?

Recall the facts about . . .

What were the characteristics of . . . ?

Which is true or false?

How many . . . ?

Who was the . . . ?

Tell in your own words . . .

Level Two: Comprehension

Why are these ideas similar?

Retell the story of . . .

What do you think could happen?

How are these ideas different?

Explain what happened after?

What are some examples of . . . ?

Who was the key character?

## Level Three: Application

What is another instance of . . . ?

Demonstrate the way to . . .

Which one is most like . . . ?

What questions would you ask?

Which factors could you change?

Could this have happened in . . . ?

How would you organize these ideas?

## Level Four: Analysis

What are the component parts of . . . ?

What steps are important in the process of . . . ?

If . . . then . . .

What other conclusions can you reach about . . . ?

The solution would be to . . .

What is the relationship between . . . ?

## Level Five: Synthesis

Design a . . .

Compose a song about . . .

Devise your own way to . . .

Develop a proposal for . . .

How would you deal with . . .

Invent a scheme that would . . .

PART THREE

Level Six: Evaluation

In your opinion . . .

Evaluate the chances for . . .

Grade or rank the . . .

What do you think should be the outcome of . . . ?

What solutions do you favor and why?

Which systems are best? Worst?

Rate the relative value of these ideas to . . .

Which is the better bargain?


## Strategy 19: Write Around

*Purpose*

Use writing to reflect on content information; use writing regularly over an extended time period; use writing to summarize and respond to content information; use writing as the basis for collaborative discussion; write in response to others' writing; use writing to extend and deepen comprehension; engage in critical thinking on a given topic.

*CCSS Connection*

Standard W.2: Write informative/explanatory texts to examine and convey complex ideas; Standard W.4: Produce clear and coherent writing; Standard W.9: Draw evidence from literary or informational texts; Standard W.10: Write routinely over extended time frames; Standard SL.1: Prepare for and participate effectively in a range of conversations and collaborations.

*Overview*

The write around strategy comes from Daniels, Zemelman, and Steineke's book *Content-Area Writing* (2007). They describe it as one of the most powerful writing-to-learn activities and note that it may be used to replace whole-class discussions. The strategy is similar to others such as the dialectic notebook and written conversation. The write around involves a group of three to five students who write about a given topic and then pass their papers to the next student. Each page then becomes a string of conversation on the topic.

*Procedure*

1. Identify a topic or create a prompt for the write around, preferably a complex topic that calls for students to raise questions, make interpretations, and express disagreements.

2. Have students form groups of about four students, moving chairs so as to face each other.

3. Each student must start with a piece of paper, placing his or her name on the heading of the paper.

4. Instruct students that they are to use all the given time for writing, and not to talk when passing the papers.

5. Students begin by writing for one minute on the topic. They may include thoughts, reactions, questions, and reflections about the prompt. The time can be extended to more than one minute if you desire.

6. Next, students pass their papers, deciding which way papers will be rotated. Then each student reads what the first student has written on the paper, and, just underneath it, he or she writes for one more minute. Stress the importance of keeping the conversation going and the need for all students to respond to what has been written on the paper.

7. Students pass their papers again, and repeat until the papers come back to the original writer.

8. When each student's own paper is returned, he or she should read through the conversation that was started with the original comments.

9. At this point in the strategy you have several options. Students could have a whole-group discussion on the topic within their group and continue any threads that developed in the written discussions. You can also assign students a new prompt and begin the write around process again, or you might have each group share one of their conversation threads with the whole class. Finally, debrief with the whole class. Ask students what worked and did not work.

Here are a couple of examples of write arounds from my sophomore American literature class. Students were partway through a reading of Barbara Kingsolver's novel *The Bean Trees* and were writing in response to this prompt: "Compare the characters of Taylor and Lou Ann in terms of background, self-esteem, and relationships." Notice how the write around allows for independent thought and generation of ideas and also serves as a written discussion as each student plays off what the previous students had written.

*Jacob:* Taylor and Lou Ann are similar in some ways and very different in others. Both Taylor and Lou Ann are single mothers at least for the time being. Each character has had some bad luck. For instance, Taylor was given the burden of Turtle without asking for it, while Lou Ann's husband left her when she was pregnant. Taylor seems to have a good sense of self-esteem and confidence, while Lou Ann does not. Lou Ann beats herself up.

*Natalia:* Lou Ann blames herself for Angel's absence. She believes she is the reason for her own problems. Taylor who prefers not to dwell in the past sees no point in taking blame for a man long gone and encourages Lou Ann to become stronger and move on. Living together, I think their different personalities combined make for a good friendship. They can both be there for each other and give strength to each other's weaknesses. They both figure out that they have to live with the life given to them, so they have to take it and make the best of what they have.

*Lily:* Good point with the bad luck bit. Didn't even occur to me. They are brought together *because* of their misfortunes. If Taylor didn't have Turtle it would be easier for her to find a job and live on less; therefore she probably wouldn't have responded to Lou Ann's ad. If Angel hadn't left, Lou Ann wouldn't have placed an ad. Maybe their "bad lucks" are the best things that ever happened to them? Lou Ann will become a strong, independent woman and Taylor will discover her inner mother bird.

*Leah:* I think Lily already covered what I was going to say! You know the saying, "One man's garbage is another's treasure"? It's sort of the same thing; one person's misfortune can be another's miracle. Taylor wasn't expecting to accumulate a child on her journey. This changed everything and it was simply "fate" if you will, that put her in the right place at the right time and the right situation to bring her and Lou Ann together.

And another example from Emily, Megan, Rachel, and Emma:

*Emily:* Although Taylor and Lou Ann are both young, new mothers, and from Kentucky, they could not be more different in terms of background and self-esteem. Taylor is tough, resourceful, and confident. Lou Ann, on the other hand, is cautious, fragile and unsure of herself. Taylor's resilient spirit is partly a product of her background. She was raised in poverty, having to "make do" with little and keep the resolve to leave Pittman County. Lou Ann, however, grew up under the influence of a controlling mother and an ignorant grandma.

*Megan:* I agree, and the words you used to describe both Taylor and Lou Ann were spot on. I also agree that Taylor and Lou Ann have very close similarities in terms of being from Kentucky and being new mothers, and how they are polar opposites when it comes to self-esteem and most parts of each woman's background (I included being from Kentucky as a background in mine, but I guess it all depends).

*Rachel:* I agree with Emily saying that Taylor and Lou Ann were very different. The words she uses to describe them are great. Taylor is very tough and confident, which is shown through many of her encounters. Lou Ann, however, is a mother by choice whereas Taylor got it thrust upon her, which is another difference between them. Lou Ann is very questioning of herself and listens to others more than she should.

*Emma:* Although Lou Ann seems to be more shy and fragile than Taylor, she is also dealing with her situation better than I expected. It shows that she is strong when she adjusts well to the divorce. Taylor, I would agree, is the more confident between the two. An example of her confidence is when she just drives away from home all by herself. Also, when Taylor chooses to keep Turtle, it shows her strength.

(Student examples used with permission.)

## Strategy 20: Written Conversation

*Purpose*

Use writing to reflect on content information; use writing regularly over an extended time; use writing to summarize and respond to content information; use writing as the basis for collaborative discussion; write in response to others' writing; use writing to extend and deepen comprehension; engage in critical thinking on a given topic.

*CCSS Connection*

Standard W.2: Write informative/explanatory texts to examine and convey complex ideas; Standard W.4: Produce clear and coherent writing; Standard W.9: Draw evidence from literary or informational texts; Standard W.10: Write routinely over extended time frames; Standard SL.1: Prepare for and participate effectively in a range of conversations and collaborations.

*Overview*

Written conversations (Daniels, Zemelman, & Steineke, 2007) are also called dialogue journals. They are a conversation on a topic that takes place in writing. Students enjoy this strategy because of their love of texting and one-on-one correspondence. It is also a good way to get everyone involved, since all students participate in the discussion of the given topic, as opposed to class discussion, in which often a handful of students tend to dominate.

PART THREE

*Procedure*

The strategy is so simple that it does not require a list of procedures. Simply have students sit next to a partner. Each one begins writing on the topic and then they exchange papers, writing back and forth to each other on the particular topic or prompt. Have students switch papers every three minutes or so. You might want to model this process with your own short piece of writing, partnering with a student volunteer to introduce the process to the whole class. You can also have students share their conversations with the whole class. The following is a short hypothetical excerpt of a written conversation that followed reading about the building of the Panama Canal. It was written in response to the prompt, "What were the benefits of the Panama Canal?"

*Juan:* The biggest benefit of building the Panama Canal was that ships no longer had to sail all the way around South America to get from the East Coast to the West Coast. The canal connects the Atlantic and the Pacific Ocean.

*Jessica:* Yes, so if I wanted to sail from New York to San Francisco, I bet the ship would go through the Panama Canal. But I was confused about how the ship gets through the canal because it has to go through a set of locks that lift the ships higher until it is in the middle of a big lake.

*Juan:* Because the land is at a higher elevation so the ship has to be lifted up by the locks until it is floating at the same level as the lake that is part of the canal. When the gates of the last lock are opened, the ship sails across the lake.

*Jessica:* Then it has to go through another channel and through more locks. This time the locks lower the ship back to the same level as the ocean on the other side. I bet there are a lot of ships that go through the canal every day, so it must be really busy.

*Juan:* There is a lot of goods and supplies that pass through the canal by ship, so things that are produced in one part of the country are taken to another part, or to another country and they have to go through the canal.

*Jessica:* I think they have expanded the canal a few times since it was built. Did you know that there are other famous canals also, like the Suez Canal? It is in the Mediterranean Sea. It is even longer than the Panama Canal.

## Strategy 21: Writing Memos

*Purpose*

Write for a specific audience and purpose; write to articulate and support a claim or argument; identify and apply the characteristics and conventions of memoranda; use writing for technical purposes; write to inform or recommend; write for a specific audience; use the writing process; revise, edit, and proofread one's own writing.

*CCSS Connection*

Standards W.1, W.2: Write arguments to support claims/informative or explanatory texts to examine and convey complex ideas; Standard W.4: Produce clear and coherent writing; Standard W.5: Develop and strengthen writing as needed; Standard W.8: Gather relevant information from multiple print and digital sources.

*Overview*

Memoranda, or memos, are technical pieces of writing used in various vocational settings and organizations. The purpose of a memo is to convey information or provide a report on a particular topic. They may also ask recipients to take some form of action (recommendation memos). They are important documents in workplace communications and provide a written archive of the activities of an organization and its people. For this reason, it is important that students learn the correct format and conventions for memos.

*Procedure*

Although memos are most common in business and organizational settings, they can be used in the classroom as class assignments. You can easily teach students the correct format of a memo, and they can write memos to you (the teacher), to other students, to historical figures, to scientists, to politicians, to community members, or to school administrators. There are numerous possibilities for real-world audiences for memos that students write. Here are some suggestions:

- Have students write memos that make a recommendation for solving a particular problem in the community or the nation.

- Have students write a memo to you to report on their progress on a term project or discuss their learning during a particular grading period or unit. Ask them to specify what grade they should receive.

- Have students write memos to you to attach to a late assignment, explaining the reason for the lateness and asking you to accept it.

- Have students write memos to other members of the class about the topic being studied.

- Have students write memos to the author of the textbook or class novel.

- Have students write memos to announce class projects or school events.

- Have students write memos to each other in the second language they are learning.

- Have students write a memo about a given topic to an imaginary figure or to themselves.

- Have students write memos to summarize class activities and learning for distribution to students who were absent.

- Have students write memos to school officials or members of the community to address problems or issues directly related to a current topic of study.

- Have students send you an electronic copy of their memo in the form of an e-mail attachment.

You can also provide students with a blank memo template such as the one in figure 3.11. Have them handwrite memos during class. When teaching students about the memo, stress that the purpose of memos is to convey information or request action in a concise way. Since readers in the real world tend to read through memos quickly, they need to get important information across quickly and directly. Teach students the following parts of the memo:

"To" line

"From" line

"Date" line

"Subject" line

Body of the memo (introduction, body, and conclusion)

Optional parts:

"Enc." (at the bottom followed by a list of enclosed documents)

"CC" (also at the bottom to indicate recipients of the memo in addition to the author).

Figure 3.10 presents the correct memo format with explanation of each part. Make a display copy of this to use in teaching students how to write memos.

Be sure to spend some time having students revise, edit, and proofread their final memos. It is best to require the final copies to be typed, since real-world, workplace memos are always in typed form.

# MEMORANDUM

**TO**:        Lists all the primary recipients with full names, each separated by a comma

**FROM**:      Author of the memo (should also initial next to the typed name)

**DATE**:       Indicates the date the memo was written

**SUBJECT**:   Concise description of the topic of the memo (Is sometimes replaced with "RE"

for "regarding")

Body of the memo:

Memoranda use a top-down structure, with the most important information listed first. In the introduction of the memo, state clearly what the memo is about. If you are writing an informative memo, give the most important information first. If you expect readers to respond in some way, let them know what they need to do and, if relevant, the deadline they need to meet, or state your recommendations and the reasons for them.

In the body paragraphs, provide further information or details regarding the subject of the memo, starting with the most important first. If you include dates, locations or other information, you can use a bulleted list.

You may have additional body paragraphs, but memos should generally be kept short so that readers can scan them quickly and access important information.

Close the memo with a short statement about how readers can request further information if any questions arise. DON'T sign the memo at the bottom. Memos do not have a signature line like letters do. However, identify any attached documents in an "enclosure" note. If you are copying the memo to secondary recipients, you should identify them also.

**Enc:** Planning Calendar

**CC:** Robert Stephens, Melissa Alberts

**Figure 3.10. Memo Format with Discussion.**

# MEMORANDUM

**TO:**
**FROM:**
**DATE:**
**SUBJECT:**

**Figure 3.11.  Memo Template.**

Strategy 22: Social Action Paper

*Purpose*

Use techniques of argument and persuasion; conduct research as necessary to write about a real-world topic, issue or problem; identify and apply the conventions of proposal writing; write clearly and coherently; conduct research on a given topic; use specific detail to support one's ideas; use the writing process; generate a claim or thesis statement; apply learning to the local community and the real world; create an organizational plan and outline for one's writing; write for a specific audience; revise, proofread, and edit one's own writing.

*CCSS Connection*

Standard W.1: Write arguments to support claim; Standard W.4: Produce clear and coherent writing; Standard W.5: Develop and strengthen writing as needed; Standard W.6: Use technology, including the Internet, to produce and publish writing; Standard W.7: Conduct short as well as more sustained research projects; Standard W.8: Gather relevant information from multiple print and digital sources; Standards L.1, L.2: Demonstrate command of conventions; Standard L.3: Apply knowledge of language to understand how language functions in different contexts.

*Overview*

When teaching writing courses, I have often tried to engage students in some type of "real-world" writing activity, often asking them to produce a document, paper, report, or editorial that will actually be sent or delivered to someone in the real world, outside of the academic setting of school. My students have completed great workplace, community, and school-related issues. This type of project is a refreshing change for students who have become so accustomed to school writing or "writing for the teacher." We don't give students enough opportunities to discover authentic writing and how writing works in the real world. When it is a topic that they are personally invested in and care about, they are more engaged and passionate and, consequently, learn more from the experience. In their book *Content-Area Writing: Every Teacher's Guide*, Daniels, Zemelman, and Steineke (2007) include a section on "public writing projects." One of the activities in this section is the "social action paper." They define this project as an activity in which students apply classroom content to real community, group, or organizational issues. These could be local, neighborhood, school, or family problems. This project also helps prepare students for future roles as active citizens in a democracy. An example presented is a group of middle school students who were studying the Vietnam War and discovered that there was no official memorial to the 612 local residents who had died in the war.

The students spent months researching the soldiers, finding public records, using the Internet, and having conversations with soldiers' friends and family members, even tracking down relatives of the soldiers for interviews. The students completed a project that involved writing biographies of all 612 soldiers and organizing a traveling memorial (Daniels, Zemelman, & Steineke, 2007).

*Procedure*

The possibilities for this type of real-world writing project are wide ranging. Students don't have to be required to undertake controversial or political issues; the projects can be more oriented toward community service activities. For example, an environmental science class creating a project to reduce electricity consumption or to save a local area waterway from pollution. These types of projects are also useful because they often include both informative and persuasive writing. The form the writing takes may depend upon the nature of the project and topic itself, and as the teacher, you will want to provide assistance with structure and format. As Daniels, Zemelman, and Steineke (2007) note, the project is a powerful tool for engaging students in responsible social action and energizes them with real purpose, real audiences, and real-world feedback.

While there are many possible ways to conduct a social action project, here are a few key ideas:

- Provide a structure for students to brainstorm ideas for possible real-world activities (or school-related activities) that are related to course content. Their brainstorming should include thinking about the resources needed to carry out the project and time available.

- Use some writing lessons or activities to help students master the kinds of written communication they will be using in the project (such as letter or report formats).

- Establish clear guidelines for how and when certain steps in the project must be completed, when students will be assigned to present the project, and when they will turn in a final project to you.

- Provide students with adequate time to complete the project, and function as a facilitator to help them make decisions, determine possible courses of action, and solve problems encountered.

- Have students complete a reflection on their learning during the project in which they explain, in writing, the connections they made between their projects and the material they have learned in class. They should also think about what they've learned overall, what challenges they faced, what strategies they used, and what they would do differently next time.

- Have students spend some time reading and responding to each other's papers. You may want to consider creating a simple rubric to be used to evaluate the final product. Have students use the rubric to revise and rewrite their papers, in addition to final editing and proofreading.

Daniels, Zemelman, and Steineke (2007) present a good example of a social action project completed at a Chicago high school based upon the book *Fast Food Nation*. The project proved to be very interdisciplinary, incorporating biology, health, economics, and political science. Students first completed a series of activities during their reading and thinking about the book, and then carried out projects to change people's attitudes about food. They prepared pamphlets, posters on diets and animal rights, and wrote letters to food service companies and to public officials. The students also drew upon other texts and nonfiction materials to supplement their learning and explore a variety of related issues.

## Strategy 23: Writing Dialogue

*Purpose*

Use writing to reflect on content information; use writing regularly over an extended time period; use writing to summarize and respond to content information; use writing as the basis for collaborative discussion; recognize and acknowledge multiple perspectives on an issue; write in response to others' writing; use writing to extend and deepen comprehension; engage in critical thinking on a given topic.

*CCSS Connection*

Standard W.2: Write informative/explanatory texts to examine and convey complex ideas; Standard W.4: Produce clear and coherent writing; Standard W.9: Draw evidence from literary or informational texts; Standard W.10: Write routinely over extended time frames; Standard SL.1: Prepare for and participate effectively in a range of conversations and collaborations.

*Overview*

This strategy involves students in writing dialogue to represent multiple perspectives. It can be used with any controversial topic, where people may disagree, or where there is a topic to debate. Dialogue writing can be used in science, history, economics, literature, the arts, math, or other areas. Students in world language can also write dialogues in the second language. The strategy is a great way for students to demonstrate that they understand different sides of complex issues. They are also practicing the rhetorical technique of exploring different sides of an issue.

*Procedure*

1. Choose a content issue that may be open ended or a question that lends itself to various viewpoints or possible outcomes. For example: Should Juliet have gone to Friar Lawrence for help in *Romeo and Juliet*? Did the United States make the right decision in invading and liberating Iraq? Is global warming caused by human activity and pollution?

2. Assign students to create a written dialogue or conversation between two people (or characters in a piece of literature). Each voice in the dialogue will take a different viewpoint or perspective on the issue.

3. Have students write a full description of each character or voice at the beginning of the dialogue, one that explains the character's position on the issue or conveys important biographical information.

4. Tell students that each character should speak at least twice for a total of at least one hundred words. Also, they should not include phrases like "I agree" or "Sounds good to me."

5. Tell students that the object is not to debate but to discuss different perspectives. Neither voice should "win" the argument.

6. Ask for volunteers or have all students share their dialogues with the class.

## Strategy 24: Writing Break

*Purpose*

Reflect on one's learning of content material; engage in writing to summarize and clarify ideas and thinking; think critically and evaluate information.

*CCSS Connection*

Standard W.10: Write routinely over extended time frames and shorter time frames.

*Overview*

This strategy comes from Daniels, Zemelman, and Steineke (2007), who note that students recall between 10 and 30 percent of what they read, hear, and see, but when we include writing at regular intervals, retention rate is between 70 and 90 percent. Writing breaks allow students to stop and reflect in writing on what they are learning and the information being presented. This activity can be used during a lecture, film, activity, or in-class reading.

*Procedure*

1. In planning your lesson, decide when students are going to stop and write. For a lecture or large group discussion, every ten to fifteen minutes is suggested. For films and reading activities, take a writing break every fifteen to twenty minutes.

2. Once you have determined where the breaks will be, generate prompts for students to use for the writing breaks.

   a. Some examples are:

      i.   What information stands out/seems really important?

      ii.  What does this remind you of?

      iii. What questions do you still have?

      iv.  What will you need to remember for a test?

      v.   What makes sense and what is confusing?

   b  You can also make the prompts more content focused:

      i.   Which character's actions surprised you the most?

      ii.  What would you do if you faced this problem?

      iii. What would have happened if the Panama Canal had not been built?

      iv.  What is the relationship between genetics and heredity?

3. Begin the activity taking writing breaks of three to five minutes at planned intervals.

4. Before the lesson ends, have students evaluate their writing, asking whether they wrote the entire time, how well they supported their ideas with specific details, and how well their writing created interesting discussion of the material.

Another possibility for this strategy is to use some of the end-of-textbook chapter questions, those that are higher-order thinking questions for your writing break prompts. They can, of course, be modified if necessary to ensure that students are responding to the major concepts as they read or participate in the activity. They can also take writing breaks after being asked to study visual materials such as charts, graphs, tables, or pictures in the text (which often get overlooked as students are reading).

## Strategy 25: Biopoem

*Purpose*
    Write creatively to share content-area learning; identify and summarize key ideas and aspects of a character, topic, place, event or concept; reflect on one's learning.

*CCSS Connection*
    Standard W.4: Produce clear and coherent writing.

*Overview*

    I decided to end this section with one of the more creative and fun writing strategies, the biopoem. The biopoem is a formula poem designed by Gere (1985) that engages students in sharing what they know or have learned about a particular character, topic, place, event, or concept. Biopoems have typically been written to describe a person or character, but there are other possible applications for the strategy. The following is Vacca and Vacca's (1993) outline formula for the biopoem. Students can write a biopoem for themselves, something I have often had my classes do as an introductory activity at the beginning of the school year. In a literature class, students might describe a character in a book or story, but the poem can also be used in other content areas to describe concepts, events, historical characters, or even scientific or mathematical elements or principles.

*Procedure*

1. Present students with the biopoem's eleven-line formula:

    a. Line 1: First name

    b. Line 2: Four traits that describe the character

    c. Line 3: Relative of (brother, sister, daughter, etc.) . . .

    d. Line 4: Lover of _____ (three things or people)

    e. Line 5: Who feels _____ (three things)

    f. Line 6: Who needs _____ (three things)

    g. Line 7: Who fears _____ (three things)

    h. Line 8: Who gives _____ (three things)

    i. Line 9: Who would like to see _____ (three things)

    j.  Line 10: Resident of _____

    k.  Line 11: Last name, nickname, or repeated name

2. Explain to students that it is important that they include information from the text or reading assignment to incorporate into the poem. Also encourage them to be creative.

3. After a particular unit of study or reading assignment, assign or have students choose a character, historical figure, or concept on which to write a biopoem.

4. It might be good to have some sample biopoems for students to use as models (such as the one included here). You might also create a sample biopoem together as a class, and model for students how to include both literal information and interpretive and inferential material in the poem.

5. After students have had time to write and polish their biopoems, ask them to volunteer to post them for a gallery walk or share them with the class by reading them aloud.

Here is a sample biopoem written about President Abraham Lincoln:

Abraham
Independent, determined, courageous, liberator
Son of Illinois, husband of Mary Todd
Lover of freedom, equality, and unity
Who feels compassion for the enslaved and downtrodden
Who needs to defend and protect the Union
Who fears rebellion, war, failure, and loss
Who gives his life in service to his country as president
Who would like to see the Union restored, to oversee Reconstruction
Resident of the White House, and forever holding a place in history
Lincoln

**PART FOUR**

# VOCABULARY STRATEGIES

## The Significance of Vocabulary

Vocabulary knowledge is fundamental to comprehension. Students' ability to understand what they read increases as their word knowledge increases (Lehr, Osborn, & Hiebert, 2004). Word knowledge is also critical for students to perform well on high-stakes tests such as the SAT and ACT. Typically, when students don't know the meaning of a word, teachers will refer them to a dictionary. Students will then look the word up in the dictionary, read a definition that they do not fully understand, and still have little or no concept of the word's meaning. Looking up words in a dictionary and writing down the definition is simply not an effective way for students to learn new vocabulary. Even if they do understand the definition, it does not help them practice using the word or learn to integrate it into their speech and writing. We need some additional strategies for helping students to work with new words and terms and learn how they are used in various contexts.

Vocabulary instruction is especially critical for students from lower socioeconomic backgrounds. Beck, McKeown, and Kucan (2002) note that "a large vocabulary repertoire facilitates becoming an educated person to the extent that vocabulary knowledge is strongly related to reading proficiency in particular and school achievement in general" (p. 1). Children from backgrounds of poverty grow up with vastly less exposure to a variety of words and language during their childhood, which proves to be a huge disadvantage to them in their later years of schooling (Hart & Risley, 1995).

Most secondary students gain about three thousand new words per year from reading of both content-area and independent materials. If students do very little reading, either for school purposes or as recreation, they are going to have much more limited vocabulary growth. The strong correlation between vocabulary and reading comprehension cannot be overlooked. Research clearly indicates that reading is the most important factor in increasing students' word knowledge (Anderson

203

& Nagy, 1991). Thus, probably the most important thing we can do for students is have them read as much as possible.

Many methods of teaching vocabulary have been recommended by experts. Vacca and Vacca (1989) recommend that vocabulary be taught and reinforced within the framework of concept development. Textbooks typically use context clues, picture clues, and typographical clues to help students understand vocabulary (Crawley & Mountain, 1988). Conley (1992) recommends selecting vocabulary terms that are important within a specific context and teaching the vocabulary at an appropriate level. He states that teachers can ask themselves three questions: Which words are important to the content objective for the lesson? Which words are unfamiliar? Which words will students see again? Vacca and Vacca (1989) note that concepts can be taught with exemplars and nonexemplars, and that individual vocabulary learning should be reinforced with a small group or the whole class. They recommend several common vocabulary strategies including word sorts, categorization, concept circles, and word analogies. Many of these are presented in this section of the book.

The new Common Core State Standards for reading and language require that students determine the meaning of words and phrases as they are used in a text (including words and phrases used in figurative ways). The CCSS language standards also include a section on Vocabulary Acquisition and Use. For example, Language Anchor Standard 4 for grades 9–12 specifies that students must be able to "determine or clarify the meaning of unknown and multiple-meaning words and phrases." The grade-specific standard then specifies "a range of strategies" for determining word meaning: use context, identify patterns of word changes, consult reference materials (i.e., dictionaries), and verify preliminary determination of word meanings. A separate language standard focuses on academic and domain-specific vocabulary; these are words such as *analyze, generate, acquire, construct, differentiate, facilitate,* and the like, which are commonly used words that cross content boundaries. A Google search for "Academic Word List" will provide you with several different lists of academic vocabulary terms to work with.

Since students need to gain an understanding of how words are used in different contexts, vocabulary instruction should help students apply these terms across numerous contexts and teach them strategies for figuring out the meanings of new words they encounter (Bryant, Ugel, Thompson, & Hamff, 1999). Word identification strategies, concept combining, semantic feature analysis, concept formation, and several other specific strategies can be employed to enhance vocabulary learning. It is important that struggling readers increase their vocabularies in meaningful ways, and practice in oral reading helps build vocabulary and increase fluency (Salinger, 2003). Research also clearly indicates that vocabulary instruction is an important part of learning across the content areas (Marzano, Pickering, & Pollock, 2001). Yet systematic vocabulary instruction is often not included in the curriculum. Marzano,

Pickering, and Pollock (2001) examine research to draw several generalizations about vocabulary instruction:

- Students must encounter words in context more than once in order to learn them.

- Instruction in new words enhances learning those words in context.

- A good way to learn new words is to associate images with them.

- Direct vocabulary instruction does work.

- Direct instruction in words and terms critical to new content produces the most powerful learning.

Salinger (2003) also points out numerous ways in which students can learn vocabulary: direct, explicit vocabulary instruction; use of dictionaries and other reference materials; focus on technical terms in content areas; use of root words to teach vocabulary; discussion of word origins; semantic mapping; and teaching of idioms and colloquial expressions. Many of the strategies in this section of the book incorporate these elements. Francis and Simpson (2003) recommend designing activities that encourage students to develop a deeper level of understanding about vocabulary words, having students evaluate their own levels of word knowledge, and teaching students how to create word maps and concept cards to build conceptual understanding.

Since the traditional method many teachers use to teach vocabulary is giving students a list of vocabulary words, having them look up the definitions and memorize them, and giving a test, vocabulary instruction is often not effective. In some cases teachers may also ask students to use the word in a sentence, but students are still unlikely to retain the words or make them a part of their own vocabularies. Typically, teachers tend to focus on too many words, overwhelming students with numerous unfamiliar words and terms. Students typically write sentences that use the word incorrectly because they don't recognize the part of speech of the word and because they lack a context or background knowledge in how the words are used. This section of the book provides you with many useful strategies that will help students master content vocabulary in meaningful ways. Many of the strategies are fun and engaging for students as well.

Tompkins and Blanchfield (2008) identify eight important elements or principles of good vocabulary instruction that can help to guide our teaching:

1. Students must learn to use context clues to uncover word meaning whenever possible.

2. Students must be actively involved in learning vocabulary.

3. Students must understand important concepts to understand related words (linking new words with those they are already familiar with).

4. Students must understand that there are various levels of word knowledge.

5. Students must learn how to use dictionaries and use word morphology (prefixes, suffixes, and roots).

6. Classroom practice should include opportunities for nonlinguistic representations of meaning (mental images, pictures, or acting out words).

7. Classrooms should promote language awareness and play.

8. Vocabulary study should include study of cognates to meet the needs of English language learners.

## Criteria for Selecting Vocabulary to Teach

Good teaching practice requires that we take time to pre-teach critical vocabulary before students read a piece of new text or learn new content material. Here are some criteria to guide your practice:

1. Select vocabulary that is critical to the meaning of the text. Choose words students must know to understand important ideas, words that are essential to comprehension. An unknown vocabulary word that appears often should be taught. There is a direct correlation between understanding of critical vocabulary and comprehension. If the student understands the key words, comprehension is more likely to happen.

2. Select only a few critical words and terms to pre-teach. Students will have better retention and not be overwhelmed with too many words at once.

3. Select commonly used words. This will help build general knowledge of academic words and language. These are also words students will encounter in other contexts.

4. Select words that are not already defined in context. Some new vocabulary will be defined within the context of the reading assignment. Terms that are central to the lesson will need to be taught using some strategy to help the student master and use the term.

In general, since we learn new words and develop vocabulary from the reading that we do, people who read more tend to have better vocabularies. As we are reading, we learn vocabulary in several different ways:

1. Context Clues: The meaning is derived from the context in which it is used.

2. Definition: Teachers can provide definitions and students can look up definitions. In textbooks, terms are sometimes defined directly.

3. Word Structure: Knowledge of Greek and Latin prefixes, roots, and suffixes can help us to determine the meaning of words.

4. Etymology: Vocabulary is learned through knowledge of the history and origin of the words.

## General Vocabulary Strategies

Before we begin focusing on specific strategies, here are some general suggestions and ideas for helping students learn and remember new words and terms:

1. Teach key words, but keep in mind that some research shows about ten new words per week is all that students can cognitively process.

2. Use nonlinguistic representations (pictures, video, objects, visuals) to help students understand new concepts.

3. When asking students to learn prefixes, suffixes, and roots, remember the "five test." If you can't think of five other words that share the same root, it's probably not useful for students to remember.

4. Make a scavenger hunt before a unit of study. Divide students into teams and ask them to find objects, models, or pictures that represent concepts that will be used during the unit.

5. Ask students to be responsible for deciding which words are important by doing a vocabulary self-collection. Divide the class into groups, and have them choose words that should be emphasized in a particular passage or chapter. Each group should present their nominations, pointing out where in the text they found the word, defining it, and justifying why they think that word is important.

6. Ask students to act out words in skits or pantomime, or draw pictures or visuals to represent the words. This is one of my favorite ways of teaching students new words. This method is presented in more detail later in this section.

7. Create space on your bulletin board for a word wall. Cut out some strips of construction paper and begin placing key vocabulary words related to a

particular unit of study on the wall. Have students add words based upon their reading. The word wall is also one of the strategies included later in this section.

8. Use graphic organizers for central ideas/concepts. This book presents several different strategies that involve graphic organizers in which students identify elements such as root words, other forms of the word, antonyms, exemplars and nonexemplars, and use of the terms in a sentence.

## A Procedure for Planning a Unit

Harmon, Wood, and Hedrick (2006) present a procedure for teachers to follow when preparing a unit that will include a focus on vocabulary:

1. Decide on the conceptual ideas for the unit or lesson.

2. Read the text and develop a word list of related terms and phrases.

3. Examine the word list to determine how the terms should be taught.

4. Develop activities to introduce, build, and refine word and phrase meanings before reading (such as a KWL chart, word wall, or graphic organizer).

5. Develop activities to support word meanings during reading.

6. Develop activities to extend and reinforce word meanings after reading.

7. Develop content-specific activities (and meaningful use of newly learned words associated with important concepts).

The rest of part 4 includes specific vocabulary strategies you can begin using in your classroom today.

## Vocabulary Strategies

Strategy 1: Daily Oral Language (DOL)

*Purpose*
    Develop written and spoken language skills; learn and use content-specific vocabulary words and academic vocabulary.

*CCSS Connection*
    Standard L.4: Determine or clarify the meaning of unknown and multiple-meaning words and phrases; Standard L.6: Acquire and use accurately a range of general academic and domain-specific words and phrases.

*Overview*

Having a DOL exercise is one way for students to build and develop their written and spoken vocabulary. Many English teachers who include DOL activities use them to teach grammar, punctuation, and sentence structure, and conduct general mini-lessons on language features. However, DOL can also be focused on content-specific vocabulary and academic words and terms as well. Most teachers choose to use the DOL as a warm-up activity at the beginning of each period. They could also be done during the last five minutes of each period (time that is often unfortunately wasted).

*Procedure*

1. Present a vocabulary word, write it on the board, and pronounce the word. Have students pronounce the word in chorus.

2. Define the term for students and give them the part of speech. For example: "*Ambiguous* means unclear or having more than one possible meaning. Because it ends with '-ous' we can tell it is an adjective and would be used to describe something someone says or an event."

3. Give students several examples of the word used in sentences so they can see a variety of ways in which the word could be used.

4. Have students work with partners to come up with synonyms, antonyms, examples, drawings, and uses of the word in context.

Here is another example:

- The teacher presents the word "meticulous," writing it on the board. The class pronounces the word.

- The word is an adjective.

- Meaning: "extremely careful about details."

- Sentences: "The meticulous student checked every math answer to make sure her calculations were accurate." "A good cashier needs to be meticulous when giving customers change." "Don't be too meticulous about sweeping the sand from the floor because everyone tracks it in from the beach."

- Ask students the following: "How many synonyms for the word 'meticulous' can you think of?" "What is the opposite of 'meticulous'?" "Use the word in a sentence of your own. Share it with the class." "Draw a visual or picture that illustrates the meaning of the word 'meticulous.'"

## Strategy 2: Context Clues

*Purpose*

Identify unknown or unfamiliar words used in text; use context clues to determine the meaning of unknown words.

*CCSS Connection*

Standard RI/RL.4: Interpret words and phrases as they are used in text; Standard L.4: Determine or clarify the meaning of unknown and multiple-meaning words and phrases; Standard L.6: Acquire and use accurately a range of general academic and domain-specific words and phrases.

*Overview*

One of the main barriers to good reading comprehension is lack of sufficient knowledge of word meanings. Good readers identify key vocabulary words in informational and technical reading material. For students who struggle with reading, there are many ways teachers can help students master critical vocabulary and learn to identify the meaning of unknown words. This three-step process helps students develop their skills in using context clues.

*Procedure*

Gather the following materials: copies of assigned textbook pages, an article, or other reading material. Identify several words in the passage or article that may be unknown to students. You will also need several highlighters in two different colors. Model the three-step process shown next. Explain to students your thinking process so students can do it for themselves.

1. First, read through the material and highlight the unknown words, concepts, or terms, especially those that you think are critical to the study of the topic.

2. Use a different color to highlight the context clue that might help you understand each word. It may be a definition, restatement, or example.

3. Now try to use the context clues to write your own definition of each word you highlighted. Don't look the word or term up in the dictionary; write your own definition using only the context clues.

Have students practice this process several times on their own after you have modeled it for them initially.

## Strategy 3: Vocabulary Carousel

*Purpose*

Use a dictionary to identify an appropriate definition for given words and terms; learn the meaning of unfamiliar vocabulary words.

*CCSS Connection*

Standard L.4: Determine or clarify the meaning of unknown and multiple-meaning words and phrases; Standard L.6: Acquire and use accurately a range of general academic and domain-specific words and phrases.

*Overview*

Tompkins and Blanchfield (2008) attribute this strategy to teacher Kathleen Markovich, who invented the vocabulary carousel, "a merry-go-round of words," as a way to expeditiously teach vocabulary for Steinbeck's novel *The Pearl*. The carousel strategy, however, can work well in many different disciplines and provides a way for students to quickly learn several new words. It has the added advantage of incorporating movement into the class period as well. If you find that you don't have a whole lot of time to teach students vocabulary, you may want to try the vocabulary carousel.

*Procedure*

1. Give each student a large sheet of white paper and a colored marker (sticky note chart paper would be ideal). Students will also need their reading assignment and a print or electronic dictionary.

2. Assign one vocabulary word, numbered in the order that it appears in the text, to each student, along with the page number from the text. If there are leftover words that are not assigned, give them to students who finish early.

3. With their markers, have students write the number of the word and the word, spelled correctly, on their chart paper. They should write large enough for everyone to see.

4. Have students locate their word in the text or reading assignment and then copy the sentence that contains the word, underlining the word on their paper. Sentences can be shortened if they are too long.

5. Next, students will look up the word in the dictionary and, if there is more than one definition, determine which is the correct one to match the meaning in the text. Then have them write the definition on their

paper. Check to be sure that students are identifying the correct definition of their words as they work.

6. Have students paste their papers to the classroom wall, extending all the way around the room in the order they appear in the chapter or reading assignment.

7. Next, position students randomly in front of a particular word with a sheet of lined paper, numbered for the specific number of vocabulary words. Have students write the word in front of them on their paper, writing down the word and its definition. So, one student will start at number eight, for example, and then move on to the next number, rotating around the classroom. Students should keep moving in the merry-go-round pattern until they have written down all the words and definitions.

8. When students are finished, they can begin reading the chapter, article, or reading assignment with their list of vocabulary words in front of them.

## Strategy 4: Class Context

*Purpose*

Identify the meaning of unfamiliar words in reading or conversation; use context clues; use and practice newly learned vocabulary words.

*CCSS Connection*

Standard L.3: Apply knowledge of language to understand how language functions in different contexts; Standard L.4: Determine or clarify the meaning of unknown and multiple-meaning words and phrases; Standard L.6: Acquire and use accurately a range of general academic and domain-specific words and phrases.

*Overview*

This strategy is not so much a specific vocabulary strategy as it is a general teaching method. In his book *The English Teacher's Companion: A Complete Guide to Classroom, Curriculum, and the Profession*, Jim Burke (2008) recommends teachers use words that challenge students during discussion, on handouts, and when giving directions. This is something that can be done in every content area.

*Procedure*

Rather than "dumbing down" your language for students, instead use complex vocabulary and sophisticated words, and expect students to learn the meaning of them. Take the opportunity to question students about the term's meaning. For example, while giving directions, I might say, "You have a *plethora* of options to choose from for this activity. Can someone explain what 'plethora' means?" Or "I will now *segue* into the next method for developing vocabulary." Talk about the word "segue" and give students the opportunity to incorporate the word into their own vocabularies.

About this strategy, Burke (2008) adds,

> Similarly, while reading or discussing a text in class, stop when it seems necessary to inquire about the use or meaning of a word. For example, while reading portions of Nathan McCall's *Makes Me Wanna Holler*, we encountered the word surrogate three times in one paragraph. I stopped and asked the class if they could understand what the author was talking about if they did not know what the word meant. "No," they said. We talked about the word in the context of a surrogate mother, an issue that was being discussed in the news at that time, then returned to reading the book. This was effective and natural because if grew out of class context.

This method of teaching vocabulary is probably most effective for second-language learners who are challenged every day by a vast new language. Don't be afraid to challenge students by presenting them with difficult words and stressing the importance of constantly working to learn new words.

### Strategy 5: Clarifying Cue Card

*Purpose*
   Identify and clarify the meaning of unknown words and terms; use context clues, identify word parts, and consult resources to determine the meaning of given words.

*CCSS Connection*
   Standard RL/RI.4: Interpret words and phrases as they are used in text; Standard L.4: Determine or clarify the meaning of unknown and multiple-meaning words and phrases; Standard L.6: Acquire and use accurately a range of general academic and domain-specific words and phrases.

*Overview*
   Clarifying cue card is a simple and easy-to-use vocabulary strategy that comes from Lubliner (2005). Figure 4.1 shows a variation of the original version by Lubliner.

PART FOUR

*Procedure*

Prepare a "cue card" or handout similar to the one in figure 4.1 and have students complete the card for new terms and concepts. Ask students to use these cards whenever they are reading new material in class (or for homework).

---

**CLARIFYING CUE CARD**

When you come across a word in your reading you don't understand, use the following

strategies:

- Mine your memory: have you ever seen the word before or can you remember what it

  means?

- Study the word structure: Do you know the root or base word? Does the word have a

  prefix or suffix that you might know? Try to use any possible clues in the word to figure

  out the meaning.

- Consider the word's context: Look at the information the sentence provides and think

  about the whole paragraph. Can you figure out the meaning of the word?

- Substitute a synonym: When you think that you know what the word means, try replacing

  it with a similar word. Does it make sense?

If the strategies above don't work:

- Ask an Expert: Does someone in your class or group know the meaning, or can they help

  you figure it out?

- Place a Post-It Note: If you can't figure out the word's meaning, put a post-it by the word

  and check with the teacher or look in the dictionary.

If you speak Spanish, try this:

- Catch a cognate: Does the word sound or look similar to some word in Spanish? See if

  the Spanish word's meaning makes sense.

---

**Figure 4.1. Clarifying Cue Card.**

## Strategy 6: Student VOC Strategy

*Purpose*

Identify and clarify the meaning of unknown words and terms; use context clues, identify word parts, and consult resources to determine the meaning of given words.

*CCSS Connection*

Standard RL/RI.4: Interpret words and phrases as they are used in text; Standard L.4: Determine or clarify the meaning of unknown and multiple-meaning words and phrases; Standard L.6: Acquire and use accurately a range of general academic and domain-specific words and phrases.

*Overview*

Similar to the clarifying cue card, use this simple vocabulary form (which could easily be reproduced on half sheets) to help students examine a word's context, predict the meaning, and demonstrate their understanding of the new word learned. The VOC strategy helps students analyze the word meaning within the context and helps them make sensory connections that relate to their learning style (Doty, Cameron, & Barton, 2003).

*Procedure*

Prepare a large number of half sheets of paper with the student vocabulary strategy (see figure 4.2). During reading assignments, either ask students to complete a specified number of strategy sheets or use them as needed during reading. Another option is to have each student prepare one or two strategy sheets during his or her reading to be placed on the document camera and shared with the class.

## STUDENT VOCABULARY STRATEGY

Vocabulary Word: _____

Write the sentence in which the word appears in the text:

_____

_____

_____

Based upon how it is used in the text, predict what the word means:

_____

_____

Consult an expert for the actual definition (a friend, teacher, dictionary, or website). Expert's

definition: _____

_____

Show your understanding of the word by using it in a sentence of your own:

_____

_____

Choose one of the following ways to help you remember the meaning: draw a picture of what

the word means to you, select an action that will remind you of what the word means, or connect

the word to something you have heard or read (story, news report, song, incident, etc.) Write

down what personal associations you have made with the word: _____

_____

_____

_____

**Figure 4.2.   Student Vocabulary Strategy. (Reprinted by permission of McREL.)**

## Strategy 7: Knowledge Rating Scale

*Purpose*

Identify unknown words and terms in text; connect background knowledge to new information learned.

*CCSS Connection*

Standard L.4: Determine or clarify the meaning of unknown and multiple-meaning words and phrases; Standard L.6: Acquire and use accurately a range of general academic and domain-specific words and phrases.

*Overview*

The knowledge rating scale was created by Blachowicz (1986) as a strategy for introducing unknown words to students. It helps students connect new information to their previous learning. This strategy can be used in any subject area and has the added benefit of establishing a purpose for reading.

*Procedure*

1. Choose a number of important vocabulary words from the reading material you are about to assign. Focus on choosing those terms that are essential to understanding the particular content.

2. Provide a handout for students with four columns, or ask them to draw four columns on a piece of paper. Label the columns in order: "Vocabulary Word," "Know It Well," "Have Heard or Seen It," and "No Clue."

3. Place students in groups of two to four and have them share what they know about the words. During their discussion they should individually place a check next to each word in the appropriate column based on how much understanding they have of the word.

4. Next, have students write sentences for each word they have listed in the Know It Well column.

5. Individually, students then complete the reading assignment.

6. After the reading, have students add definitions for their unknown words and confirm or revise their previous placement of checks. Students should also be assigned to write additional sentences for those words they now have a better understanding of.

PART FOUR

## Strategy 8: Vocabulary Log

*Purpose*
Identify unknown words and terms in text; identify parts of speech of unknown words; use context clues and consult dictionaries to determine meaning of unfamiliar words; incorporate newly learned words into one's own language.

*CCSS Connection*
Standard RL/RI.4: Interpret words and phrases as they are used in text; Standard L.4: Determine or clarify the meaning of unknown and multiple-meaning words and phrases; Standard L.6: Acquire and use accurately a range of general academic and domain-specific words and phrases.

*Overview*
The vocabulary log is another strategy recommended by Jim Burke (2008). Have students keep a special section in their notebook, journal, or on paper for a vocabulary log.

*Procedure*
As they are reading and learning new content information, instruct students to record all the words and terms they do not understand. Give students the following directions:

1. When you come across a word you don't understand, write down the word. Be sure to include it in its original sentence with the word underlined.
2. Write down the part of speech (noun, verb, adjective, etc.).
3. Identify the source (e.g., physics textbook) and the page number where the word is used.
4. Define the word using the following procedure:
   a. Make your own guess, using contextual clues.
   b. Write down the dictionary definition that best describes the way the word was originally used.
   c. Use your own words to define it, so if you were asked to explain the meaning of the word, you could do it.
5. List any other variations of the word (other forms) or synonyms. So, for example, if the word is "profane," you would write down "profanity" as well as "swearing" and "cursing." Also list any antonyms, such as "revere" and "respect."
6. Write your own original sentence using the word in the same way it was used in the original.

218

## Strategy 9: Word Cards

*Purpose*

Identify and clarify the meaning of unknown words and terms; use context clues, identify word parts, and consult resources to determine the meaning of given words; incorporate newly learned words into one's own language.

*CCSS Connection*

Standard RL/RI.4: Interpret words and phrases as they are used in text; Standard L.4: Determine or clarify the meaning of unknown and multiple-meaning words and phrases; Standard L.6: Acquire and use accurately a range of general academic and domain-specific words and phrases.

*Overview*

This strategy is another easy and useful way to help students learn and study new vocabulary words. It can also be varied in numerous ways to fit your particular content area. It is best at first to identify the ten or so key words or terms from the reading material that you will ask students to identify and define. After students have done the strategy a few times, you could then have them identify words themselves while reading.

*Procedure*

1. First, determine the central concepts and key words in a unit or reading assignment. Try to limit the list to ten words.

2. Give students half sheets of paper or index cards, one for each word. Have students write each word in the center of one of the cards (see figure 4.3).

3. Have students locate the word in the text and try to figure out the meaning by examining context and root words. Then have them check the meaning in a dictionary.

4. Students write the definition in the upper-right-hand corner of the card. (This can be done together as a class, which may be a good idea when first introducing the strategy.)

5. Have students create a sentence using the word in context and write it in the lower-right-hand corner of the card.

6. Have students identify possible synonyms for the word and write them in the upper-left-hand corner of the card.

7. Have students come up with a symbol, picture, drawing, or stick figure to demonstrate the meaning of the word. Draw the visual in the lower-left-hand corner.

8. Model this process with the first few cards and then gradually release students to work on their own. It is a good idea for the class to agree on the definition that is written in the upper-right-hand corner.

| Synonyms | Definition |
|---|---|
| **WORD** | |
| Symbols/Pictures | Sentence |

**Figure 4.3. Word Card.**

## Strategy 10: Sequencing Instruction for Multiple Exposure

*Purpose*

Identify and clarify the meaning of unknown words and terms; use context clues, identify word parts, and consult resources to determine the meaning of given words; use visual representations to learn and remember newly learned words and concepts.

*CCSS Connection*

Standard RL/RI.4: Interpret words and phrases as they are used in text; Standard L.4: Determine or clarify the meaning of unknown and multiple-meaning words and phrases; Standard L.5: Demonstrate understanding of figurative language, word relationships, and nuances; Standard L.6: Acquire and use accurately a range of general academic and domain-specific words and phrases.

*Overview*

One of the most powerful ways to teach students new terms is to design a series of instructional activities that allows students to be exposed to the terms in several different ways. Marzano, Pickering, and Pollock (2001) present a process for teaching new terms and phrases using this method.

*Procedure*

1. Present students with a brief explanation or description of the new term or phrase.

2. Present students with a nonlinguistic representation of the new term or phrase (a visual).

3. Ask students to generate their own explanation or description of the term or phrase. These can include students' own examples and may be based upon their prior knowledge of the term.

4. Ask students to create their own nonlinguistic representation of the term.

5. Periodically ask students to review the accuracy of their explanations and representations.

To illustrate this process, let's suppose that Mrs. Miller, an English teacher, wants her students to understand the terms "dynamic character" and "static character." She begins step one by asking students to compare two characters in a short story the students have recently read. She asks them to think about which character has changed and developed and which one has stayed the same. She then explains the terms to students: a *dynamic character* is one who changes, grows, and develops during the course of a story; a *static character* is one who stays the same or does not go through any process of development. She explains that dynamic characters are those who are more like real human beings. Next, she presents a nonlinguistic representation by drawing a stick figure on the board to illustrate a static character, one who is not fully developed or characterized and may only represent one trait or characteristic. She then draws (or shows a photograph) of a more artistic, rounded character with features such as hair, eyes, facial and physical features, jewelry, and distinctive articles of clothing, one who looks more like a real person, growing and changing through life's experiences. For the third step, Mrs. Miller asks her students to come up with their own explanations of the terms and what they mean and give some examples of characters they have seen in stories that are either dynamic or static. For part four, Mrs. Miller asks students to make a poster that includes pictures of various people from magazines and magazine ads to illustrate dynamic characters. Students will include on their posters descriptive words and phrases they make up to describe what the character in the picture is like. For the final part of this strategy, during the next two weeks, while reading a novel as a class, students will be asked to think about which characters in the novel are dynamic and which are static to reinforce their learning of the two terms.

## Strategy 11: Analogies

*Purpose*
    Understand the parts and characteristics of an analogy; understand and identify relationships among words; create analogies to help clarify understanding of words, terms, and concepts.

*CCSS Connection*
    Standard RL/RI.4: Interpret words and phrases as they are used in a text; Standard L.3: Apply knowledge of language; Standard L.4: Determine or clarify the meaning of unknown and multiple-meaning words and phrases; Standard L.5: Demonstrate understanding of figurative language, word relationships, and nuances; Standard L.6: Acquire and use accurately a range of general academic and domain-specific words and phrases; Standard SL.1: Prepare for and participate effectively in a range of conversations and collaborations.

*Overview*
    Analogies are comparisons of two unlike things. Because analogies can help us understand something unfamiliar by comparing it to something familiar, they can serve as a bridge between familiar and new concepts. Harmon, Wood, and Hedrick (2006) recommend using analogies to help students understand new concepts.

*Procedure*

1. Begin by teaching students how analogies work. To interpret analogies, students will need to understand how the parts of the analogy relate to each other, and they will need to see lots of examples:

    a. ":" refers to the words "is to"

    b. "::" refers to the "as"

2. Use several simple analogies such as the following to help students understand how analogies work:

    a. word : sentence :: page : book ("word is to sentence as page is to book")

  b.  mitten : hand :: sock : foot

  c.  gas : car :: wood : fire

  d.  day : month :: minute : hour

  e.  wheel : bike :: tire : car

3.  Students need to understand that because words can have various relation-ships with other words, there are several different types of analogies. Harmon, Wood, and Hedrick (2006) present the following analogy types:

  a.  Part to whole (finger : hand :: toe : foot)

  b.  Person to situation (Roosevelt : Great Depression :: Lincoln : Civil War)

  c.  Cause and Effect (aging : facial wrinkles :: sunbathing : tan)

  d.  Synonyms (master : expert :: novice : apprentice)

  e.  Antonyms (naive : sophisticated :: alien : native)

  f.  Geography (Rocky Mountains : west :: Appalachian Mountains : east)

  g.  Measurement (inches : ruler :: minutes : clock)

  h.  Examples (Folgers : Maxwell House :: Cheerios : Corn Flakes)

  i.  Functions (switch : lamp :: key : door)

4.  Using these examples or others like them, model the thinking processes used to understand them. If you talk through a few of the analogies to demonstrate for students how you think through them, it will be very helpful to students who may have difficulty with this at first. Explain that analogies can help us to understand new concepts in a particular subject matter such as science.

5.  Come up with some examples of analogies from the lesson or from the reading material students are working with. For example: gas : engine :: food : digestive system.

Here are some variations for working with analogies:

1.  Have students create a certain number of analogies while reading a text-book chapter.

2.  Use a given list of vocabulary words and terms and ask students to write a certain number of analogies using the words.

3.  Have students work in groups to create analogies and also provide ratio-nale for their choice of terms.

PART FOUR

Here are some examples (figure 4.4) showing how analogies could be used in computer science (computer science terms are in bold print) (Harmon, Wood, & Hedrick, 2006).

---

For each analogy, state the relationship, provide a reasonable term, and justify your answer:

ignite: fire :: _____: computer

    relationship: action done to an object

    term: **boot**

    justification: You start a fire by igniting it and you start a computer by booting it.

jam: lock :: **freeze** : computer

    relationship: _____

    Term: _____

    Justification _____

word : sentence :: **byte** : computer information

    Relationship: _____

    Term: _____

    Justification: _____

letter : word :: **bit**: byte

    Relationship : _____

    Term : _____

    Justification: _____

---

**Figure 4.4. Analogy Example. (Reprinted with permission from the Association of Middle Level Education [formerly National Middle School Association], www.amle.org.)**

Strategy 12: Association in Word Recognition

*Purpose*
   Use prior knowledge and associations to identify word meaning; analyze and identify word parts.

*CCSS Connection*
   Standard L.3: Apply knowledge of language to understand how language functions in different contexts; Standard L.4: Determine or clarify the meaning of unknown and multiple-meaning words and phrases.

*Overview*
   Association in word recognition is a strategy that encourages students to make associations between their prior knowledge and new information and terms (Punch & Robinson, 1992). This approach helps students identify the word parts in terms. This technique does not work across the board with all vocabulary, but for many words and terms, it is effective.

*Procedure*
   First, identify important terms that students will need to know, the critical vocabulary from a passage of text. Next, try to identify smaller words that are spelled within the word, which might be used to make an association with the meaning of the word. Develop an explanation to show the connection between the vocabulary word and smaller words within it. After students become familiar with this strategy, have them identify the smaller words within vocabulary concepts and create their own explanations and associations (Harmon, Wood, & Hedrick, 2006).
   The following examples from social studies come from Punch and Robinson (1992).

- Amendment: To "mend." To fix or change. Ask students to connect this to a change that adds or takes out a part as in the Bill of Rights or a Constitutional Amendment.

- Segregate: Note the word "gate," which separates or keeps apart. This word provides a good example for discussion of and learning about the word and its meaning to describe groups of people who are excluded or kept apart from others.

- Monopoly: The "o" vowel has control of this word. It contains no other vowels, other than the "y" at the end used as a vowel sound. A monopoly is a business with no competition, or exclusive control of a product or service help by one company. (Reprinted with permission from the National Council for the Social Studies.)

Harmon, Wood, and Hedrick (2006) present some additional examples from math:

- Perimeter: Contains the small word "rim." Have students think about how the rim is the outside edge of something. Have them make the connection to the perimeter, which is the sum of the sides of the polygon.
- Horizontal: A horizontal line looks like the horizon in the sky. It also goes in the same direction as the crossed line in "H" and the top line in "T."
- Measurement: Has the word "sure" in it. Measurements are sure things. You are sure of your numbers if you have measured correctly.

### Strategy 13: Concept Definition Map

*Purpose*

Identify features of key terms and concepts, including categories, properties and illustrations; build conceptual understanding of key terms and concepts.

*CCSS Connection*

Standard L.3: Apply knowledge of language; Standard L.6: Acquire and use accurately a range of general academic and domain-specific words and phrases.

*Overview*

The concept definition map comes with many variations. It was designed by Schwartz and Raphael (1985) as a way to help students understand a central concept. It has been adapted into many different forms and variations, but in general it is a graphic organizer for helping students consider the various features of a single term. Use it when there is a key term or concept that all students need a solid understanding of. The features of the framework include categories, properties, and illustrations. It can also be extended to include purpose or "How do you do this?" depending on the concept. It helps students internalize the features and generally works best with nouns rather than verbs. Some examples of concepts from various disciplines might include imperialism, capitalism, scientific notation, realism, regionalism, endocrine system, internal combustion, or mutation.

*Procedure*

1. Explain to students that concepts can be defined by their features, such as categories, properties, or examples.

2. Introduce the concept definition map. Explain each part.

3. As a class or with partners, have students complete the concept definition map for the particular term.

4. Place a blank concept definition map on the overhead or document camera and ask students to share information to contribute to a whole-class map for the term.

Several years ago, I created my own version of a concept map, which I called the "graphic for word study." It asks students to use the word in a sentence, provide antonyms, synonyms, roots, other forms of the work, an illustration or visual representation, and also provide examples of people or things related to the word. I use this map often with students when I want them to master key concepts. I have also used it with a vocabulary list, assigning each student (or a pair) one word, having them complete the graphic for their particular word, and then asking them to present their graphic organizer to the class, which helps the whole class review and think more deeply about all the vocabulary words.

Figures 4.5, 4.6, and 4.7 all present various versions of the concept map. The version in figure 4.7 may be more appropriate for disciplines such as science, math, and technical subjects. Figure 4.8 presents an example of a completed concept definition map. Figure 4.9 presents my own graphic for word study.

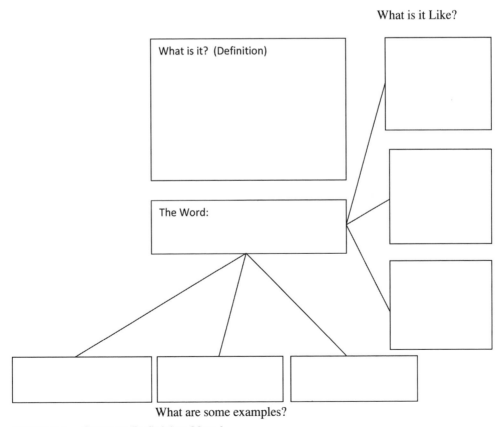

**Figure 4.5. Concept Definition Map I.**

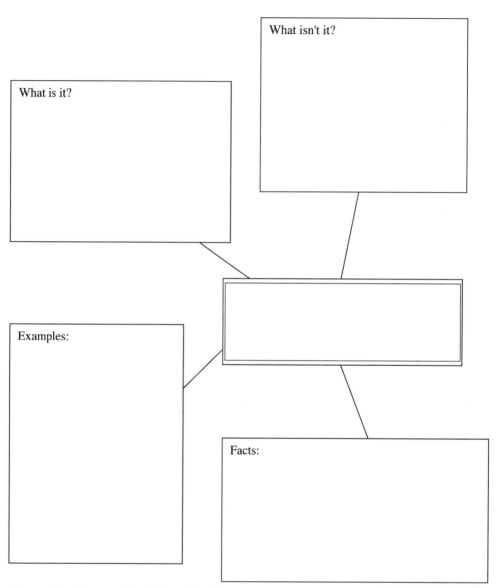

What isn't it?

What is it?

Examples:

Facts:

**Figure 4.6.   Concept Definition Map 2.**

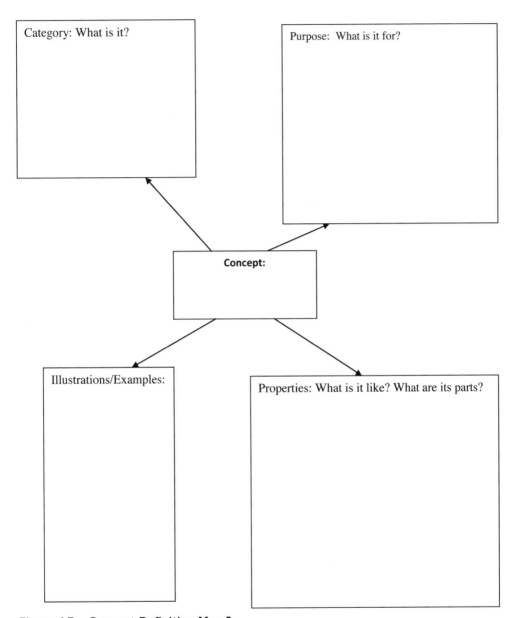

**Figure 4.7. Concept Definition Map 3.**

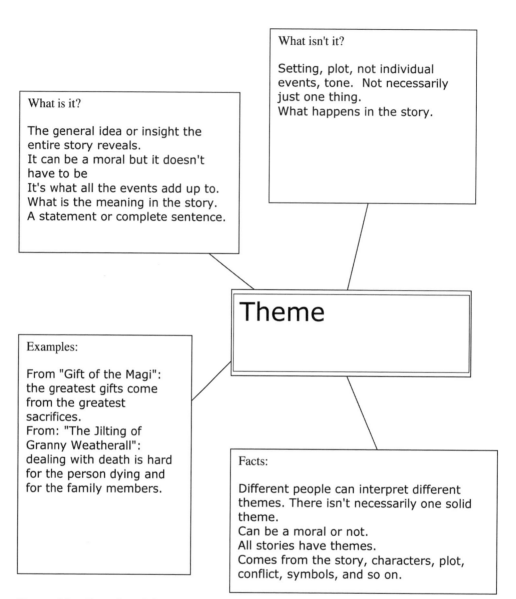

What isn't it?

Setting, plot, not individual
events, tone. Not necessarily
just one thing.
What happens in the story.

What is it?

The general idea or insight the
entire story reveals.
It can be a moral but it doesn't
have to be
It's what all the events add up to.
What is the meaning in the story.
A statement or complete sentence.

Theme

Examples:

From "Gift of the Magi":
the greatest gifts come
from the greatest
sacrifices.
From: "The Jilting of
Granny Weatherall":
dealing with death is hard
for the person dying and
for the family members.

Facts:

Different people can interpret different
themes. There isn't necessarily one solid
theme.
Can be a moral or not.
All stories have themes.
Comes from the story, characters, plot,
conflict, symbols, and so on.

**Figure 4.8. Completed Concept Definition Map.**

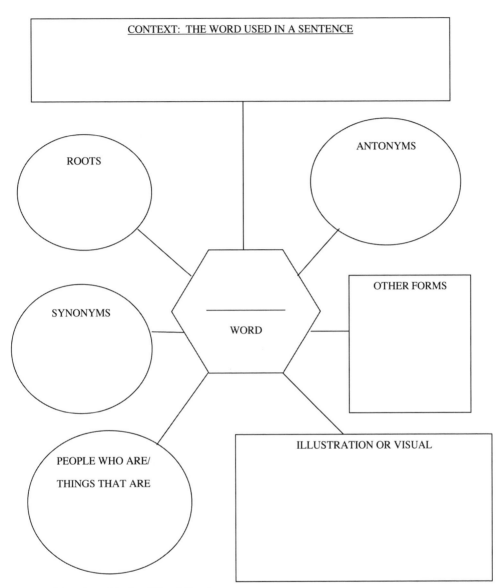

CONTEXT:  THE WORD USED IN A SENTENCE

ANTONYMS

ROOTS

OTHER FORMS

SYNONYMS

WORD

ILLUSTRATION OR VISUAL

PEOPLE WHO ARE/
THINGS THAT ARE

**Figure 4.9.   Graphic for Word Study.**

## Strategy 14: Text, Organize, Anchor, Say, and Test (TOAST)

*Purpose*

Use an organizational system for learning new vocabulary; learn new words and terms; assess one's own learning of new words and terms.

*CCSS Connection*

Standard L.3: Apply knowledge of language; Standard L.4: Determine or clarify the meaning of unknown and multiple-meaning words and phrases; Standard L.6: Acquire and use accurately a range of general and domain-specific words and phrases.

*Overview*

The TOAST strategy (Dana & Rodriguez, 1992) provides students with a system for learning new vocabulary words, which they can use in any subject area. Students learn the meaning of new words and phrases at varying levels and rates, and this strategy allows them to work at their own pace. It is an especially effective strategy for struggling readers.

*Procedure*

1. Text: Choose vocabulary words and terms from reading material or class context that students need to know. Give students a number of index cards and have them write the words on one side and the definition and a sentence using the word on the other (one word for each card).

2. Organize: Have students organize the cards into categories that make the most sense to them.

3. Anchor: Have students work individually or with a partner, using the cards to quiz each other.

4. Say: Emphasize that it is important for students to pronounce the words and definitions out loud to themselves or their partner.

5. Test: Have students complete a practice test on the words to identify which of the words they still need to learn. They can then pull out cards for those words and continue the process.

## Strategy 15: Frayer Model

*Purpose*

Identify features of key terms and concepts, including categories, properties and illustrations; generate examples and nonexamples of key terms and concepts; build conceptual understanding of key terms and concepts.

*CCSS Connection*

Standard L.3: Apply knowledge of language; Standard L.6: Acquire and use accurately a range of general academic and domain-specific words and phrases.

*Overview*

The Frayer model is also a graphic organizer and a categorizing activity that helps students develop conceptual understanding (Frayer, Frederick, & Klausmeier, 1969). Students may be asked to provide a definition, characteristics, examples, and nonexamples.

*Procedure*

1. Assign students to complete the model for a particular idea, term, or concept they are studying.

2. Explain the parts of the Frayer model graphic organizer (see figure 4.10).

3. Use a simple term to illustrate how to complete the Frayer model. Instruct students to write the definition in their own words and include examples and nonexamples from real life or from their own lives and experiences.

4. Have students complete the model using the concept assigned. They may work with partners or complete the model individually and then share their work with a partner.

5. You can also have students display their Frayer models or create poster-size versions to be displayed.

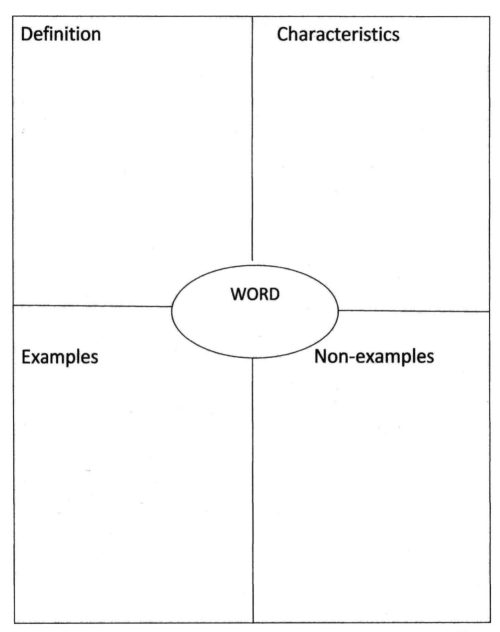

Figure 4.10. The Frayer Model. (From D. A. Frayer, W. C. Frederick, and H. J. Klaus-meier [1969], *A schema for testing the level of concept mastery* [Working Paper No. 16]. Madison, WI: Wisconsin Research and Development Center for Cognitive Learning.)

## Strategy 16: List-Group-Label-Write

*Purpose*

Use prior knowledge to identify meanings of unfamiliar words; build conceptual understanding; categorize and classify concepts; use prior knowledge to comprehend text; use key words and concepts in writing.

*CCSS Connection*

Standard RL/RI.4: Interpret words and phrases as they are used in a text; Standard L.3: Apply knowledge of language to understand how language functions in different contexts; Standard L.4: Determine or clarify the meaning of unknown and multiple-meaning words and phrases; Standard L.6: Acquire and use accurately a range of general academic and domain-specific words and phrases.

*Overview*

List-group-label-write is a strategy in which students use their prior knowledge to improve their vocabulary, comprehension, and writing skills (Harmon, Wood, & Hedrick, 2006). Begin by asking students to brainstorm and make a list of all the words and terms they know related to a particular topic. For example, for the term "data," a student might brainstorm a list similar to this one: mean, histogram, mode, median, data set, compute, bar graph, circle graph, add, scatter plot, divide, distribution. Next, students will group or categorize the terms according to their similarities. Using the following procedure, start with a reading assignment or passage from a text that students will be reading.

*Procedure*

1. Select a passage on a particular topic that students will reading during the class period.

2. Ask students to brainstorm a list of everything that comes to mind on the topic. Display these terms on the overhead.

3. Have students independently or in pairs or small groups categorize the terms. Ask them to be able to explain why they decided to categorize the words as they did.

4. Have students read the selected passage and add to their list of terms or make changes in their original categories as needed.

5. Have each student choose a category of terms and write a paragraph about that category, using the terms included. It may be necessary to model this writing activity at first before having students write their own.

The example in figures 4.11a and 4.11b is from Harmon, Wood, and Hedrick (2006). Figure 4.11a shows the grouping and labeling, and figure 4.11b shows the written paragraph.

---

**Topic:  Middle Ages: Feudalism**

Brainstorming (whole class):

| | | | |
|---|---|---|---|
| Feudalism | Chivalry | Knights | Manor |
| Lord | Religion | Royalty | Serf |
| Middle Ages | Kingdom | | |

Grouping and labeling (small groups):

| Concepts and Ideas: | Places: | People: | Time Periods: |
|---|---|---|---|
| Feudalism | Castle | Lord | Middle Ages |
| Chivalry | Kingdom | Kings | |
| Religion | | Knights | |
| Royalty | | Serf | |

Post reading: Adding new terms (whole class or small group)

| | | | | |
|---|---|---|---|---|
| Secular | Vassal | Manor | Peasants | Fief |
| Clergy | Serfs | Tithe | | |

Grouping and Labeling new terms with old terms (small groups):

| Concepts and Systems: | Places | People | Time Periods | Things "Given" |
|---|---|---|---|---|
| Feudalism | Castle | Lord | Middle Ages | Tithe |
| Chivalry | Kingdom | Kings | | Fief |
| Religion | Manor | Knights | | |
| Royalty | | Serfs | | |
| Secular | | Clergy | | |
| | | Vassal | | |
| | | Peasants | | |

---

Sample Writing: The structure of feudalism is like a pyramid of distinct roles and classes. At the top of the pyramid, with the most power, is the king. Next are the wealthy landowners and high-ranking clergy such as bishops. At the next level of power are the knights--warriors on horseback who defend their lords' lands in exchange for fiefs or land. At the bottom of the pyramid are the landless peasants or serfs who work the land for their lords.

**Figure 4.11.   Example of List-Group-Label-Write. (Harmon, Wood & Hedrick [2006]. Reprinted with permission from the Association of Middle Level Education [formerly National Middle School Association], www.amle.org.)**

Strategy 17: Vocabulary Pictures

*Purpose*

Define word meaning using dictionaries or other resources; create visual representations to clarify the meaning of new words; incorporate newly learned words into one's own speaking and writing.

*CCSS Connection*

Standard L.4: Determine or clarify the meaning of unknown or multiple-meaning words and phrases; Standard L.6: Acquire and use accurately a range of general academic and domain-specific words and phrases.

*Overview*

This simple and effective vocabulary strategy asks students to define vocabulary words and then create nonlinguistic representations to understand and remember the words.

*Procedure*

Students begin by folding a blank piece of paper into, or drawing, a number of squares (two, four, or six per page). You can also have students use a number of note cards instead. In each square students do the following:

1. Write the vocabulary word.

2. Write the definition of the word.

3. Draw a picture to show the word's meaning or cut a picture out of a magazine.

4. Write a sentence using the word.

Figures 4.12a and 4.12b show two examples of vocabulary squares.

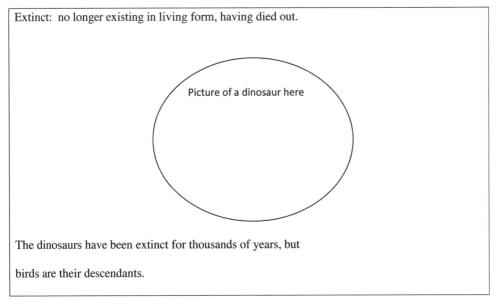

Extinct: no longer existing in living form, having died out.

Picture of a dinosaur here

The dinosaurs have been extinct for thousands of years, but

birds are their descendants.

**Figure 4.12a. Vocabulary Square 1.**

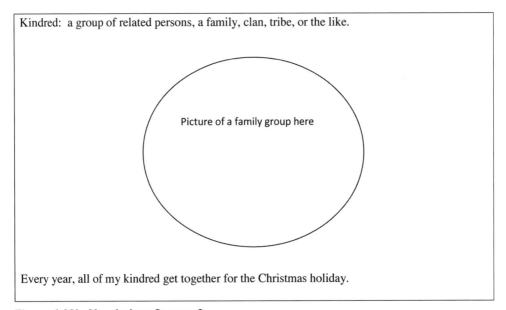

Kindred: a group of related persons, a family, clan, tribe, or the like.

Picture of a family group here

Every year, all of my kindred get together for the Christmas holiday.

**Figure 4.12b. Vocabulary Square 2.**

## Strategy 18: Contextual Redefinition

*Purpose*

Use context clues and root words as well as prior knowledge to determine word meaning; use dictionary skills to clarify word meaning; use newly acquired vocabulary in one's writing.

*CCSS Connection*

Standard L.3: Apply knowledge of language; Standard L.4: Determine or clarify the meaning of unknown and multiple-meaning words and phrases; Standard L.6: Acquire and use accurately a range of general academic and domain-specific words and phrases.

*Overview*

The contextual redefinition strategy (Readence, Bean, & Baldwin, 1998) is a useful strategy for helping students use prior knowledge to figure out the meaning of words. As opposed to random guessing at the meaning, this activity helps students use important clues about the word's meaning.

*Procedure*

1. First, locate several words or terms related to the assigned reading material, especially those you can predict students will find challenging.

2. Determine to what extent the context provides clues to the word's meaning.

3. Review the list of words with students and have them write the words in the first column of the chart. Ask them to try to use their prior knowledge to figure out what the word might mean as well as using word roots and guessing at the word's meaning as they complete the second column of the chart.

4. Next, students use the word in a sentence, either one from the text or a sentence of their own. Have students complete the third column.

5. Finally, students write their own prediction of the word's meaning in the fourth column and then check the textbook, glossary, or dictionary to confirm. The actual word meaning is to be written in the last column of the chart.

The example in table 4.1 comes from Harmon, Wood, and Hedrick (2006).

**Table 4.1. Contextual Redefinition Chart Example**

Terms: seismology, fault, tsunami
Instructional contexts for the each word:

- "The history of *seismology* dates back to the 1750s when a major earthquake caused great damage to Lisbon, Portugal. This catastrophe prompted scientists of that time to learn more about earthquakes, including the effects, locations, and timing of these natural occurrences."
- "After the San Francisco earthquake of 1906, scientists learned that the forces that create earthquakes find weak areas in the earth's crust to relieve this gradual buildup of stress. These *fault* lines are sometimes located a great distance away from the source of the earthquake."
- "Coastal cities located in earthquake-prone areas are always in danger of the devastating effects of the ocean brought on by *tsunamis*."

| Word | Word Level Clues | Context Clues | Predicting Word Meaning | Actual Word Meaning |
|---|---|---|---|---|
| Seismology | Clues: -ology means "study of" Guess: Something in science | Clues: earthquakes; learning more about earthquakes | Study of earthquakes, including the effects, locations, and timing | Study of earthquakes |
| Fault | Clues: Guess: Did something wrong | Clues: weak areas | Weak area in the earth's crust where an earthquake occurs | A fracture in the continuity of a rock formation caused by a shifting or dislodging of the earth's crust in which adjacent surfaces are displaced relative to one another and parallel to the plane of fracture |
| Tsunami | Clues: Has "sun" in it Guess: sun has something to do with earthquakes | Clues: coastal cities; ocean | City flooded because of the water from the ocean | A very large ocean wave caused by an underwater earthquake or volcanic eruption |

*Source*: Harmon, Wood, & Hedrick (2006). Reprinted with permission from the Association of Middle Level Education (formerly National Middle School Association), www.amle.org.

## Strategy 19: Finding Common Roots

*Purpose*

Identify multiple-meaning words during the reading process; contrast words' common meanings versus subject-specific meanings; use dictionary skills to identify word meaning; identify word parts to clarify word meaning.

*Overview*

In many content areas, terminology may consist of words that have multiple meanings. Some words even have the same spelling but may have different meanings depending on how they are used (e.g., "bass" is a type of fish in science [or cooking] and a deep singing voice in the area of music; "advocate" can be pronounced with a long "a" sound and mean "to speak or write in support of" but can also be pronounced with a short "a" sound and refer to a person who supports or pleads the cause of another). Think of how the word "compound," for example, can be used in many different ways in different content areas. In English class, "compound" is a grammatical term referring to a particular type of sentence structure; in math it may describe a mathematical function or process; in science it may refer to a mixture of different chemicals or substances; in social studies it may refer to an event that creates additional problems or difficulties, or a fenced-in area. Finding common roots is a strategy that helps students identify multiple word meanings within or across given subject areas (Harmon, Wood, & Hedrick, 2006).

*Procedure*

1. After activating students' prior knowledge and engaging in prereading activities, assign students to read a given passage or textbook section. While they are reading, have students look for and highlight all the words that may have more than one meaning in the passage.

2. Begin a whole-class discussion following the reading in which you ask students to share words they have identified. Discuss the common meanings of the word versus the content-specific meaning. Define for students the word "homograph" as "words that have the same spellings but different meanings and origins." Also point out that these words will have dictionary entries for each definition.

3. Have students work in pairs to complete the finding common roots map (figure 4.13). Tell them they are assigned to determine whether the particular word is a homograph. Students can complete additional maps on separate paper for additional terms.

4. Have students discuss their findings with the whole class.

You may need some additional examples to help students understand the concept of homophones:

accent—stress or emphasis/a manner of speaking or pronunciation influenced by the region in which one lives or grew up

agape—wide open/a Greek word meaning "love"

attribute—a characteristic or quality/to think of as belonging to or originating in some person, place or thing

axes—the plural of ax or axe/the plural of axis

bass—a deep voice or tone/a kind of fish

bat—a piece of sporting equipment used in baseball/a winged animal associated with vampires

bow—to bend at the waist/the front of a boat/a pair of tied loops/an instrument used to play a string instrument such as a violin

buffet—to hit, punch, or slap/a self-serve food bar

compact—small/to make small/a small case for holding makeup

compound—to mix or combine/an enclosed area with a building or group of buildings inside

You can find additional examples of homographs online.

# FINDING COMMON ROOTS

Word: _____

<table>
<tr><td>Content Meaning:</td><td>Common Meaning:</td></tr>
</table>

Content Meaning:

Common Meaning:

Word Origin

Word Origin

Are these words homographs?

Figure 4.13. Finding Common Roots Map. (Harmon, Wood & Hedrick [2006]. Reprinted with permission from the Association of Middle Level Education [formerly National Middle School Association], www.amle.org.)

## Strategy 20: Using Prefixes, Roots, and Suffixes

*Purpose*

Use prefixes, roots, and suffixes to clarify and define words; learn common prefixes, roots, and suffixes; identify unfamiliar words from reading of text and identify word parts to clarify meanings; create a list of self-selected vocabulary words.

*CCSS Connection*

Standard RL/RI.4: Interpret words and phrases as they are used in a text; Standard L.4: Determine or clarify the meaning of unknown and multiple-meaning words and phrases.

*Overview*

Critical to good reading comprehension in any subject area is the ability to recognize common prefixes, root words, and suffixes in English, which is helpful in clarifying word meaning. Having students use a list of prefixes, roots, and suffixes allows students to record unfamiliar terms and determine their meanings by analyzing the word parts. Students should continue using the word part list for as long as necessary, until they realize they have learned most common word parts that are used in English.

*Procedure*

1. Provide students with their own copy of a word part list such as the one that follows (table 4.2). Ask them to keep the list in their notebook and to use it when they are completing reading assignments. You might also consider making a poster-size copy of the list to display in your classroom. Most dictionaries include good lists of prefixes, roots, and suffixes students can use. Lists of common prefixes, suffix, and roots can also be found easily with a simple online search.

2. Spend some time discussing with students how to use the word. Share with students simple examples such as this one:

   "un-" is a prefix. "Unprepared" means to not be prepared; "unusual" means something out of the ordinary; "unavailable" means to not be present or available. Therefore, the prefix "un-" means "undone" or "not." It is a prefix that makes the meaning of the term negative.

   Ask students how many other words they can name that begin with the prefix "un-." Practice with the word list by using some of the word parts and asking them to brainstorm a list of as many words as they can think of that use that prefix, root, or suffix.

3. Have students use the word list to determine the meanings of words they encounter in the context of class work and reading assignments. Have them create a space or section in their journal or notebook where they can write down all of the words they find from lectures, discussions, films, or readings that use particular word parts.

4. At the end of a unit, or periodically during the unit, have students discuss and share the words they have found.

Table 4.2 presents a list of some common prefixes, suffixes, and roots. You will notice each item includes the word part, the definition and examples of words that include the particular part.

**Table 4.2.  Common Prefixes, Roots, and Suffixes**

*Prefixes*

| | | |
|---|---|---|
| ad | to, toward | advance, adhere, adhesive |
| ante | before, in front of | antebellum, antediluvian, antecedent |
| anti | against, opposite | antithesis, antipathy, antagonist |
| bi | two | biannual, bicentennial |
| centi | one hundred | century, centennial, centenary |
| circum | around | circumvent, circumnavigate |
| co | together, with | cooperate, coordinate |
| com/con | together, with | committee, convene, combine, compound |
| contra | against | contradict, contraindicate |
| deci | ten | decimate, decimal, decade |
| dia | apart, opposite | diametric, diagonal, dialogue, diagnosis |
| dis | away, from, not | discount, disavow, distance |
| equi | equal | equality, equipoise, equidistant |
| extra | in addition | extraordinary, extrasensory, extraterrestrial |
| ex | out of, former, away | exclude, exhume, exhale |
| hyper | above, beyond excessive | hyperactive, hypertension, hyperextend |
| hypo | under, less than normal | hypothermia, hypoglycemia |
| im, ir | not in, into without | immoral, irredeemable, irreplaceable |
| inter | between, among | interrupt, intervene, interregnum |
| intra | within | intramural, intranet |
| kilo | thousand | kilometer, kilogram |
| mega | large, million | megalopolis, megatrends |
| milli | thousand | millipede, millionaire |
| mis | wrong, bad | mistake, misinterpret, misplace |
| multi | many, several | multitude, multiple, multiplication |
| non | not, negative | noncompliant, nonresponsive |
| over | too much | overspend, overextend, overdo |
| peri | around | periscope, perimeter, periphery |
| pre | before, in order | preview, predate, preclude |
| pro | before, forward in favor of | prospect, provide, profess, project |
| re | again, back | revisit, retell, return |
| retro | again, back | retroactive, retrograde |
| sub/sur | under, beneath | substitute, surrogate |
| sug/sup | under, beneath | suggest, supplant |

*(continued)*

**Table 4.2.** (*continued*)

| | | |
|---|---|---|
| super | above, over, in addition | supervisor, superior, superfluous |
| syn | with | synonym, synchronize, syncopate |
| trans | across, through, change | transgress, transport, transform |
| tri | three | trio, trilogy, trimester, triangle |
| ultra | excessive, beyond | ultramarine, ultrasound |
| un | not, the opposite of | unnecessary, undone, untie |

*Roots*

| | | |
|---|---|---|
| act | to do | active, action, actuate |
| aero | air | aerodynamics, aeronautical |
| anthro | man | anthropology, philanthropist |
| aqua | water | aquarium, aquatic, aquifer |
| astro | star | astronomy, astrological |
| aud | to hear | audible, audition, auditorium |
| bellus | war | bellicose, belligerent |
| bene | good | beneficial, benefit, beneficiary, beneficent |
| biblio | book | bibliography, bibliophile |
| bio | life | biography, biology, biosphere |
| cap | head | captain, capitol, capital |
| capto | to take or seize | capture, captive, captivate |
| cide | to kill | homicide, suicide, pesticide |
| cite | to call | incite, recite, recitation |
| chronos | time | chronological, chronometer |
| cogno | to know, recognize | recognize, recognition, cognizant, cognitive |
| crat | rule | democrat, autocrat, bureaucrat |
| cred, creed | believe | incredible, creed, credulous |
| cycl | circle | bicycle, cycle, cyclical |
| demo | the people | democracy, demography |
| dent, dont | tooth | dental, orthodontics |
| dicto | speak | diction, contradict, predict |
| duct | to lead | deductive, aqueduct |
| facto | to do or make | manufacture, factory |
| fid | trust | fidelity, infidel, fiduciary |
| fin | end | final, finish |
| formo | shape | form, perform, formative |
| frater | brother | fraternal, fraternity, fraternize |
| gen, gene | race, family | genetics, gene, genealogy |
| geo | earth | geography, geology, geopolitics |
| gon | angle | polygon, pentagon |
| graph, gram | to write | graphology, telegram, monogram |
| greg | flock, herd | gregarious, egregious |
| luc, lumen | light | lucid, illuminate |
| hydra | water | hydrant, hydrophobia |
| jud/jus | law | judge, justice, judicial |
| legis | law | legislature, legitimate, legislate |
| liber | free | liberty, liberation |
| loc | place | location, locale |
| logos | word, study, speech | biology, chronology, chronological |
| macro | large | macrobiotics, macroeconomics |
| magn | great, large | magnificent, magnate, magnify |
| mal | evil | malevolent, malignant, malediction |
| mand | order | command, demand, commandment |

| manus | hand | manuscript, manual, manicure |
| mar | sea | marine, marina, maritime |
| mater | mother | maternal, alma mater, matrimony |
| mech | machine | mechanism, mechanic, machinery |
| mem | mindful | memory, memorial, commemorate |
| meter, metr | measure | metronome, meter, metric |
| micro | small | microphone, microbiology |
| min | small | minute, miniature, miniscule |
| mob/mov | to move | movement, mobility, motion |
| mono | one | monotonous, monocle, monogram |
| morph | form | morpheme, amorphous, anthropomorphous |
| mort | dead | mortal, mortician, mortify |
| nat | born | prenatal, innate, nature |
| naut | ship, sailor | nautical, astronaut, cosmonaut |
| nova | new | novel, innovation, innovate |
| omni | all | omnipotent, omniscient |
| opt | eye | optic, optician, optometrist |
| ortho | straight | orthodontist, orthography, orthodox |
| pater, patri | father | patrimony, patrician, paternity, patricide |
| pathos | feeling | pathetic, empathy, pathology |
| ped | foot | pedestrian, pedal, pedometer |
| phil | love | bibliophile, philanthropic, philosophy |
| phob | fear | phobia, acrophobia, agoraphobia |
| phon | voice | telephone, phonics, gramophone |
| photo | light | photosynthesis, photography |
| phys | nature | physical, physician, physiology |
| pod | foot | podiatrist, tripod |
| polis | city | politician, metropolis |
| poly | many | polygamy, polymorphous |
| prim | first, basic | primary, primal, primitive |
| psycho | mind | psychotic, psychology, psychiatrist |
| pug | first | pugilist, pugnacious |
| quir, ques | to ask or say | inquiry, question, inquire |
| rect | straight, right | correct, rectangle, rectify |
| scop | to see | telescope, microscope, periscope |
| sect | to cut | section, transect, intersect |
| sign | mark | signature, signage, signify |
| son | sound | sonar, sonic |
| soph | wise | sophomore, sophist |
| pec | to see | spectacle, spectator, spectacular |
| spir | to breathe | inspire, respiration |
| struct | to build | construct, structure |
| syn/sym | with, together | synonym, sympathy |
| tech | skill | technology, technician |
| tele | far | telecast, telephone, telemarket |
| terr | land | terrain, terrestrial |
| theo | god | theology, theological, atheist |
| therm | heat | thermal, thermos, thermometer |
| tract | to pull | tractor, intractable |
| turb | trouble | turbulence, disturb, perturb |
| uni | one | unify, uniform, universe |
| vac | empty | vacant, vacate, vacation |
| var | different | variety, variation, variable |
| ver | truth | veracity, verity |

*(continued)*

**Table 4.2.** *(continued)*

| | | |
|---|---|---|
| vert | to turn | convert, reverse, conversion |
| vit, viv | live | survive, vital |
| vid, vis | to see | visual, video |
| voc | to call | vocal, vocation, evoke |
| volv | to roll or turn | revolve, involve |
| vor | eat or consume | carnivore, voracious |
| zoo | animal | zoo, zoology |

*Suffixes*

| | | |
|---|---|---|
| -able, ible | worthy of or inclined to, able to | understandable, edible |
| -acy, -acity | having the quality of | voracity, authenticity |
| -ance | quality, state, or condition of | assurance, acceptance |
| -archy | government | anarchy, monarchy, oligarchy |
| -ate | state, office, or function | candidate, delegate, inviolate |
| -ation | quality, state, or condition | abomination |
| -ation | action or process of | creation, retaliation |
| -ative | pertaining to | relative, pejorative |
| -bility | state or quality of being | nobility, fragility |
| -chrome | pigment or color | monochrome, codachrome |
| -cide | act of killing | genocide, fratricide, suicide |
| -crat | ruler | autocrat, plutocrat |
| -dom | quality, state or condition | freedom, kingdom |
| -ed | forms the past tense of a verb | debated, legislated |
| -escent | becoming | fluorescent, evanescent |
| -est | most | kindest, hardest, biggest |
| -ferous | bearing, producing | cruciferous, vociferous |
| -fold | multiplied by | manifold |
| -form | having the form of | uniform, cruciform |
| -ful | full of, having the quality of | fanciful, mournful |
| -gram | item written | telegram |
| -graphy | something written about | geography, biography |
| -ics | science or art of | mechanics, biometrics |
| -ify | to make | rectify, unify, modify |
| -ing | a continuing action | progressing, undergoing |
| -ish | pertaining to | feverish, childish, foolish |
| -ism | quality, state or condition | determinism, atheism, barbarism |
| -ist | one who, doer, agent | propagandist, chemist |
| -itious | pertaining to | fictitious, repetitious |
| -itis | inflammation | bursitis, appendicitis |
| -ive | pertaining to | conducive, receptive |
| -ize | to make | prioritize, civilize, economize |
| -less | lacking, without | artless, fatherless, homeless |
| -ly | in the manner of | lovely, forcefully, happily |
| -ment | quality, state or condition | bereavement, movement |
| -meter | measuring device | altimeter, monometer |
| -metry | process of measuring | geometry, trigonometry |
| -mony | quality, state or condition | matrimony, ceremony, parsimony |
| -ness | state, condition, quality | openness, kindness, fullness |
| -nomy | study or science of | astronomy, economy, taxonomy |
| -ology, logy | science or theory of | philology, physiology |
| -ory | place where | crematory, laboratory, directory |
| -ous, ose | possessing, full of | porous, monotonous, copious |
| -phobia | fear of | agoraphobia, arachnophobia, hydrophobia |
| -scope | instrument for observing | telescope, microscope, periscope |
| -tion | quality, state or condition | conception, perception, recognition |
| -wise, ward | manner, direction, position | lengthwise, likewise, lengthwise |

## Strategy 21: Animal Creations

*Purpose*

Use prefixes, roots, and suffixes to clarify and define words; learn common prefixes, roots, and suffixes; apply knowledge of word parts to create something new.

*CCSS Connection*

Standard L.3: Apply knowledge of language; Standard L.4: Determine or clarify the meaning of unknown and multiple-meaning words and phrases.

*Overview*

This creative strategy was adapted by Harmon, Wood, and Hedrick (2006) from the original idea by Johnson and Pearson (1984) and Cecil and Gipe (2003). It helps students learn to use knowledge of prefixes and roots. It is great for scientific and technical subject areas because scientific terminology is heavily dependent upon prefixes and roots. Students must create an imaginary creature that can be identified by its invented scientific name. For this activity, have students use the prefixes, suffixes, and roots from the list of common prefixes, roots, and suffixes in the previous strategy. They will also need some poster paper, strips of paper, and markers.

*Procedure*

1. Refer students to their list of prefixes, roots, and suffixes to use during this activity.

2. Using some scientific terms that contain prefixes and roots, have students create an original creature or monster by choosing from the prefixes and roots and then writing the scientific name of this creature on a strip of paper.

3. Students then draw a picture of their creation on the top part of their poster paper.

4. At the bottom of the paper students will write a sentence that shows the connection between the name of their creature to a real scientific term they have learned in class.

5. Students should hang their posters around the room and share their creations with the class.

This process can also be completed in pairs or small groups.

Here is an example from Harmon, Wood, and Hedrick (2006):

> My creature, *Lineatusbicornis monocephalustquadropod*, has no problem using a monocular microscope. (p. 114)

### Strategy 22: Incidental Morpheme Method

*Purpose*

Use prefixes, roots, and suffixes to clarify and define words; learn common prefixes, roots, and suffixes; apply knowledge of word parts to clarify meaning; use newly acquired vocabulary in one's writing; use dictionary skills to clarify word meaning.

*CCSS Connection*

Standard L.3: Apply knowledge of language; Standard L.4: Determine or clarify the meaning of unknown and multiple-meaning words and phrases; Standard L.6: Acquire and use a range of general academic and domain-specific words and phrases.

*Overview*

The incidental morpheme method is another strategy that requires students to make use of their knowledge of word prefixes and roots to figure out the meaning of words. It is a strategy that the teacher can use at any time during the course of teaching whenever a word requires attention to its particular word parts to identify the meaning (Manzo & Manzo, 1990).

*Procedure*

1. Write the word on the chalkboard or overhead and divide it into its parts. For example: peri + scope.

2. Ask students to try to explain each word part: peri- means "around." Scope means "to see." Write the definition of each part under the word.

3. If students have trouble coming up with the meaning, give them some other words with the same prefixes and roots to offer clues: For "peri," perhaps "perimeter" or "periphery." For "scope," perhaps "microscope," "telescope," "optical," or "optometrist."

4. Discuss the clue words with the class and ask them to make a guess as to the meaning of the target word.

5. Ask students to help you write a sentence that defines the meaning of the term: "A periscope is a device that allows one to see around an area."

6. Next, ask students to look up the meaning of the term for a more detailed definition: "A periscope is a tubular instrument containing a series of mirrors and lenses used to view objects that are above the line of direct vision as when submerged in a submarine or a trench."

7. This is a great, easy strategy that you can use at any time during your teaching. You can also ask students to write down the definitions in their word list or in their notebooks.

### Strategy 23: Word Pie

*Purpose*

Use prior knowledge to identify word meaning; identify synonyms and antonyms in order to clarify word meaning; use nonlinguistic representation as a means of learning new words; use newly learned words in one's own writing.

*CCSS Connection*

Standard L.4: Determine or clarify the meaning of unknown and multiple-meaning words and phrases; Standard L.6: Acquire and use accurately a range of general academic and domain-specific words and phrases.

*Overview*

Word pie is a variation of the Frayer model strategy. It asks students to learn a new word by defining it in their own words, providing a synonym and antonym for the word, drawing a graphic representation of the word, and using the word in a sentence. This is also an easy-to-use strategy that can be done at any time and helps students remember key vocabulary (see figure 4.14).

*Procedure*

You can give students a number of different word pie figures on a single sheet, or multiple sheets so that they can complete many different word pies. Have students complete one or more word pies.

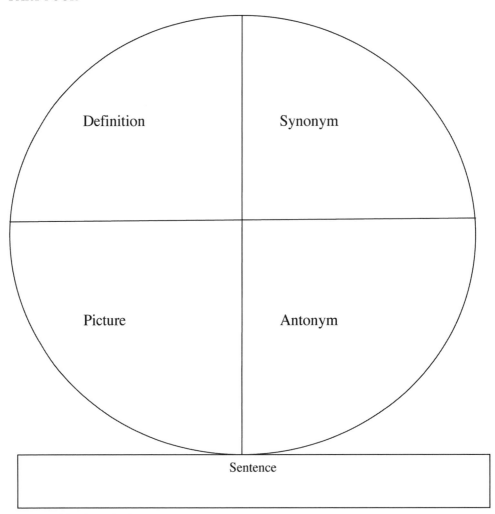

**Figure 4.14.  Word Pie.**

## Strategy 24: Word Sorts

*Purpose*
    Identify relationships among words; use critical thinking to classify and categorize words and terms into groups using a set of justifiable criteria; clarify the meaning of unfamiliar words and terms.

*CCSS Connection*
    Standard L.4: Determine or clarify the meaning of unknown or multiple-meaning words and phrases.

*Overview*

A slightly different version of the word sort was presented earlier in the book as a postreading strategy. Word sorts, however, are also a great vocabulary development strategy. Word sorts come from Gillet and Kita (1979) and Gillet and Temple (1983). They help students to identify the relationships among key concepts. You may remember from part 2 that they may be "open" word sorts or "closed" word sorts. With the "closed sort," the teacher provides students with the categories into which they will sort the words. With the "open sort," which is slightly more challenging and a better critical-thinking activity for students, students group the words and come up with their own titles or labels for each category.

This activity can be used as a review activity at the end of the unit or reading, or it can be done during a unit to help students gain a deeper understanding of the central concepts and ideas being taught. The process of sorting requires students to review or learn the meaning of each term or concept. For example, in math, students might sort a series of problems into groups according to types of functions needed to solve the problem. In English, students might sort the names of all of the characters from a novel into groups and determine a label for each category. In social studies, terms could be grouped according to places, historical periods, regions, or ideas. In shop class, students might sort a large number of different tools into categories based on their functions.

*Procedure*

1. List each of the terms in the group on one 3" × 5" note card or strip of paper. You will need one set for each student group.

2. Have students work in groups to sort the terms into categories, either open or closed. You may want to model this process for students with a simple set of words—such as common vegetables—prior to having students start.

3. Once the categorizing is finished, have each group make sure that each category is labeled (if it is an open sort) and that they have not labeled any of the categories "Miscellaneous" or "Other." Then have each group present their word sort to the rest of the class, explaining their reasons for sorting the terms as they did.

Table 4.3 shows an example of a historical character sort (Doty, Cameron, & Barton, 2003).

**Table 4.3.  Character Sort**

| American Revolution | Civil War | World War II |
|---|---|---|
| George Washington | Abraham Lincoln | Franklin Roosevelt |
| Benedict Arnold | Ulysses Grant | Gen. D. Eisenhower |
| Lord Cornwallis | Robert E. Lee | Winston Churchill |
| King George III | Jefferson Davis | Adolph Hitler |
| Marquis de Lafayette | Stonewall Jackson | Joseph Stalin |
| Alexander Hamilton | General Sherman | Benito Mussolini |
| | | Gen. D. MacArthur |
| | | Hideki Tojo |

*Source:* Reprinted by permission of McREL.

## Strategy 25: Semantic Feature Analysis

*Purpose*
  Identify relationships among words; use critical thinking to classify and compare words and phrases; clarify the meaning of unfamiliar words and terms.

*CCSS Connection*
  Standard L.4: Determine or clarify the meaning of unknown or multiple-meaning words and phrases.

*Overview*

Semantic feature analysis (Baldwin, Ford, & Readence, 1981) is a strategy in which students identify characteristics of a concept by comparing it to others in the same category. Students organize the words into a relationship grid. Any task in which students could categorize features of various similar concepts is ideal for use of this strategy. Students can gather information about concepts and identify the similarities and differences.

*Procedure*

1. Identify a category for study. For example: States of the United States.

2. Develop a matrix or grid such as the one in figure 4.15. On the left side, list terms, places, concepts, people, events, ideas. Along the top of the grid, list features that the concepts might share. For example, if students are analyzing US states, the left side would list Alaska, California, Colorado, New York, Arizona, and Minnesota. The top of the grid would list various features: mountainous, desert, Western, landlocked, population greater than five million, industrial, and so on.

3. Have students place an X in the grid if the feature applies. They may need to do research and gather information to do this part, or it can be completed while they are doing a reading assignment on the topic or during the course of a unit.

4. Have students discuss in small groups and come to consensus. Students should also look for patterns and identify the rationale behind their choices.

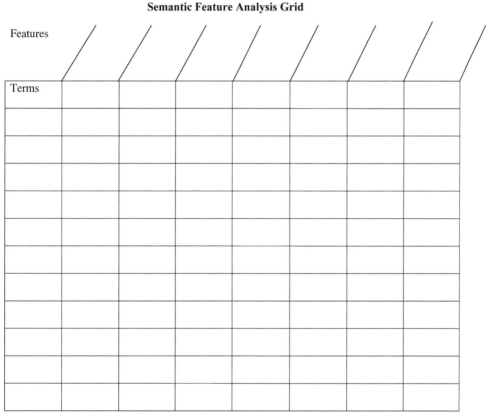

**Semantic Feature Analysis Grid**

**Figure 4.15.  Semantic Feature Analysis.**

## Strategy 26: Semantic Map

*Purpose*
Use background knowledge to identify word meaning; identify relationships among key ideas and concepts; make predictions about word meaning; clarify understanding of word meaning during reading of text.

*CCSS Connection*
Standard RL/RI.4: Interpret words and phrases as they are used in a text; Standard L.3: Apply knowledge of language; Standard L.4: Determine the meaning of unknown and multiple-meaning words and phrases; Standard L.5: Demonstrate understanding of figurative language, word relationships, and nuances.

*Overview*
Semantic maps are visual tools that help students activate their background knowledge on a central idea or concept. The maps are a visual display of the relationships among key ideas and terms related to the central concept (Doty, Cameron, & Barton, 2003). The best way to use semantic maps is at the beginning of a lesson or unit to help students activate their prior knowledge of the topic. Then later, they can refine their understanding as they progress through the reading material or unit.

*Procedure*
1. Choose a major concept of the lesson or unit. Write it in the center of a piece of poster paper and circle it. For example: totalitarianism, climate change, romanticism, realism, Stalinism, the Enlightenment, or real numbers.

2. Have students brainstorm a list of terms that relate to the concept and record their responses on the chart paper.

3. Have students work in groups to place the terms they have brainstormed into categories. Each group can create its own version of the semantic map. The semantic map helps to build a network of ideas that reveals how the key terms and ideas are related.

4. Have students return to the maps frequently during the reading and after the reading, or at the end of the unit, to add additional information and details to them as they learn new content.

Figure 4.16 shows an example of a semantic map from Doty, Cameron, and Barton (2003).

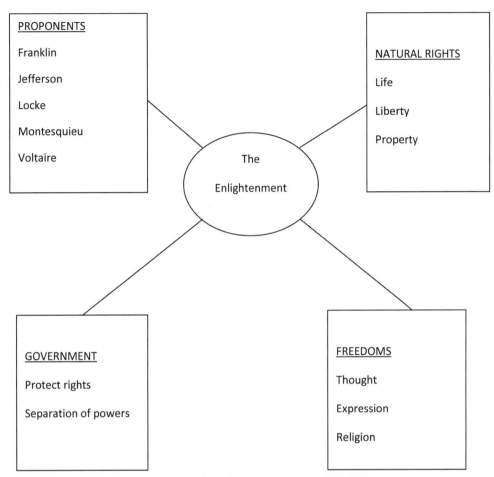

PROPONENTS

Franklin

Jefferson

Locke

Montesquieu

Voltaire

NATURAL RIGHTS

Life

Liberty

Property

The

Enlightenment

GOVERNMENT

Protect rights

Separation of powers

FREEDOMS

Thought

Expression

Religion

**Figure 4.16.  Semantic Map. (Reprinted by permission of McREL.)**

Strategy 27: Context-Content-Experience Map

*Purpose*
   Use context clues to determine word meaning; identify and clarify word meaning; recognize and clarify the meaning of multiple-meaning and domain-specific words and phrases; use personal associations to identify and remember newly learned words.

*Overview*

Similar to the concept definition map, the context-content-experience map comes from Janet Allen (1999). It is a graphic organizer that helps students to come up with possible definitions based on their analysis of the context, and then identify the actual definition. It's a good way to help students see cross-disciplinary meanings of words and also helps them identify personal associations with the concept.

*Procedure*

As an illustration, Allen (1999) presents an example of the term "metamorphosis" in the context of someone losing a great deal of weight. Students were able to identify the common definition of "metamorphosis" as "a change" and then provide examples from various disciplines such as physical education, math, and science. In an English class, I might use the map for the concept of romanticism as a literary movement. Students would then be asked to come up with a possible definition, analyze the context from a reading assignment, and then come up with a common definition such as the following: "an artistic movement of the 19th century that emphasized individualism, emotion, and imagination." Specialized examples might include areas such as art, music, literature, and perhaps history. Students then make some personal connection to the concept. Figure 4.17 shows the context-content-experience map.

**Context-Content-Experience**

Context:

_____

_____

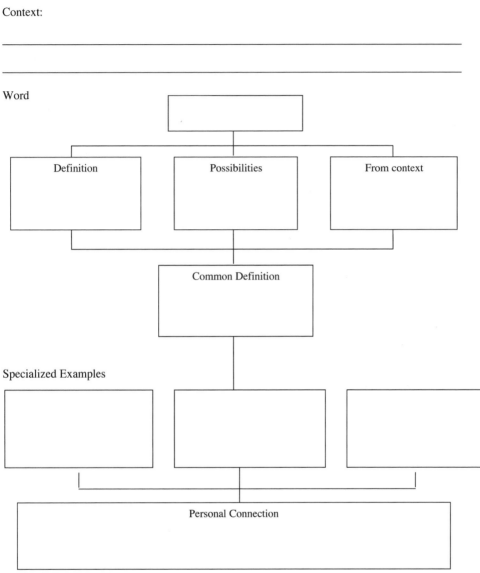

Figure 4.17. **Context-Content-Experience Map. (From Janet Allen, *Words, Words, Words,* Copyright © 1999. Reproduced with permission of Stenhouse Publishers, www.stenhouse.com.)**

## Strategy 28: Word Questioning

*Purpose*

   Make predictions about word meaning; use analysis, evaluation, and synthesis to build conceptual understanding of key terms; use word parts and context clues to identify word meaning.

*CCSS Connection*

   Standard L.3: Apply knowledge of language to understand how language functions in different contexts; Standard L.4: Determine the meaning of unknown and multiple-meaning words and phrases; Standard L.6: Acquire and use a range of general academic and domain-specific words and phrases.

*Overview*

   This strategy is similar to others presented in this section. It uses a graphic organizer to help students analyze a concept or word at different levels, including comprehension, application, analysis, synthesis, and the knowledge and evaluation level (Allen, 1999).

*Procedure*

   Begin by reading with students the target word or concept in context. Have students begin the word questioning organizer with the "Analysis" box and then proceed clockwise through the boxes. Figure 4.18 shows the word questioning organizer.

**WORD QUESTIONING**

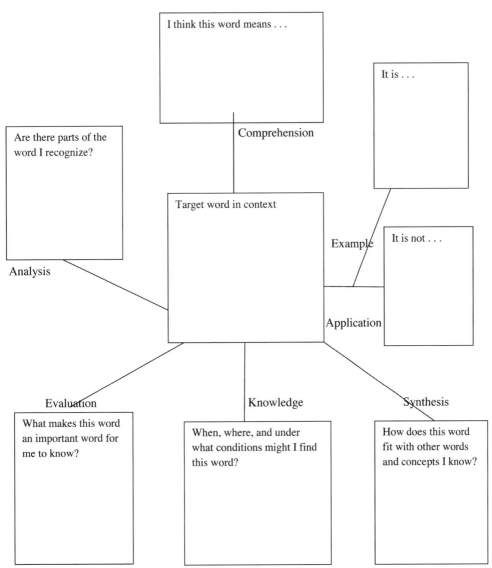

I think this word means . . .

Comprehension

It is . . .

Are there parts of the word I recognize?

Target word in context

Example

It is not . . .

Analysis

Application

Evaluation

Knowledge

Synthesis

What makes this word an important word for me to know?

When, where, and under what conditions might I find this word?

How does this word fit with other words and concepts I know?

**Figure 4.18. Word Questioning. (From Janet Allen, *Words, Words, Words*, Copyright © 1999. Reproduced with permission of Stenhouse Publishers, www.stenhouse.com.)**

## Strategy 29: The Prereading Plan (PreP)

*Purpose*

Use prior knowledge to comprehend text and identify meaning of unfamiliar words; clarify understanding based on active reading of text.

*CCSS Connection*

Standard RL/RI.4: Interpret words and phrases as they are used in text; Standard L.3: Acquire knowledge of language to understand how language functions in different contexts.

*Overview*

The PreP is a strategy that helps students discover what they know about a topic and extend their thinking. It also helps teachers identify students' levels of prior knowledge about a topic. The strategy comes from Langer (1981).

*Procedure*

1. Identify the textbook section or reading passage you are assigning to students and the key concepts that students will need to understand.

2. Use a film, quotation, online video, or display artifact to introduce the topic to students.

3. Ask students questions about the term, such as the following: "What do you think of when you . . . ?" "What might you see, hear, or feel . . . ?" "What comes to mind?" "What does this remind you of?" Make a list of students' ideas on the board, chart paper, or projector. During this process, ask students to reflect on their thinking about the word.

4. Reformulate the knowledge generated by asking if students wish to make any changes to the ideas that have been listed. They can delete or add to the list. As the teacher, analyze students' responses. Do they have:

   a. little understanding (can only identify basic word parts or roots, only think of similar sounding words),

   b. some prior information (they can identify examples, attributes, or defining characteristics), or

   c. a lot of prior knowledge (high-level thinking, analogies, definitions, super-ordinate concepts)?

5. Come back to the PreP after the reading assignment or unit is completed. Have students continue to add to, change, or delete the ideas. Harmon, Wood, and Hedrick (2006) present the following PreP from a biology class studying mammals and their characteristics (see figure 4.19).

**DIAGNOSTIC ANALYSIS OF STUDENTS' RESPONSES TO PreP**

General Topic: Mammals

Key Topic: Characteristics of Mammals (pictures of various mammals)

| Student | Responses | Level |
|---|---|---|
| Megan | 1. no eggs | some-attribute |
| | 2. mammals have hair | little association |
| | 3. dogs, cats, horses | |
| Bill | 1. They are intelligent and must be able to perform complex behavior | much--superordinate |
| | 2. limbs, legs | |
| | 3. diaphragms for breathing | some--attributes |
| Eric | 1. mammals nurse their babies, but reptiles do not | much--analogies |
| | 2. mammals can keep a constant body temperature so they can survive in extreme climates | much--superordinate |
| | 3. mammals have different ways to gather food. | some--attributes |
| Latiesha | 1. jungle animals, pets | little-- association |
| | 2. weird mammals--bats porcupines | some--attributes |
| | 3. some mammals have camouflage | |

**Figure 4.19. The Prereading Plan Example. (Wood, Harmon & Hedrick [2006]. Reprinted with permission from the Association of Middle Level Education [formerly National Middle School Association], www.amle.org.)**

## Strategy 30: KIM Chart

*Purpose*

   Identify word meaning; elaborate upon the meaning of key terms and concepts; create visual representations to learn and memorize new words.

*CCSS Connection*

   Standard L.4: Determine or clarify the meaning of unknown and multiple-meaning words and phrases.

*Overview*

   The KIM chart is a great, simple strategy for teaching vocabulary words and new concepts. The original source of the KIM chart is unknown. The KIM chart has three columns:

   K—Key idea
   I—Information that goes along with the key idea
   M—Memory clue, a picture or visual representation of the concept

*Procedure*

   The key idea may be a new vocabulary word or concept that students need to learn. Students can use a KIM chart with several different terms or vocabulary words. The information column can be an actual definition or a detailed explanation of the concept. It may also be something more technical for certain content areas. The memory clue is what students will picture in their minds in order to remember the word. Making a simple drawing helps students synthesize and apply the new word, making it their own. Figure 4.20 presents a KIM chart.

| K | I | M |
|---|---|---|
| Key Idea | Information | Memory Clue |
| pioneer | Someone who forges a way for others to follow | (Picture) |
| abolitionist | One who is morally opposed to slavery | (Picture) |
| secession | To withdraw formally from a group, organization, or union | (Picture) |

**Figure 4.20. KIM Chart.**

## Strategy 31: Preview in Context

*Purpose*

Use prior knowledge to determine word meaning; use context clues to define and clarify the meaning of words and terms; use word parts, synonyms, and antonyms to help clarify word meaning; use dictionary skills to define vocabulary words.

*CCSS Connection*

Standard RL/RI.4: Interpret words and phrases as they are used in a text; Standard L.3: Apply knowledge of language to understand how language functions in different contexts; Standard L.4: Determine the meaning of unknown and multiple-meaning words and phrases; Standard L.5: Demonstrate understanding of figurative language, word relationships, and nuances; Standard L.6: Acquire and use a range of general academic and domain-specific words and phrases.

*Overview*

The preview in context is a strategy for introducing students to new vocabulary words by using the original context. It comes from Tierney and Readence (1999). The strategy involves students exploring meanings and using discussion and context to determine the correct meaning.

*Procedure*

1. Select key vocabulary terms from the text passage or reading assignment.

2. Present the words to students on the board or overhead. Pronounce each word and ask students if they have any idea what each word may mean.

3. Have students study how the author uses the terms in the reading passage. It is best to do this in the context of a whole-class reading of the passage.

4. Use questions such as the following:

    a. What does the sentence tell you about the word?

    b. What questions do you have about the word?

    c. Do you recognize any of the roots or word parts?

    d. Can you think of any synonyms or antonyms for the word?

    e. What do you think is probably the meaning of the word?

5. For those words that do not provide enough context information, ask students to look up the dictionary definition of the word. I often have a student use his or her Smartphone to quickly look up the definition. Have students compare the dictionary definition with the way that the word is used in the context.

Harmon, Wood, and Hedrick (2006) present an example of a class exploring the meaning of the term "extravagant" as it was used in a history textbook (see figure 4.21).

---

*Teacher: Look at the word "extravagant." From the way the author uses the word, what*

   *do you think it might mean?*

*Students: It sounds like it has something to do with getting France into debt.*

*Teacher: Why do you say that?*

*Students: The first sentence says that the government was in debt; the second sentence*

   *says that the spending that the king and queen did was part of the problem. So*

   *maybe they spent too much money.*

*Teacher: "Extravagant" has the prefix "extra," which means what?*

*Students: "To go beyond," "More than," "To be outside of . . ."*

*Teacher: Can you think of any other words that begin with "extra"?*

*Students: Extraordinary.*

*Teacher: Good. What does "Extraordinary" mean?*

*Students: Going beyond what is ordinary.*

*Teacher: So how would you describe extravagant spending by the king and queen?*

*Students: They spent more money than they had. They went beyond their means.*

---

**Figure 4.21. Preview in Context Example. (Harmon, Wood, & Hedrick [2006]. Reprinted with permission from the Association of Middle Level Education [formerly National Middle School Association], www.amle.org.)**

## Strategy 32: Word Walls

*Purpose*

Identify unfamiliar words and terms in reading and discussion; identify and clarify the meaning of words; use newly learned words and terms in one's own writing.

*CCSS Connection*

Standard L.4: Determine or clarify the meaning of unknown and multiple-meaning words and phrases; Standard L.6: Acquire and use accurately a range of general academic and domain-specific words and phrases.

*Overview*

As mentioned earlier in this section, word walls are a powerful method of teaching and reinforcing vocabulary. Consider designating a section of bulletin board in your classroom for a "word wall," a place to display vocabulary words in the classroom. You and your students can add words and concepts to the word wall as the unit proceeds.

*Procedure*

When a new unit begins, start a new word wall. The word wall becomes a permanent location for high-frequency words and those you want to continually reinforce. Here are some guidelines for word walls:

1. Choose the location carefully. You want the word wall to be visible to students. Keep some strips of paper and markers nearby to write down new words in large black letters.

2. Ask students to try to use the words from the word wall in their written assignments, graphic organizers, and discussions.

3. While you can do word walls for general vocabulary terms and general unfamiliar words encountered, they can also be topical and thematic, with the words related to a particular course topic, unit, or reading selection.

4. Ask students to help you in determining what words should go up on the word wall. Don't add any more than a few per week.

5. A good way to begin a word wall is to go through the textbook section for a particular unit and choose a number of key concepts and ideas that you know students will need to understand, and also some general or academic vocabulary words that you predict students will have trouble with when they encounter them in their reading.

### Strategy 33: Vocabulary Self-Selection

*Purpose*

Monitor one's own reading and use active reading strategies to identify unknown words and terms; use context clues to identify word meaning; use dictionary skills or other resources to identify and clarify word meaning; recognize which words and terms are essential to understanding.

*CCSS Connection*

Standard RL/RI.4: Interpret words and phrases as they are used in text; Standard L.4: Determine the meaning of unknown and multiple-meaning words and phrases; Standard L.5: Demonstrate understanding of figurative language, word relationships, and nuances; Standard L.6: Acquire and use a range of general academic and domain-specific words and phrases.

*Overview*

The vocabulary self-collection strategy (Haggard, 1982) actively engages students in identifying important words from their reading to share with the class. Students are introduced to the process before they begin reading.

*Procedure*

1. When presenting students with the particular reading assignment, tell them they will be expected to find new and unfamiliar words as they read.

2. Model how to do this for students by choosing a word from a particular passage, explaining why understanding the word may be a key to understanding the particular sentence or the passage around it. Then show them how you would use context, a glossary, or a dictionary to help figure out the meaning of the word. Write the word down on the board along with the sentence from the reading passage and the definition.

3. Have students read the first section of the reading assignment and choose a word they wish to select. This part can be done in small groups. Each student or group should develop a reason for selecting the word, writing it down on their own piece of paper.

4. Have them continue the reading process in small groups or individually. For each word, selected students should identify the word, why they would select it as an important word to learn, identify how the word was used by writing the sentence in which the word was used, and identify the meaning of the word.

5. Each student or small group will be asked to present two words to the class by writing them down on a large piece of chart paper in the front of the room.

6. Another option is to have students write each word down on a two-column chart, with one column indicating the word and its definition and the other column explaining why the words are important. You might have each group complete its own two-column chart and then share the words they identified with the rest of the class.

## Strategy 34: Forced Associations

*Purpose*
   Identify connections and relationships among words; identify domain-specific words as well as those that are cross-curricular; clarify understanding of words and terms through collaborative discussion.

*CCSS Connection*
   Standard L.3: Apply knowledge of language to understand how language functions in different contexts; Standard L.4: Determine the meaning of unknown and multiple-meaning words and phrases; Standard L.6: Acquire and use a range of general academic and domain-specific words and phrases; Standard SL.1: Prepare for and participate effectively in a range of conversations and collaborations.

*Overview*
   Forced associations is a creative vocabulary strategy designed by Middleton (1991). This strategy asks students to make connections between two terms or concepts. These may be random words that teachers choose to help students connect the specific content terms they have been studying, or they may be words that students choose to make cross-curricular concepts based on content they have recently been learning.

*Procedure*
1. Choose some content vocabulary words students have been studying recently.

2. Find some unrelated words either from another content area or from a dictionary.

3. Write each word on a note card and keep them in two separate piles, one for content words from your class and one for words from the diction-

ary or other content areas. You might want to use different-colored note cards for each pile.

4. Place students into groups of four and have each group member select one card from each pile. Allow them to trade cards with other students if they wish.

5. Have students think about their understanding and knowledge of each term and how the two terms might be connected together.

6. Have group members work together to write sentences that correctly use both words. These sentences should then be shared with the whole class.

Figure 4.22 shows an example of forced association across two content areas, history and science (Harmon, Wood, & Hedrick, 2006).

| HISTORY TERMS FOR A UNIT ON THE HOLOCAUST | SCIENCE TERMS FOR A UNIT ON AIR POLLUTION |
|---|---|
| racism | contaminants |
| propaganda | toxic |
| censorship | ambient air |
| disenfranchised | chronic |
| extermination | greenhouse gases |
| deportation | fossil fuels |

*Racism* is vile and can hurt people. *Toxic* substances are vile and can hurt people.

*Propaganda* and *fossil fuels* both pollute. *Propaganda* pollutes information people receive and *fossil fuels* pollute the environment.

*Censorship* and things that are *chronic* have the potential to influence outcomes over time.

*Disenfranchised* people are marginalized (or external) in relation to the group of people considered mainstream. *Ambient air* is air that surrounds (or is external to) a given object.

People who experience *deportation* are "expelled" from a certain place or country. *Greenhouse gases* are "expelled" from any kind of combustion engine, such as vehicles, and other gas-driven machines.

**Figure 4.22. Forced Association. (Harmon, Wood, & Hedrick [2006]. Reprinted with permission from the Association of Middle Level Education [formerly National Middle School Association], www.amle.org.)**

Forced associations actually makes use of another strategy called concept combining, in which students are asked to combine two or more vocabulary words or concepts into one sentence. Anytime I have students use vocabulary words in sentences, I ask them to write a certain number of sentences that use more than one of the vocabulary words. For example:

Dark, ominous looking clouds are harbingers of spring storms.

The rock concert was attended by a raucous audience that filled the auditorium with a cacophony of stomping, cheering, and screaming.

Lily had such an aversion to peas that she became astute at picking them out of her food despite her mother's painstaking efforts to hide them.

When things are too abstruse for me to understand, I become very soporific and doze off.

Next time you are teaching students multiple vocabulary words, have them extend their thinking and use their creativity to make associations between words. Then have them write some sentences that make use of concept combining.

## Strategy 35: Play Ball

*Purpose*

Review and reinforce learning of new vocabulary.

*CCSS Connection*

Standard L.4: Determine or clarify the meaning of unknown and multiple-meaning words and phrases.

*Overview*

Play Ball comes from Brunner (2011). It is a simple, fun activity for students that promotes movement and physical activity while reinforcing learning by reviewing the meanings of newly learned words. It is also a great strategy for students who are kinesthetic learners, and a good one to use at the end of a unit for review. This strategy does require some type of soft, plastic, or cloth ball.

*Procedure*

1. Following a reading assignment or at the end of a unit, prepare a list of vocabulary words and concepts that students have been learning along with their definitions.

2. Clear desks and chairs to the side and have students stand in a circle.

3. Explain to students that they will be tossing a ball to other students. Each student will receive one point for catching the ball and two points for correctly answering the question. (You may want to assign one student as a scorekeeper, so that you are free to monitor the process.)

4. Begin the game by tossing the ball to a student and asking him or her to define a vocabulary term from the unit. The other option, of course, is to provide the definition of the word and ask students to identify the term.

5. The student will gain points if he can correctly identify the word or definition. Then the student will toss the ball to another student in the group. You might need to set up some rules of the game for this strategy: the ball must be tossed gently, no student may be tossed to a second time until every student has received one toss, students must participate politely, and students are not allowed to question the final decision about how many points they will receive.

6. Continue the game for as long as desired, but do not stop until everyone has had a chance to participate. You might arrange some sort of simple prize for the two or three top scorers in the game.

## Strategy 36: Vocabulary Skits

*Purpose*
    Identify and clarify word meaning; apply knowledge of word meaning; use movement and dialogue to demonstrate understanding of word meaning; use newly learned words and terms in one's own writing and speech; work effectively with others in a collaborative group.

*CCSS Connection*
    Standard L.4: Determine or clarify the meaning of unknown and multiple-meaning words and phrases; Standard L.5: Demonstrate understanding of figurative language, word relationships, and nuances; Standard L.6: Acquire and use accurately a range of general academic and domain-specific words and phrases; Standard SL.1: Prepare for and participate in a range of conversations and collaborations.

*Overview*
    This section of the book ends with a simple strategy that my students always enjoy doing. I call it "vocabulary skits." It's a variation on the game of charades in which students create a brief, dramatic scene or skit to illustrate the meaning of a vocabulary word. Unlike charades, they can use words and dialogue, but cannot use the actual vocabulary word itself.

*Procedure*

1. Identify a number of different vocabulary terms from a reading assignment or a particular unit of study that students need to know.

2. Depending on the number of vocabulary words, have students work in pairs or in small groups. Assign one word to each group or pair. Their assignment is to prepare a scene or skit of one to two minutes to illustrate the meaning of the vocabulary word. Their skit must illustrate or enact the meaning of the word without actually using the word itself. They can use synonyms for the word or build into the scene explanatory material or action but *cannot* use the word itself or any form of it. You could choose to assign students to actually write out a script for their scene; however, because the scenes are so short, I do not require a written script.

3. Give students some time to discuss the word, plan out a scene that would effectively portray the meaning of the word, and then practice their skits a couple of times.

4. Once student skits are prepared, have each group or pair present their skit for the class. After each skit is over, have the other students guess which vocabulary word has been presented in the scene. Require that the rest of the class wait until the skit is finished before guessing at the word presented.

This strategy is effective for a number of reasons. It requires students to understand the meaning of the word well enough to adequately illustrate the meaning with a skit, it allows students to use their energy and creativity, and it builds conceptual understanding in a visual and kinesthetic way, requiring students to not only construct dialogue but also include movement and action to convey the meaning of the word. Students are more likely to remember all of the vocabulary words because they will remember the student-created scenes.

## PART FIVE
# USING TECHNOLOGY TO SUPPORT LITERACY LEARNING

Most of my students today were born in the last years of the twentieth century. They have grown up surrounded by various forms of technology and multimedia. As teachers, we need to recognize the importance of learning to use new forms of technology and consider the potential impact of incorporating various forms of technology into our teaching. Brooks-Young (2010) points out that many students today are disenchanted with current educational programs: "They view educators who use traditional teaching methods as being out of touch. They rankle at completing the same projects and assignments their parents and even grandparents did when they attended school. They believe that the technology tools that are banned on campus are, in fact, the keys to success in their future" (p. 1). In the information age that we live in, the world around us is rapidly changing, and various forms of new technology are appearing every few months. These new forms provide enormous benefits for students when integrated into our teaching in meaningful ways.

Biancarosa and Snow (2006) argue in favor of including technology in literacy programs, noting that technology is both "a facilitator of literacy and a medium of literacy" (p. 19). To adequately incorporate technology tools into our teaching of literacy in all disciplines, many of us need additional training. In a newly published book *Reading and Writing Digital Texts: An Activity-Based Approach*, Beach, Anson, Breuch, and Reynolds (2014, in press) argue that both students and teachers need to become better educated in the potential uses of digital reading and writing tools. The ability to engage with and use various forms of technology, as well as to read, interpret, and comprehend online and multimedia text, is an important element of literacy in the twenty-first century. Yet many of us, for multiple reasons, are resistant to incorporating technology into our teaching. Sometimes we may feel the benefits to students simply are not worth the extra time and effort to learn and integrate the technology. Beach, Anson, Breuch, and Reynolds (2014, in press) note that teachers are often overwhelmed by the need to learn more about how to use digital reading

275

and writing tools, and often feel they are not provided with ample professional de-velopment resources or time to learn about new tools.

Let me begin this section with a disclaimer: I am not by any stretch of the imagina-tion an expert in technology. However, I have come to recognize the increasing impor-tance that technology holds in the lives of my students and I have tried to experiment with new forms of technology in the classroom. Our students today are often referred to as "digital natives" because they have been surrounded by technology since birth. Diamond Hicks (2011) argues that teachers must embrace technology to meet the needs of these learners: "The saturation of technology in students' lives has produced an entirely different type of student, shaping the way they think, learn and experience the world around them" (p. 188). She goes on to argue that because technology is so prevalent in students' everyday lives, their learning styles have become more visual and they are less likely to respond well to traditional methods such as textbook reading. The use of technology can also increase students' enthusiasm and motivation to learn.

Students today use technology to engage in multiple forms of reading and writ-ing, including text messaging, postings on blogs and other interactive sites, status updates on various forms of social media, online reviews of videos, music, books and other products, e-mail messages, online collaboration and co-construction of text with tools such as Google Docs, and various forms of citizen journalism. There are a number of ways that teachers in all content areas can use various forms of technology to support good teaching and literacy learning, and they can be accomplished without high-tech classrooms full of computers, iPads, and Smart boards. This section of the book will offer a few suggestions and strategies.

The Common Core State Standards address technology and multimedia in sev-eral of the anchor standards and at certain grade levels. Anchor standard 7 indicates that students should be able to "integrate and evaluate content presented in diverse formats and media, including visually and quantitatively, as well as in words." In the Reading Standards for Informational Text, grade-specific standards for anchor standard 7 include the following:

- Grade 7: Compare and contrast a text to an audio, video, or multimedia version of the text, analyzing each medium's portrayal of the subject.

- Grades 9–10: Analyze various accounts of a subject told in different me-diums determining which details are emphasized in each account.

- Grades 11–12: Integrate and evaluate multiple sources of information presented in different media or formats as well as in words in order to address a question or solve a problem.

The grade-specific standards for writing (6–12) also make clear that in their writ-ing of informative/explanatory text, students should be able to include graphics and multimedia. Most importantly, writing standard 6 specifies that students must be able to use technology and the Internet to produce and publish writing, and to interact and collaborate with others. The grade-specific standard for grades 9 and 10 state, "Use technology, including the internet, to produce, publish, and update individual or shared writing projects, taking advantage of technology's capacity to link to other information and to display information flexibly and dynamically." Speaking and listening standards also specify students should "make strategic use of digital media in presentations."

It is obvious that the authors of the CCSS recognize the important role of technology in education, and the importance of teaching students to learn from technology and to read and write with technology, as a vital college and career readiness skill. As teachers, we are going to be required in the coming years to make more use of technology and multimedia in our teaching. There are some suggestions and strategies in this section of the book that will provide you with some help.

## General Suggestions

Let's start with some general suggestions and some dos and don'ts. First of all, do whatever you can to get your classroom set up to accommodate as much technology as possible. Find space in the back of the room where you can bring in a couple of older computers. Talk with your school's technology specialist to see if there might be a couple of computers available or in storage that you could bring into your classroom. Arrange for providing network connection for them also. (More and more school buildings now have Wi-Fi coverage.) These extra computers will provide options for students who may write better if they can use a computer, who need to prepare presentations or use presentation software, or who must conduct research. It will also provide a valuable resource for your students who may not have access to a computer and Internet access at home. Request a document camera to replace your old-fashioned overhead projector. Also, get your own classroom computer hooked up to a projector (or arrange for a laptop to connect to it). Using a splitter will allow you to leave your computer hooked up to the projector and still use it as your personal computer. This will allow you to integrate more multimedia and Internet resources into your day-to-day teaching.

Second, and perhaps one of the most important pieces of advice I can offer, is to use technology as nothing more than a strategy or vehicle to support good teaching. It should be a means to an end. There's no need to try to change the way we do everything in our classrooms. We should rather find ways to use technology to support what we already do. In other words, various tools and forms of technology should not just be added into your curriculum and lessons to provide "bells and whistles" or because students may like using them. Instead, they should have a viable purpose in that they support your objectives and help students meet learning targets. It is easy enough to find a film, video, website, or something related to the unit or topic we are teaching, but always ask yourself: How is this increasing students' learning or mastery of the content?

The third general suggestion is that we should never assume a certain level of knowledge about technology with our students. Our students may supposedly be "digital natives," but you will no doubt find that although many of the students in your classroom have expert-level knowledge and understanding of computers, various hardware and software tools, social media, online gaming, and all manner of things technology related, we can't necessarily assume that all of our students have expert or even basic-level knowledge. I have been surprised to find that some students do not know even the most basic principles of word processing. For example, I have seen students who do not know how to change the line spacing or font style in a basic Microsoft Word document. I have also noticed that students are often not very skilled at navigating the Internet or doing Internet searches. They also tend to lack understanding of the various features of online text (such as hyperlink) and have trouble identifying the purpose of or evaluating material on websites. (This topic is addressed more in the sections on reading online text and multimedia.) We also cannot assume that students know how to put together a PowerPoint presentation or use other presentation software. You may need to spend some time teaching students how to use these resources.

Next, it's important to recognize that many of your students do have expert-level knowledge about many aspects of technology. They can be very helpful in assisting you and other students in learning to use new tools and technology-related resources. I often observe students helping others navigate websites or software programs, sharing tips, and offering advice. I can also think of several times when I have called upon students I knew were taking advanced levels of computer science courses to help me with something I was trying to do. When I first set up my own teacher website a few years ago, it was a student who designed it for me and helped me learn to navigate it. It's important for us to be open to asking knowledgeable students for help.

Another piece of advice is this: Focus on the software rather than the hardware. There are many ways you can have students learn about and use various forms of software, often free and available to you through your school and district resources that do not depend upon specialized computer equipment. You can incorporate technology into your teaching without having a computer for every student, a Smart board, a classroom set of iPads, or expensive and complicated equipment.

Additionally, your success in incorporating technology into your teaching depends upon your willingness to explore and experiment with various bits and pieces of technology. We are all busy every day with teaching, planning, grading, and the innumerable other tasks that we have to attend to. Sometimes trying to do something new or different seems like just one more thing added to your to-do list. But try to establish a mind-set that allows for learning to incorporate some new technology-related strategies into your classroom. Try to spend a few minutes each week, or perhaps a couple of hours during the evening once a week, in which you focus on learning about a new resource or piece of software that might be useful for you when you teach a particular unit or lesson. Also, enlist the help of others. If you participate in a professional learning community (PLC), get help and suggestions from your PLC colleagues, especially those who may know more about technology than you do.

Finally, some general cautions about use of technology resources, especially with the Internet and social media: Technology, as we all know, has been and can be used by students for inappropriate purposes. Cell phones, MP3 players, websites, social media sites, and virtual spaces have been used for cheating, sexual harassment, and cyber-bullying. Inappropriate photos are taken and posted online; threatening messages are sent, and the privacy of others can be violated. We may worry about everything from safety and privacy issues to inappropriate content or use and placement of advertisements. Educators obviously need to take on a parent-like role in terms of educating students about appropriate uses of technology and appropriate behavior in general. None of us wants to unintentionally promote any of these negative behaviors, and cyber-bullying has become a very serious and difficult problem in schools, so it is important for us to have appropriate measures in place before employing use of technology for academic purposes. We have a responsibility to help students learn to use technology appropriately and ethically, in part because it is an important workplace skill (Brooks-Young, 2010).

We need to have in place very strict requirements that students clearly understand, including the following: students are expected to use technology appropriately and professionally in an academic setting, and they are to be consistently respectful in their comments and interactions in online spaces and forums. Most school networks have security systems and filters in place that block inappropriate websites from being viewed or downloaded, but it is also important for teachers to monitor classroom social networking sites. If using social networking for academic purposes, use one of the platforms designed for schools and students such as Edmodo (this one and others are discussed later in this section). We also need to provide students with lots of cautions about the fact that social networks are public spaces and they need to exercise caution and restraint in terms of what they post online, whether it's on Facebook or on a classroom social network. The other thing we must do is check our school and district policies to make sure that our use of technology or online platforms is not violating acceptable use policies that are in place. Check with your school administrators and make sure that they clearly understand the learning objectives and support the project you are planning to do with students and that they approve of the safeguards you have in place.

This final section of the book will provide you with some suggestions for using various tools to help students conduct research effectively. It also contains some information and suggestions for reading and comprehending online text and multimedia, offers some useful online resources, and recommends some good strategies that help to build literacy and promote content-area learning while also making use of technology.

## School and Local Library Resources

In addition to resources most schools have available, such as computer labs and audiovisual equipment, to help promote information literacy and help students master research skills, you will want to make use of your school library or media center. Librarians, or media specialists, are highly trained and knowledgeable professionals who can help both teachers and students access books, online materials, and various other resources to support your teaching. They not only help students learn to value and love reading, but they can also help students learn how to conduct research on various topics. I am certain that school libraries and media centers are often undervalued and underused. They offer a wealth of resources that, as twenty-first-century teachers, we should be taking advantage of. Schedule a period to take your class to the school library and have your librarian or media specialist give a presentation to help orient students to the school library's research resources.

Obviously, libraries contain books, and most students have learned how to use an online catalog to search for books by author, title, or subject. If not, however, the librarian can easily teach them. Whatever subject area you teach, consider taking your class to the school library and requiring them to check out a book with some relationship or connection to your content area or a particular topic of study. Require them to read the book, using the first ten minutes of each class period, or as homework, and then have them write some variation of a book report or critique, an online review, or present an oral report on the book. Many school libraries are now also offering e-books, or books in electronic format, which can be downloaded to laptops or cell phones.

Another important research skill, and one that students definitely need to learn to be prepared for college, is citation styles. Whether your subject area requires students to cite sources using MLA, APA, or Chicago style, students need to have some experience in writing with sources and learning how to correctly cite their sources. I often point out to teachers that we could eliminate most of the plagiarism issues we deal with by teaching students how to correctly use and cite sources. Many library webpages now have MLA guides and citation makers. Teach students how to use an easy online citation maker. Bibme.com and easybib.com are both easy-to-use bibliography and citation generators. There are numerous others as well. Our high school library's website also has a variety of college and career resources that students should be aware of. For example, ACT, SAT, and AP test practice is available through Learning Express.

Most school districts now subscribe to one or more online databases that offer a vast number of journal articles and other resources for research. Learning to use the library databases is another indispensible skill students will need to know to be prepared for college. My school district subscribes to several databases, one of which is EBSCO. EBSCO is actually a large collection of databases that collectively contain thousands of magazine articles, books, journal articles, documents, and encyclopedia resources. Most schools have a student version of EBSCO as well as the full EBSCO version. I have my older high school students use the full version because I want them to be exposed to the kinds of complex and scholarly materials they will be expected to read in college. EBSCO allows users to choose which databases in the collection you want to search, or you can select all of them at once. Expensive subscription databases such as EBSCO mean that some districts probably subscribe to fewer databases than others. EBSCO has databases related to a variety of content areas and topics:

| | |
|---|---|
| Business | Health |
| Computer Science | Law |
| Education | Newspapers |
| Encyclopedias | Psychology and Behavioral Sciences |
| Environment | Science and Technology |
| General Academic Databases | |

These databases will bring up both abstracts and full-text articles and documents. When I am doing research using the databases, I usually have them bring up only full text articles. There are also advanced search options available so one can look only for certain types of articles, or further narrow the search through cross-referencing or by date published. Some articles may be only available in HTML but the more recent ones in PDF. Articles can also be saved to student files or flash drives, or e-mailed and, of course, printed.

Your district may subscribe to the Gale databases in place of or in addition to EBSCO. The Gale databases are very similar to EBSCO, but one particular Gale resource I find particularly valuable is "Opposing Viewpoints." This database within the Gale collection offers information and opinion pieces on hundreds of social issues, many of them full text articles, news, and editorials. I have students use Opposing Viewpoints when writing argument essays or research papers, often just to get ideas for topics. Just by skimming through the variety of topics, which are classified into several main categories, students can usually come up with an interesting research topic or an idea for a paper. The main subject areas included in Opposing Viewpoints are:

| | |
|---|---|
| Business and Economics | National Debate Topics (somewhat like |
| Energy and Environment | current issues) |
| Health and Medicine | Science, Technology, and Ethics |
| Law and Politics | Society and Culture |
| | War and Diplomacy |

Each one of these is broken into subcategories that bring up links to various articles related to the topic.

Other databases available through Gale are these:

Academic One File (a common database for scholarly research in a variety of areas)
Agriculture Collection
Business
Communication and Mass Media
Computer Science
Criminal Justice
Culinary Arts
Education
Environment
Fine Arts and Music
Gardening, Landscape, and Horticulture
General One File (news articles)
Health
Home Improvement
Hospitality, Tourism, and Leisure
Law
Newspaper Index
Nursing
US History in Context

Gale also has junior and student editions for younger students. Like EBSCO, Gale databases include advanced search options, and articles can be saved, e-mailed, or printed.

Check out the other resources that your particular school district may have available. My school district offers a couple of other online resources that can be very useful for any content area. One is *World Book Encyclopedia Online*. This is a student version of *World Book* that allows students to search by topic or subject. There is also a Spanish version. Many of the articles also have links to videos on the topic, which may make them more appealing to some students. It also includes atlases, dictionaries, timelines, and other features. Another valuable resource that I use quite often is Discovery Education Streaming. This is a collection of streaming videos on a variety of educational topics. You can easily search for video clips by topic and also search by grade-level categories, grades 6–8 or 9–12. The general subject areas are English, math, science, social studies, and health. Discovery includes both short videos, five to ten minutes long, and longer videos.

Many district and school library websites now offer all or most of these online resources even when students or staff are not at school. They can be accessed at home or anywhere else with a password, which your media specialist can provide. In some districts, students may also be required to enter their student identification number or code. The first step in incorporating these great resources into your teaching is to familiarize yourself with them, and then enlist the librarian and his or her staff to help your students learn to access and use them. These resources may be one of the best ways to not only incorporate more reading and writing into your teaching but also teach students essential research and information literacy skills.

Don't overlook your local library or libraries as sources of other valuable resources as well. Most local libraries also offer various electronic resources, collections of digital materials, and books and materials on topics that your school library may not have. If your district library media department does not subscribe to many databases, you may be able to access Gale, EBSCO, or others at the local library, and it usually requires no more than a library card. For younger students, the local libraries often offer tutorials on technology, conducting research, and even homework and tutoring programs. Our local library also offers book groups, writing workshops, and talks and lectures on a variety of topics. Some also offer summer programs for students. A recent ASCD *Education Update* article makes some additional recommendations for accessing public library resources: check YouTube to see if the library has a video channel, follow local libraries on Facebook, Twitter, and Pinterest, and look into the library's special displays and events related to historical celebrations such as Black History Month or Women's History Month ("Extend Learning," 2013).

## Useful Online Resources

The World Wide Web offers a vast and unlimited source of material for both entertainment and information. We should definitely take advantage of many of the great online resources available for both teachers and students to help increase student learning in your classroom. Here are some sites that I recommend for you and your students:

- Official State Websites: Your state's official website may offer many opportunities for student learning and research that you may not be aware of. There are usually materials available that would be useful in a number of different content areas. If you live close enough to your state capital, you can probably also take your students to your state library or on tours. Some of our school's government students here in Oregon's capital recently had the opportunity to learn about the legislative process by presenting a bill in the state senate. State governments offer resources and opportunities to learn about local history, government, business, science, environmental issues, education, careers, and other topics. Since I live and teach in Oregon, I recently researched what is available at www.oregon.gov, the official website of our state. I was amazed by the volume of materials and topics available. Students can access historical materials such as a hyperlinked historical chronology of the state with primary documents. Business and social studies teachers may want to take advantage of various employment and workforce opportunities; labor market information; articles on economics, business, and industry; and demographic and statistical information. Psychology students will find a range of materials on topics such as substance abuse, children's and teen's health, and mental health. The website also includes materials related to natural resources, public safety, transportation, education (including various teacher resources), and legislative materials. Check out what's available on your state's website.

- Library of Congress: The Library of Congress (www.loc.gov) is the national library of the United States and the largest library in the world. It contains millions of books, as well as photographs, maps, and various manuscripts in its various collections. Many of them are available electronically. The Library of Congress is simply a great source of historical materials and primary texts, audio archives, and photographs. One can also find recordings and webcasts by well-known authors and experts. The Library offers training sessions for teachers, and you can sign up for the Teaching with the Library of Congress blog. Also, sign up for training sessions available in your area. In the Northwest, the Northwest Council of Computer Education sponsors Library of Congress training sessions for teachers (www.ncce.org/training/loc-workshops.html).

- Project Gutenberg: Project Gutenberg (www.gutenberg.org) contains the largest single collection of free electronic books. Michael Hart, founder of Project Gutenberg, began the project in 1971 and the site continues to promote and make available 42,000 free e-books for downloading and reading online. The site does request a small donation from users. You can search the online book catalog, view the top one hundred books and also find audiobooks, CDs, and DVDs. Free Kindle books are also available.

- Annenberg Foundation Learner Program: This is an excellent online source for teachers and students (www.learner.org). The Annenberg Project's mission is to advance excellence in teaching in American schools. As stated in the website, "Annenberg Learner uses media and telecommunications to advance excellent teaching in American schools. This mandate is carried out chiefly by the funding and broad distribution of educational video programs with coordinated Web and print materials for the professional development of K–12 teachers. It is part of The Annenberg Foundation and advances the Foundation's goal of encouraging the development of more effective ways to share ideas and knowledge." The site includes video series, professional development for teachers, numerous lesson plans, and interactives for both teachers and students. Disciplines include the arts, foreign language, literature and language arts, math, science, social studies, and history. The interactives are a particularly fine feature of this site. You can select interactives by grade level, including grades 6–8, grades 9–12, and college level.

- Top Documentary Films: This website (www.topdocumentaryfilms. com) is where you can access hundreds of documentary films on a variety of topics. Teachers of history, psychology/sociology, language arts, fine arts, science, health, and technology can all find useful materials to use with your students. The main webpage features some recommended documentaries. Some are also available for purchase at very reasonable prices. Some of the categories include biography, comedy, crime, drugs, economics, environment, health, history, media, nature, performing arts, philosophy, politics, psychology, religion, science, sports, and technology.

- PBS: Public Broadcasting System's website (www.pbs.org) includes a wealth of resources for teachers. Videos and feature stories are included on the home page. Students can explore materials in arts and entertainment, news, and public affairs. The teachers' link (www.pbslearning media.org) features thousands of classroom-ready digital resources including videos, games, audio clips, documents, and lesson plans. Resources are arranged by grade level and subject and are aligned to CCSS. Lesson plans are included in the areas of science, math, English language arts, literacy, the arts, health and physical education, social studies, and world languages. There are thousands of lesson plans on a variety of topics in each subject area plus staff development resources. To access some of the material, you will have to create a PBS account.

- National Geographic: National Geographic's website (www.national geographic.com) is also an excellent source of videos and photos. Access materials related to the environment, travel, adventures, and also regular feature stories. This is a great source for science teachers and those who teach geography or global studies. There is a "For Educators" link that will provide you with classroom resources, and you can sign up for professional development courses in areas including reading, science, social studies, ELD/ELL, literacy, Spanish, and other areas. Courses are delivered live, onsite, or by webinar.

- National Gallery of Art (NGA): The National Gallery of Art (www.nga .gov) is a great resource for art teachers, but for teachers of other content areas as well. You can search the National Gallery's collection online, and educational resources are provided for teachers, families, young kids, and teens. The site features an interactive art zone where students can create their own artwork while learning about techniques, styles, and historical periods. Lesson activities, teaching packets, and videos are available for teachers. There is also information about various NGA site programs and school tours available. The lesson plans are organized by grade level and aligned to National Art Education Association Visual Arts Curriculum

Standards. Some integrated curriculum materials are also available on the site, which combine art with other areas such as ecology, literature, mythology, and mathematics.

- American Association for the Advancement of Science (AAAS): This AAAS website (http://sciencenetlinks.com) is an outstanding resource for science teachers with science lessons and tools for all grade levels. Featured recent lessons are posted on the main page. For example, when I recently visited the website there was a feature lesson on ocean sunlight in which students could learn about photosynthesis in the context of marine life. A search tool at the top of the main page allows you to search for lessons by grade. You can also refine your search by themes or strands such as chemistry, earth science, engineering math and statistics, and also by content. Content features include lessons, tools, collections, after-school resources, or science updates.

- MERLOT: MERLOT stands for Multimedia Educational Resources for Learning and Online Teaching. This website (www.merlot.org) is designed for educators and allows you to build course content with peer-reviewed online learning materials. You can also network with colleagues within or across disciplines. You can find online learning materials in different disciplines, access other teachers' personal collections, find exercises to use with students, and network with colleagues. Collections are available in the areas of art, business, education, humanities, math and statistics, science and technology, and social sciences. There are various "disciplinary communities" in even more areas including teacher education, world languages, library media, and more. Webinars and phone apps are also available through MERLOT.

- TeacherTube: TeacherTube is a teachers' version of YouTube (www.teachertube.com). The online information provides the mission of TeacherTube: "Our goal is to provide an online community for sharing instructional videos. We seek to fill a need for a more educationally focused, safe venue for teachers, schools, and home learners. It is a site to provide anytime, anywhere professional development with teachers teaching teachers. As well, it is a site where teachers can post videos designed for students to view in order to learn a concept or skill." On teachertube.com you can access videos, collections, photos, audios, and documents. Documents include various classroom and learning materials such as assessment items, student materials, course syllabi, vocabulary cards and so on. Also, upload your own videos and lessons.

- ReadWriteThink.org: ReadWriteThink.org is a useful site cosponsored by the International Reading Association and National Council of Teachers of English. Most of the materials are for English language arts teachers but they do have some materials useful for history and social studies teachers and lots of interdisciplinary lessons available. The site includes not only classroom resources and lesson plans but also professional development opportunities such as a professional library and online professional development options. You can search for lesson plans by grade level, lesson plan type (standard lesson, mini-lesson, or unit), learning objective, and theme.

- Free Technology for Teachers Blog: The website features an online blog (www.freetechforteachers.com) by educator Richard Byrne. In addition to the blog, you can access iPad and Android apps, find tutorials for using Google tools, and access a compilation of resources for videos under the "Alternatives to YouTube" link. Also find information on creating blogs, websites, and videos.

- New York Public Library (NYPL): NYPL is an excellent library website with lots of resources for teachers as well as kids and teens (www.nypl.org/events/teaching-learning). Participate in blogs, and find teaching materials, videos, podcasts, lesson ideas, and much more.

- For Math Teachers: KUTA Software (www.kutasoftware.com) is an excellent resource for math teachers. Math teachers at my school are making good use of the resources available. There are lots of free worksheets and materials even if you don't purchase the software itself. You can create math questions, differentiate instruction, print multiple versions of tests, and create multiple choice and free response questions for testing in various levels of algebra and geometry. In addition to the free worksheets and materials, a free fourteen-day trial is available. If you find this software useful, ask your school administrators to purchase it. School packages allow unlimited use for one school campus for three years, priced according to the number of programs purchased.

- Math Forum: Another site for math teachers, http://mathforum.org, allows students of all levels to work on math skills (and the reading skills involved in math content) through sample problems and activities.

- For History Teachers: This is an interactive website (www.ushistory.com) that uses music to enhance learning about history. It tells stories of the great events and figures in US history.

- For English Teachers: On the website www.bibliomania.com, you can access classic literature including poetry, fiction, nonfiction, and full text versions of Shakespeare's plays. Students with disabilities who may need to use adaptive technology or text-to-speech programs might benefit from this site. You can also access study guides and other material related to the literary pieces included.

## Reading Online Text

Much of the reading that students do today is in various online formats including social networking sites. Students also frequently access various websites for information or research; many of them, however, are not very skillful at recognizing and using various online text features, nor have they been taught very much about how to evaluate the quality of material on the web. As twenty-first-century teachers, we need to help students build skills in reading, interpreting, and evaluating material from websites and in various multimedia formats because it is an important part of information literacy in the modern world. This section will provide you with some suggestions and strategies. Julie Coiro (2005) observes that students vary greatly in their ability to locate, understand, and use online information, and that the challenges faced by less capable readers are compounded when online material is being read because they tend to interact more passively with text and may be unsure where to focus their attention. She goes on to point out that online text requires knowledge about how information is organized within websites, and its format requires "higher levels of inferential reasoning and comprehension monitoring strategies that help readers stay on task" (p. 31).

First, it's important to teach students some of the language surrounding online text. They need to understand terms like "link," "search engine," "URL" and "hypertext." (Most students have no clue that URL, which stands for "Universal Resource Locator," is the technical term for the Web address.) Before having students do research or read online text, spend some time teaching them these terms. Students also need to understand the differences between various domain names such ".com," ".edu," ".org," and ".gov." They should be aware that ".com" sites are primarily commercial, and that ".org" and ".gov" sites may be more reliable sources of information. Coiro (2005) also recommends having students preview the website's home page to gain a sense of the structure and organization, scanning menu choices (usually at the top of the page), exploring the interactive features of the site, and making predictions about where various links may lead. Many websites are also designed to accommodate the needs of various types of readers, so they may provide information and links for the general public, for people looking for answers to specific questions, and for people with a greater level of expertise.

In addition to some lessons on how to navigate within a website and understand the various levels of interactivity available, we also need to help students learn to assess the validity and accuracy of online information. Coiro (2005) recommends a

"Think and Check" activity to help students check the validity of the information. It involves asking the following questions:

- Does this information make sense?

- Where else can I look?

- Who created the website and why? (Look for an "About Us" link.)

- Who is the author? (Search online for the author's name.)

- Who is linking to the site? (This can be discovered by typing "Link:" followed by the URL of the website into the search box.)

Roger Sevilla (2012) from Project Look Sharp at Ithaca College created a useful tool for evaluating websites called "Criteria for Examining the Credibility of Information on the Internet" (see www.ithaca.edu/looksharp/criteria.pdf for the complete document). I often assign students to use this document or one very similar to write an evaluation of one or more websites they are considering using for research. The document provides questions to ask and clues to look for in assessing websites in terms of five areas: authority, accuracy, objectivity, currency, and coverage:

- Authority: Is there an author? Is the author qualified and/or reputable? Who is the sponsor? Is there any other way to determine the origin? Are there links to other sites?

- Accuracy: Is the information reliable? Is there an editor or someone who verifies or checks the information? Can the information be cross-checked with another source?

- Objectivity: Does the information show a minimum of bias? Is the page designed to sway opinion? Is there any advertising on the page?

- Currency: Is the page dated? When was it last updated? How current are the links? Have some expired?

- Coverage: Is there an indication that the page has been completed and is not still under construction? Is there a print equivalent? What topics are covered? How in-depth is the material? (Sevilla, 2012)

## Digital Text and Multimedia

Students today are engaging in writing and reading in various forms of digital media. They can now collaborate online to create documents and projects, create films and movies, incorporate video and music into other documents, participate in blogs and online forums, and create webpages with multimodal features. When these various forms of communication are being used to help students to engage in reading and writing and to learn and master content material, they become very powerful learning experiences. Online reading can build on traditional forms of reading, but it also requires learning new comprehension skills such as how to navigate online text, how to synthesize information, and how to engage in critical thinking and evaluation.

It is clear that part of the literacy skills today's students need involve learning how to read, understand, and evaluate information in a variety of different media and formats. Students are also engaging in lots of new forms of writing. New technologies in the classroom have led to new forms of writing. The technological tools that writers use have changed dramatically in recent years with new media and digital technologies. Kathleen Blake Yancey (2004) refers to this as "textured literacy—the ability to comfortably use and combine print, spoken, visual, and digital processes in composing a piece of writing" (p. 38). As teachers, we must help students not only to learn to be active readers and viewers of various forms of media but also to create presentations and multimedia text using new forms of technology.

It is important that our students recognize and identify characteristics of the various forms of media they will encounter in print and online formats. One of my colleagues, instructional coach Laurelin Andrade, recently designed a series of scaffolds for helping students read and comprehend various forms of multimedia including video news reports, images, narrative films, documentaries, novels, and speeches. She has graciously allowed their publication in this book. Each of Laurelin's scaffolds is in two parts, including a graphic organizer that students can use to gather information while viewing followed by a scaffold providing a format for students to follow to summarize the text. (These types of writing scaffolds are very useful especially for students who struggle with writing.) Similar scaffolds could be designed for other forms of media as well, such as websites, charts, graphs, diagrams, and so forth. These scaffolds can be used to help students build the skills they need to "comprehend" various media, both print and nonprint, and, of course, they can be adapted to fit the particular content or elements you want students to identify. The scaffolds may be especially useful for struggling students and special-needs students who may have difficulty identifying what elements they need to be looking for when observing, viewing, or reading. The following sections present the comprehension scaffolds for summarizing a video news report (figure 5.1), summarizing an image (figure 5.2), summarizing a narrative film (figure 5.3), summarizing a documentary (figure 5.4), and summarizing a speech (figure 5.5). Each one is preceded by an introduction and some possible applications.

## Video News Report

Have students watch a news report on a current issue or a story that relates to course content or the particular unit or topic of study. News clips can be recorded from network news stations and are also available online at national news network

Title _____

| Setting |
| Where? |
| When? |

Main Characters: Name (characteristics)

- 
- 
- 

Central Problem

| Detail 1 | Detail 2 | Detail 3 | Detail 4 |

Resolution to the Problem

My Reactions

**Figure 5.1.   Summarize a Video News Report. (Reprinted with permission from Laurelin Andrade, instructional coach, Salem-Keizer School District.)**

PART FIVE

The news story _____ takes place _____
                          (title)

_____ .
              (setting)

The report tells about_____
                          (characters)

_____

who _____ .

At first, _____
                          (central problem)

Then _____
              (details 2-4)

_____

_____

_____

_____ .

In the end, _____
                          (resolution)

_____ .

On the whole, this news story was _____ because _____
                          (adjective)

_____ .
          (your reaction)

**Figure 5.1—Continued**

websites such CNN.com and MSN.com, and most local television stations also
post recent news reports on their websites. Since most video news reports are fairly
short and present the information rapidly and concisely, you may need to show the
clip multiple times for students to complete all the parts of the scaffold with the
necessary information.

## Summarize an Image

This scaffold is a great way to support visual literacy. Use the scaffold to have students view, interpret, and summarize any visual image, which could include a piece of
art, painting, photograph, or other image created by someone. In language arts classes,
various pieces of art can be used to prompt descriptive writing or explore the themes
in a work of literature. Social studies teachers can use historical images, photographs,
or artwork to teach about historical periods or geographical regions. Math teachers can
have students examine images that relate to mathematical concepts or present a visual

Title _____

---

Subjects:  Name/Descriptor (characteristics)
- 
- 
- 
- 

---

Setting

Where?

When?

What else was going on then?

---

What was the artist trying to accomplish or say?  What was his/her purpose?

---

| Detail 1 | Detail 2 | Detail 3 | Detail 4 |
|---|---|---|---|
|  |  |  |  |

---

Why is this image significant? What impact did it have?

---

My Reactions

---

**Figure 5.2.   Summarize an Image. (Reprinted with permission from Laurelin Andrade, instructional coach, Salem-Keizer School District.)**

PART FIVE

The painting/photograph/drawing _____
                                                        (title)
depicts _____.
                        (subjects)
It was taken/ created _____
                                    (setting)
_____

During this time _____

_____.

In the image, the artist tries to _____
                                            (artist's purpose)
_____

This is evident in _____
                        (describe two details that support the purpose)

_____

_____

_____

_____.

This piece is significant because _____

_____

On the whole, this image is _____ because _____
                                (adjective)                              (your reaction)
_____.

**Figure 5.2—Continued**

math problem. Science teachers can also use images and photographs that demonstrate, reveal, or display topics of study or scientific principles. Of course, art teachers
can teach students to use this scaffold as a means of summarizing and evaluating elements in paintings, drawings, and other works of art. You can also use this scaffold to
have students examine the pictures and photographs that appear in their textbooks.

## Summarize a Narrative Film

In my English classes, students are quite frequently assigned to read novels and
stories. The CCSS anchor standard 7 for Reading Literature states that students
should be able to "analyze the representation of a subject or a key scene in two different artistic mediums, including what is emphasized or absent in each treatment"
(grades 9–10). Obviously, the CCSS recognize media literacy as an important skill.
Following whole-class reading, I typically show a film or movie version of the novel

Title _____

| Setting |
| --- |
| Where? |
| What else was going on then? |

| Main characters: Name (characteristics) |
| --- |
| • |
| • |
| • |

| Central Problem |
| --- |
| |

| Event 1 | Event 2 | Event 3 | Event 4 |
| --- | --- | --- | --- |
| | | | |

| Resolution to the Problem |
| --- |
| |

| My Reactions |
| --- |
| |

**Figure 5.3. Summarize a Narrative Film. (Reprinted with permission from Laurelin Andrade, instructional coach, Salem-Keizer School District.)**

PART FIVE

The film _____ takes place _____
          (title)                                                     (setting)

_____.

During this time _____
                      (details about time period)

_____.

The film tells the story of _____, a _____ who
                    (main character's name)

_____.
                    (central problem)

At first, _____
               (event 1)

Then, _____
               (events 2-4)

_____

_____

_____

In the end, _____
               (resolution)

_____.

On the whole, this film was _____ because _____
                    (adjective)                     (your reaction)

_____.

**Figure 5.3—*Continued***

and ask students to identify similarities and differences between the two versions. For example, following reading of the 1920s novel *The Great Gatsby*, I now have three movie versions to choose from. I have used film versions of numerous other pieces of literature over the years: *To Kill a Mockingbird*, *Great Expectations*, *A Lesson before Dying*, *Lord of the Flies*, and *Romeo and Juliet*, among others. Many shorter works of fiction are also made into film versions. Even if students read novels or stories independently, they can still be assigned to locate and watch the film version and do some comparison. I often hear students discussing some of the movies and films they are watching in their other classes as well. Social studies and history teachers often use movies that portray historical periods or events. A great example and option for teachers of US history would be the new Spielberg movie *Lincoln*. Students in other courses are often assigned to watch films and movies that may involve moral problems or dilemmas, reflect cultural differences or psychological principles, or focus on social problems and issues, economics, current events, and so on. The narrative film scaffold can be used to help students "read," analyze, and evaluate a film or movie.

## Summarize a Documentary

Much like narrative films, documentary films are often used in various ways to supplement content material. Students in my writing classes are often assigned to watch a documentary on a particular topic. My college writing students recently watched a documentary news report about the working poor in America. Viewing of the documentary film *Food, Inc.* in the context of one of their other classes generated much discussion among my students. In short, documentary films are a great resource for content-area teachers, because they can be used to give students a better understanding of topics and also make obvious for students the real-world connections and implications of the content they are studying. Great documentaries are available that are appropriate for one or more disciplines: psychology, mental health, poverty, industry, science, the environment, politics, sociology, health and medicine, business, economics, world events, and so forth. As recommended earlier, make use of www.topdocumentaryfilms.com as a valuable source for high quality documentaries.

## Summarize a Speech

The final scaffold included here is one for helping students listen to, comprehend, analyze, and summarize a speech. Outside of their obvious use in a public speaking course, speeches can also be used in many different content areas to reinforce and extend learning. Ideally, you would want students to see and hear the speech being delivered, in audiovisual form (or even in person if attending a live event). However, this scaffold can be used with the written transcript of speeches as well. Students could be assigned to read a written transcript of the speech and then use the scaffold to summarize and analyze it. One can find speeches by famous scientists, authors, scholars, public figures, athletes, celebrities, world leaders, civil rights leaders, and even ordinary people that you might consider bringing into the classroom. These may be audio version only or both audio and visual. I have always enjoyed listening to famous historical speeches, and I still get chills when I hear the voice of Dr. Martin Luther King Jr. delivering his "I Have a Dream" speech or FDR delivering the famous Pearl Harbor "Day of Infamy" speech. Speeches by presidents and other world leaders are great sources for history classes, but also can also be used to teach students speaking skills, literary elements, argument-persuasion techniques, and elements of rhetoric. The subject matter of various speeches can also be used to reinforce content material.

There are several good online sources for speeches. I recommend www.americanrhetoric.com for MP3 audio recordings of famous speeches. The site features the top one hundred famous American speeches, most of them in audio format. YouTube is also a great source of video recordings of speeches. A good source of speeches for history is www.history.com/speeches. A useful source for written transcripts of speeches is www.greatamericandocuments.com/speeches.

Title _____

Filmmaker: name, qualifications, past films, etc.

Subject

Setting

Where?

When?

What else was going on then?

What stance does the filmmaker take on the subject?

| Detail 1 | Detail 2 | Detail 3 | Detail 4 |
|---|---|---|---|
| | | | |

Why is this documentary significant? What impact did it have?

My reactions:

**Figure 5.4. Summarize a Documentary. (Reprinted with permission from Laurelin Andrade, instructional coach, Salem-Keizer School District.)**

The documentary _____
　　　　　　　　　　　　　　　　　　(title)

by _____ is about _____
　　　(filmmaker's full name)　　　　　　　　　　　　　　(subject)

_____.

The film takes place _____
　　　　　　　　　　　　　　(setting)

at a time when _____

_____.

_____ takes the position that _____
(Filmmaker's last name)　　　　　　　　　　　　　　(stance)

This is evident in _____
　　　　　　　　　(describe the details that support the stance/purpose)

_____

_____

_____

_____.

The documentary is significant because _____

_____

_____.

On the whole, this documentary is _____ because _____
　　　　　　　　　　　　　　　　　(adjective)　　　　　　　　　　　(your reaction)

_____

_____.

**Figure 5.4—*Continued***

Title/Occasion_____

| Speaker |
|---|
|  |

| Setting |
|---|
| Where? |
| Audience? |
| When? |
| What else was going on then? |

| What was the speaker's purpose? |
|---|
|  |

| Detail 1 | Detail 2 | Detail 3 | Detail 4 |
|---|---|---|---|
|  |  |  |  |

| What was the impact? |
|---|
|  |

| My Reactions |
|---|
|  |

**Figure 5.5. Summarize a Speech. (Reprinted with permission from Laurelin Andrade, instructional coach, Salem-Keizer School District.)**

This recording of _____was made on
(speaker)

_____
(setting)

During that time _____
(occasion)

_____.

_____ was addressing _____
(speaker's name)                                        (audience)

He/she wanted to _____
(speaker's purpose)

_____.

To do this, he/she _____
(most important detail)

_____.

In addition, _____
(additional details)

_____

_____.

As a result of this speech, _____
(impact)

_____.

On the whole, this speech is _____ because _____
(adjective)                                    (your reaction)

_____.

**Figure 5.5—*Continued***

Many of students' literacy practices today happen through their reading and writing in multimedia and online contexts, and we need to better equip students with comprehension strategies for both new media and online text. The International Reading Association (2009) notes, "To become fully literate in today's world, students must become proficient in the new literacies of 21st century technologies. As a result, literacy educators have a responsibility to effectively integrate these new technologies into the curriculum, preparing students for the literacy future they deserve" (p. 1). I would suggest modifying this statement to acknowledge that all educators are literacy educators, and we must all share in the responsibility of helping students become literate in new forms of media. As noted, the CCSS also recognize the importance of nonprint text and new media. Hopefully, this section has presented you with some useful strategies and ideas for doing so. The final section will present some additional tools and strategies for incorporating technology into your teaching.

## Other Resources and Strategies

### Cell Phones

Many schools are now reassessing their strict policies prohibiting cell phones and electronic devices in the school and classroom. This is partly a result of growing awareness of the increasing usefulness of cell phones as an educational technology tool. Today's phones are essentially mini-computers with Internet access and recording capabilities. Few classrooms provide a computer for every student but most students today carry Smartphones and other high-tech cell phones. The challenge, of course, is keeping students focused on the assignment or task at hand. What are some of the things students can use cell phones for? They can do research online, use the camera function to take pictures and videos for multimedia assignments, send each other practice test questions via instant messaging, access research databases, and refer to online dictionaries. Chadband (2013) recommends using "Celly," a group messaging service as a means of communicating with students through their phones. This requires starting a cell group by texting "start" to Celly, setting up a username and group name, and then texting group members' cell phone numbers. Students can then text the new group to join. Students can use Celly to set up study groups and receive homework assignments or reminders from the teacher (Chadband, 2013).

### Presentation Software

Media literacy is a critical form of literacy for today's students that cannot be overlooked. As Brooks-Young (2010) points out, we should teach students to become not only consumers but also creators of various forms of media. Teachers often don't have students give oral classroom presentations because of the amount of time it takes for every student to present. However, it is important to teach students not only how to prepare a good presentation but also some techniques for effectively presenting it. The CCSS include speaking and listening standards for grades 6–12. For example, the grade 9 and 10 anchor standards include the following:

Standard 2: Integrate multiple sources of information presented in diverse media or formats (e.g., visually, qualitatively, orally) evaluating the credibility and accuracy of each source.

Standard 4: Present information, findings, and supporting evidence clearly, concisely, and logically such that listeners can follow the line of reasoning and the organization, development, substance, and style that are appropriate to purpose, audience, and task.

Standard 5: Make strategic use of digital media (e.g., textual, graphical, audio, visual, and interactive elements) in presentations to enhance understanding of findings, reasoning, and evidence and to add interest.

Following a particular unit or research project in your class, consider having students prepare a presentation using some form of presentation software. Even if you do not want to take the time to have every student present to the class, students will still gain the experience of creating a presentation, and you can assess their prepared presentation in electronic format. They can also deliver their presentation in small groups, or post them on a class website or Google Docs where other students can view them. Even if students create a photo or video project, they can share these by posting them online or on a class or school website. There is, of course, much additional value in giving students public speaking experience by having them actually prepare and deliver a presentation.

Most of us probably know how to make a PowerPoint presentation, which is fairly simple and easy to learn. Many of our students are familiar with PowerPoint, but many are not. Conduct a few mini-lessons to show students some of the basic features of PowerPoint. The following list includes some of the things you can do with PowerPoint and other presentation software:

1. Use color, shading, and textures in your slides.

2. Import clip art, photographs, and images.

3. Create animated text and images and dynamic transitions between slides (flashing images, and sliding and dissolving text).

4. Create speaker's notes that the audience cannot see.

5. Move slides into various sequences.

6. Time your presentation precisely.

7. Show your presentation in multiple formats (on computer, large-screen format, projector, online, or printed handouts) (Lannon & Gurak, 2012).

Give students additional presentation tips such as starting with a slide that provides an overview of the presentation and what it will cover, not overusing visuals, how to present without simply reading what's on the slides, and ending with a concluding slide.

In addition to PowerPoint, there are other great presentation tools you may want to consider. Brooks-Young (2010) recommends a couple of presentation tools that make it easy for students to organize their images and use templates. The slides can also be captioned and narrated. One of these is http://edu.glogster.com/, which makes it easy to get started with creating presentation materials. Google Docs also includes presentation tools (see the next section on Google Docs). Another resource is http://show.zoho.com, which has lots of great online presentation tools (Brooks-Young, 2010). Some of my colleagues are now using Prezi as an alternative to PowerPoint (www.prezi.com). It is more visually creative and dynamic than Power-Point and includes fun slide transitions that are appealing.

## Google Docs

Google Docs is a set of online collaborative tools that many teachers are now using in the classroom. Google Docs has features that allow students to share their work and receive quick feedback from the teacher and other students. Google Docs also makes it easy to access simple tools to support writing and research. It is very easy, for example, to create citations and connect to Easybib.com to prepare a works cited page. Google Docs also features a drawing component and other features that make it easy for students to work collaboratively on group projects. Teachers can also use Google Forms to create simple, self-grading quizzes with a few multiple choice questions. The application generates a spreadsheet showing class results. You can also easily create templates for particular assignments and distribute them to students. There are also user-submitted ones available for public use. When using Google Docs for collaborative work, you can see the revision history of the document, which is also useful for grading. Perhaps one of the biggest benefits of Google Docs is that students can access their documents from any computer.

To get started, follow this procedure:

1. Open the Google Docs website at www.docs.google.com. Create a user-name and password.

2. Create a document by clicking "New Document" and choosing from "document," "spreadsheet," or "presentation." Create the document the same way you would any other Word, Excel, or PowerPoint document. Google Docs has most of the same features.

3. Save your document by choosing "Save" in the file menu. Use "Rename" to give the document a name. Google does not use folders, so you will want to be able to retrieve your document easily by tagging it. Click on "Tags" at the bottom of the page. The drop-down menu will provide suggested tag names or you can choose your own.

4. To share a document with others, open the Google Docs page. Click on the "Share Now" button for the particular document title, and then enter the e-mail addresses of those with whom you want to share the document. These individuals can be "viewers" who are only allowed to read the document, or "collaborators" who can read, edit, and contribute to the document. Obviously, for group projects, students would want to indicate their group members as collaborators so that all of the group members can work together on the paper or project.

5. To publish the document, open the document from your list and then click on "Publish" at the top right. You can also save or print the document as a file or PDF.

Try using Google Docs with your class. Have them set up Google accounts and then experiment with using Google Docs to write and publish their papers, do research, and participate in online collaborative groups.

## Blogs

One of the ways teachers can use technology to encourage students to write and communicate is through the use of blogs, a term that is a shortened version of "web logs." They are made up of dated entries that are posted most recent first. Entries can be made up of text alone, or can include links and images (Brooks-Young, 2010). Essentially, a blog is a set of discussions or commentaries on a particular topic. Blogs have become a popular form of online discussion for people with similar interests. Several websites now offer free, simple classroom blogs that only require the teacher to initiate a blog. Once the classroom blog is registered, students can sign up, compose pieces of writing related to the assignment, and post it to the blog. The teacher can also moderate and approve blogs for posting. All members of the class can then read and reply to the postings (Brozo & Puckett, 2009). Blogs also include an RSS feed (really simple syndication), which means that readers who are subscribed to the blog are notified when a new posting appears (Brooks-Young, 2010).

Brozo and Puckett (2009) note that "blogs are a great way for students to express themselves, improve their writing skills, share what they know, and learn from others" (p. 199). Consider the possibility of using a blog as an alternative to a classroom website, and ask students and parents to participate by posting questions. Use blogs to have students respond to writing prompts as well. Other classes can even be invited to join the discussion. Some teachers have used blogs in place of a traditional study guide for reading of a book or classroom novel. Consider setting up a classroom blog and assigning students to respond to some prompts by blogging, as well as responding to other students' posts. There are several good blog-hosting sites that Brooks-Young (2010) recommends: Google's blog-hosting site is www.blogger.com. Other good options are http://edublogs.org/ and http://wordpress.com. Blogmeister (http://classblogmeister.com) is also a good option for classroom use because of several built-in security features.

You may have also heard the term "microblogging," which refers to blogs that limit the length of the message. Twitter.com, of course, is the most famous microblog and limits users' messages to 140 characters. Also, try Plurk at www.plurk.com and Jaiku at www.jaiku.com (Brooks-Young, 2010). These sites, of course, especially Twitter, have become increasingly popular as forms of social media and sources of information. Students who may not find traditional classroom writing very appealing may develop greater interest in their work when allowed to write and discuss class topics in blog form.

### Wikis

Another technology tool to encourage online writing is the wiki. Wikis are "community encyclopedias that allow anyone to add to or edit the content of a listing" (Lannon & Gurak, 2012). Of course, the most common wiki is Wikipedia, an online encyclopedia in which users can edit the content. They are based on the theory that over time, incorrect information will be corrected and the material will become highly accurate. Of course, this is debatable, and since anyone can add any information to Wikipedia articles, one cannot verify the accuracy of the information at any given time; therefore, I do not allow students to use Wikipedia as a research source, although I do point out that it is still a useful source for general information and for locating additional sources on the topic. Useful wiki host sites include PBWorks (http://pbworks.com), Wikispaces (www.wikispaces.com), and Wetpaint (www.wetpaint.com) (Brooks-Young, 2010). Other useful sites are MediaWiki (http://mediawiki.org) and PBWiki (pbwiki.com).

Classroom wikis can be a very useful online tool for teaching purposes because they create a space for collaboration among students and can enhance writing instruction. Wiki host sites provide templates that allow the user to create personal wikis. The user can also add graphics and other elements (Brooks-Young, 2010).

Morgan and Smith (2008) describe their school-college partnership using classroom wikis. Students researched topics of their choice and then created online media reports using wiki technology. Morgan and Smith (2008) note, "The ease of collaboration strengthened students' abilities to engage with text as writers and readers" (p. 81). Teacher Tracy J. Tarasiuk (2010) used wikis during whole-class reading of a novel as an alternative to more traditional worksheets and packets. Students were assigned to groups that each set up a site on PBWorks. Students then collaborated with each other while studying vocabulary, writing summaries and analyzing characterization as they read. Tarasiuk (2010) noted that students put more work into their wikis because they knew others could view the site. They downloaded and added images to vocabulary and summary pages, and even logged into Wikipedia (wikipedia.org) to add and correct information about the novels they had read.

Consider using wikis in place of a class website, or having students create their own wikis to share projects and information following a specific unit (and view and edit others' wikis). Brooks-Young (2010) offers some great suggestions for classroom projects that can be enhanced by use of a wiki: "Besides posting written work, students can upload related photos and embed podcasts and online presentations. Consider using a wiki for students to create a class glossary or a math problem solution guide or to document a field trip" (p. 74).

## Podcasts

The term "podcast" is a combination of the words "iPod" and "broadcast." It is an audio recording that is uploaded to an Internet site and can then be downloaded on a portable digital player such as MP3 player. There are many potential classroom uses for podcasts. Teachers can post lectures, assignment, and presentations in podcast format and students can access them on their iPods. Students can also, of course, develop their own podcasts (Brozo & Puckett, 2009).

At first, those who made podcasts had to have a computer, microphone, and software program to record the audio file. Once it was recorded, it was then posted online. Today most people can use their cell phones (if they have recording capability) or an MP3 player to record the audio. These audio recordings can then be easily posted on the Internet (Brooks-Young, 2010). To listen to the podcasts, one only needs a media player program such as RealPlayer or iTunes, which most people have on their personal computers.

Brooks-Young (2010) notes that many educators have begun recording lectures that students can listen to. They also have realized the potential involved with having students create and publish podcasts, which can help build literacy skills and reinforce content learning. A good podcast requires the student to conduct research, write a script, rehearse the recording, create a clear recorded version, and edit before the podcast is uploaded.

Borgia and Owles (2012) discuss a podcasting project during reading of a class novel in which students were asked to choose a favorite passage from the novel and practice reading the passage with a partner until it was polished and ready to record. They used the Apple software GarageBand to create the podcasts and then exported the podcasts to iTunes. They also note that completing the project with partners and using the podcasting technology helped to motivate students and allowed them to practice reading skills.

Here are some other ideas for possible classroom uses of podcasting:

1. The teacher can record podcasts for students who are absent or to help students study for a test. (Some teachers are now recording all of their lectures in podcasts and requiring students to listen to the lecture for homework, reserving class time for other activities.)

2. Students can practice their reading and fluency skills by recording excerpts from textbooks, reading assignments, novels, poems, or conversations.

3. Students can respond to discussion questions in podcast format.

4. Students can use voice recording during lectures or field trips to save notes for later review.

5. Students can conduct interviews recorded in a podcast.

6. Students can study for a test by answering sample test questions.

7. Students with disabilities or injuries that prevent them from writing can create a podcast in place of a written assignment or test.

## Social Networks

You might consider some possible uses for social networking to build upon classroom activities and content learning. Social networks began gaining popularity in the 1990s and their popularity has exploded since with networks such as MySpace, Friendster, Facebook, and Twitter. (MySpace, which quickly declined in popularity with the rise of Facebook, has now been redesigned as a social network for the arts and entertainment industry and includes lots of streaming music.) Some social networks such as Facebook are banned in many school districts, and it's important to be cautious what platforms you use for classroom social networking. Brooks-Young (2010) recommends that educators check their school's acceptable use policies and, if social networking is banned, meet with your principal or site administrators to explain the educational purpose of the activities you are proposing, clearly explaining the academic benefits for students. Social networks have great potential for providing an online space for students to collaborate, work on classroom projects, share their work, build literacy skills, and reinforce content learning. There are several platforms that are specifically designed for teachers and schools. These include:

1. Edmodo (www.edmodo.com), which includes applications for assignments, quizzes, and polling, also allows students to submit their homework on the site. Teachers can post questions, comments, and updates, much like status updates on popular social networking sites.

2. Elgg (http://elgg.org) is open-source software for schools to use to create their own in-school social networks.

3. Ning (http://ning.com) allows users to create their own personal networks. It also removes ads when members are students.

## Digital Video

Digital video and movie making have a number of potential uses for content-area teachers. Through making films, documentaries, and videos students can reinforce their content learning as well as learn to think critically and communicate effectively in an alternative format. Brooks-Young (2010) observes that the development of digital camcorders allowed anyone to create videos, and when combined with increased Internet connection speech and video-sharing sites, users could easily upload and share videos online. Video has always been appealing to students, however, especially to those who are more visual learners. Students today can even record and upload videos from their cell phones, and, of course, YouTube is one of the most popular sources of video for students.

There are two common video editing programs: Windows' Movie Maker and Mac's iMovie, both of which are either preloaded in the computer software package or available for download. They are also user friendly and allow edited clips to be combined with other video clips and audio tracks. They can also easily be incorporated into presentation programs like PowerPoint (Brozo & Puckett, 2009). Consider some of the following possibilities for digital video in your curriculum:

1. Have students create photo and video slide shows or films to share their learning in a particular unit.

2. Assign small groups to make a video for a designated academic purpose, such as to provide instructions, create a proposal, create an argument in video format, or dramatize a scene.

3. Have students create a video to accompany a written report or to document their progress.

4. Have students create a documentary film that illustrates a community problem or issue such as a local health concern, a scientific or environmental issue, a social problem such as poverty or crime, mathematical principles and applications, art and creativity in the community, or a local history topic.

5. Brooks-Young (2010) offers some additional suggestions: have students create a short video tour of the school, a public service announcement, a

videotaped interview with someone, or video tutorials for concepts they have learned to be shared with other students.

If you consider the possibility of asking your students to create and upload videos, be sure to follow this advice of Brooks-Young (2010):

> Site administrators must be kept informed by teachers who plan to have students post photos and videos and information about the instructional units or lessons should be shared with parents as well to ensure that all interested parties understand how this work relates to academic and media-literacy skills. (p. 83)

## Voicethread

Voicethread (www.voicethread.com) is a great media conversation platform where users create conversation "threads" incorporating and integrating videos, images, and other features. Simple directions are provided to create a "one-minute voicethread." It requires simply finding the image of the document on your computer, uploading it, commenting on the images, and adding a title and description. The user then selects "Share" and invites others to view the thread. Comments can be made by telephone, text, or microphone (a tutorial is included to show you how to set up a microphone). People who listen to and view your thread can make comments that will fill in around the edges of the original. If you want to make revisions to your thread, simply delete the comments and rerecord. The thread creator can also choose to moderate and approve all comments under "publishing options."

On the Voicethread webpage, you can view and browse through example Voicethreads. There are also several online tutorials that clearly explain how to use and create threads. In order to set up Voicethread to use with your classes or groups of students, you will want to download one of the Education Guides (PDF files) provided on the site, which will give you all the information you need to get started.

The Voicethread website includes lots of examples of ways that teachers in various content areas have used Voicethread. Browse through these examples to get some ideas for your own classes. Seventh-grade students studying radio advertising created their own advertisements and uploaded them, with students providing feedback and commenting on each other's work. Eighth-grade students created historical fiction picture books that were written, illustrated, and told by the students. In place of a written test, seventh graders used their learning of Edgar Allan Poe to create the "What do you know about Poe?" thread. Tenth-grade Chinese language students used Voicethread to practice pronunciation and create sentences using their newly learned words. Eleventh-grade French students responded to the teacher's questions using Voicethread. Seventh-grade math students shared their knowledge of measurements and ratios with students at an elementary school. Seventh-grade science students created a thread on the water cycle and one to promote environmental issues. High school social studies students used Voicethread for research, biographical study, and to create historical narratives.

Voicethread is a powerful online tool that is user friendly and has a great deal of potential for facilitating learning in many different content areas.

### E-Portfolios

English teachers and teachers of other content areas often have students keep a portfolio to document their work and progress toward meeting course goals. An electronic portfolio is a variation on the traditional file-folder portfolio and can serve as a powerful form of authentic assessment that capitalizes upon technology. In general, portfolios are used not only to provide a record of students' work but also as a metacognitive tool to help students reflect upon their own learning. I use portfolios in my writing classes not only as a form of self-assessment but also to encourage student goal setting. In her review of using technologies to teach writing, Kathleen Blake Yancey (2004) notes several ways in which teachers have incorporated digital technology into students' writing portfolios. One teacher has students create e-portfolios that include a hyperlinked table of contents for the portfolio. Students can also add images, photos, and audio files to their portfolios. They can also include links to other websites or resources.

E-portfolios are useful as a self-reflection tool, to help students identify their strengths and weaknesses. Students can create portfolios using websites, blogs, wikis, Google Docs, or other platforms as a place to collect examples of their writing over time (Beach, Anson, Breuch, & Reynolds, 2014, in press). The advantages of an e-portfolio over a traditional one are that the pieces included can be organized into categories and students can import images and videos, use hyperlinks, and add material over an extended time period. They also expand the potential audience for the students' work (Beach, Anson, Breuch, & Reynolds, 2014, in press).

## Conclusion

My hope is that this final section of the book has given you some ideas and things to think about in terms of incorporating technology into your teaching and helping students better use technology and digital media to enhance their learning. While I believe that there are some very good resources, suggestions, and strategies included here, they are certainly only scratching the surface of what technology has to offer both teachers and students. In the coming years, technology will continue to revolutionize the way that we teach and the way that students learn. We must not only make use of good teaching strategies but also continue to learn in order to keep up with the pace of change and meet the needs of our students in the twenty-first century.

# REFERENCES

Alfassi, M. (2004). Reading to learn: Effects of combined strategy instruction on high school students. *Journal of Educational Research, 97*(4), 171–184.

Allen, J. (1999). *Words, words, words: Teaching vocabulary in grades 4–12.* Portland, ME: Stenhouse.

Allen, J. (2000). *Yellow brick roads: Shared and guided paths to independent reading 4–12.* Portland, ME: Stenhouse.

Alvermann, D. E. (1991). The discussion web: A graphic aid for learning across the curriculum. *The Reading Teacher, 45,* 92–99.

Alvermann, D. E., Phelps, S. F., & Ridgeway, V. G. (2007). *Content area reading and literacy: Succeeding in today's diverse classrooms* (5th ed.). Boston: Pearson.

Anderson, R. C., & Nagy, W. E. (1991). Word meanings. In R. Barr, M. L. Kamil, P. B. Mosenthal, & P. D. Pearson (Eds.), *Handbook of reading research* (Vol. 2, pp. 690–724). New York: Longman.

Aronson, E. (2013, July 6). Jigsaw classroom: Jigsaw in 10 easy steps. Retrieved from www.jigsaw.org/steps.htm.

Association for Supervision and Curriculum Development (Producer) (2002). *Reading in the content areas* (DVD). Available from http://shop.ascd.org/VIDEOS.aspx.

Baldwin, R. S., Ford, J. C., & Readence, J. E. (1981). Teaching word connotations: An alternative strategy. *Reading World, 21,* 103–108.

Beach, R., Anson, C., Breuch, L., & Reynolds, T. (2014, in press). *Reading and writing digital texts: An activity-based approach.* Lanham, MD: Rowman & Littlefield.

Bean, T. W., Bean, S. K., & Bean, K. F. (1999). Intergenerational conversations and two adolescents' multiple literacies: Implications for refining content area literacy. *Journal of Adolescent and Adult Literacy, 42*(6), 438–449.

Beck, I. L., McKeown, M. G., Hamilton, R. L., & Kucan, L. (1997). *Questioning the author: An approach for enhancing student engagement with text.* Newark, DE: International Reading Association.

Beck, I., McKeown, M., & Kucan, L. (2002). *Bringing words to life.* New York: Guilford.

Bedard, B. (2003, Nov./Dec.). Sticky situations. Retrieved from www.teachingK-8.com

Beers, K. (2003). *When kids can't read, what teachers can do: A guide for teachers 6–12.* Portsmouth, NH: Heinemann.

Biancarosa, C., & Snow, C. E. (2006). *Reading next—A vision for action and research in middle and high school literacy.* A report to the Carnegie Corporation of New York (2nd ed.). Washington, DC: Alliance for Excellent Education.

# REFERENCES

Blachowicz, C. L. Z. (1986). Making connections: Alternatives to the vocabulary notebook. *Journal of Reading, 29*, 539–543.

Blake Yancey, K. (2004). Using multiple technologies to teach writing. *Educational Leadership, 62*(2), 38–40.

Borgia, L., & Owles, C. (2012). Terrific teaching tips. *Illinois Reading Council Journal, 37*(3), 48–54.

Braunger, J., & Lewis, J. P. (2006). *Building a knowledge base in reading* (2nd ed.). Newark, DE: International Reading Association and National Council of Teachers of English.

Brooks-Young, S. (2010). *Teaching with the tools kids really use: Learning with web and mobile technologies.* Thousand Oaks, CA: Corwin.

Brown, A. L., Day, J. D., & Jones, R. (1983). The development of plans for summarizing texts. *Child Development, 54*, 968–979.

Brozo, W. G., Moorman, G., Meyer, C., & Stewart, T. (2013). Content area reading and disciplinary literacy: A case for the radical center. *Journal of Adolescent and Adult Literacy, 56*(5), 33–357. doi: 10.1002/JAAL.153

Brozo, W. G., & Puckett, K. S. (2009*). Supporting content area literacy with technology.* Boston: Pearson/Allyn & Bacon.

Brozo, W. G., & Simpson, M. L. (1998). *Readers, teachers, learners: Expanding literacy across the content areas* (3rd ed.). Upper Saddle River, NJ: Prentice Hall.

Brozo, W. G., & Simpson, M. L. (2003). Writing as a tool for active learning. In *Readers, teachers, learners: Expanding literacy across the content areas* (4th ed.) (pp. 253–302). Upper Saddle River, NJ: Merrill/Prentice Hall.

Brunner, J. T. (2011). *I don't get it! Helping students understand what they read.* Lanham, MD: Rowman & Littlefield.

Bryant, D. P., Ugel, N., Thompson, S., & Hamff, A. (1999). Instructional strategies for content area reading instruction. *Intervention in School and Clinic, 34*(5), 293–305.

Buehl, D. (2001). *Classroom strategies for interactive learning* (2nd ed.). Newark, DE: International Reading Association.

Burke, J. (2008). *The English teacher's companion: A complete guide to classroom, curriculum, and the profession* (3rd ed.). Portsmouth, NH: Heinemann.

Caverly, D.C., Mandeville, T. F., & Nicholson, S. A. (1995). PLAN: A study reading strategy for informational text. *Journal of Adolescent and Adult Literacy, 39*(3), 190–199.

Cecil, N. L., & Gipe, J. P. (2003). *Literacy in the intermediate grades: Best practices for a comprehensive program.* Scottsdale, AZ: Holcomb Hathaway.

Chadband, E. (2013). Teaching with today's tech: How to use social media effectively with students. *NEA Today, 31*(3), 26–27.

Ciborowski, J. (1992). *Textbooks and the students who can't read them: A guide to teaching content.* Cambridge, MA: Brookline Books.

Coiro, J. (2005). Making sense of online text. *Educational Leadership, 63*(2), 30–35.

*Confronting the Crisis: Federal investments in state birth-through-grade-twelve literacy education* (2012). Policy Brief. Washington, DC: Alliance for Excellent Education. Retrieved from www.all4ed.org

Conley , M. W. (1992). *Content reading instruction: A communication approach.* New York: McGraw-Hill.

Council of Chief State School Officers and National Governors' Association (2010). Common Core State Standards for English Language Arts and Literacy in History, Social Studies, Science, and Technical Subjects. Retrieved from www.corestandards.org

Crawley, S. J., & Mountain, L. H. (1988). *Strategies for guiding content reading.* Boston: Allyn & Bacon.

Dana, C., & Rodriguez, M. (1992). TOAST: A system to study vocabulary. *Reading Research and Instruction, 31*, 78 81.

Daniels, H., & Zemelman, S. (2004). *Subjects matter: Every teacher's guide to content-area reading.* Portsmouth, NH: Heinemann.

Daniels, H., Zemelman, S., & Steineke, N. (2007). *Content-area writing: Every teacher's guide.* Portsmouth, NH: Heinemann.

Davey, B. (1983). Think aloud: Modeling the cognitive process of reading comprehension. *Journal of Reading, 27*(1), 44–47.

Denti, L., & Guerin, G. (2004). Confronting the problem of poor literacy: Recognition and action. *Reading and Writing Quarterly, 20*(2), 113–122.

Diamond Hicks, S. (2011). Technology in today's classroom: Are you a tech-savvy teacher? *The Clearing House, 84*, 188–191.

Dillon, S. (2010, September 28). 4,100 students prove small is better rule wrong. *New York Times*, p. A1.

Donahue, D. (2003). Reading across the great divide: English and math teachers apprentice one another as readers and disciplinary insiders. *Journal of Adolescent and Adult Literacy, 47*(1), 24–37.

Doty, J. K., Cameron, G. N., & Barton, M. L. (2003). *Teaching reading in social studies.* Aurora, CO: Mid-continent Research for Education and Learning.

Extend learning with public library resources (2013). *Education Update* (ASCD), *55*(4), 2.

Fang, Z., & Coatoam, S. (2013). Disciplinary literacy: What you want to know about it. *Journal of Adolescent and Adult Literacy, 58*(8), 627–632. doi: 10.1002/JAAL.190

Francis, M. A., & Simpson, M. L. (2003). Using theory, our intuitions, and a research study to enhance students' vocabulary knowledge. *Journal of Adolescent and Adult Literacy, 47*(1), 66–78.

Frayer, D. A., Frederick, W. C., & Klausmeier, H. J. (1969). *A schema for testing the level of concept mastery* (Working Paper No. 16). Madison, WI: Wisconsin Research and Development Center for Cognitive Learning.

Gallagher, K. (2006). *Teaching adolescent writers.* Portland, ME: Stenhouse.

Gere, A. R. (Ed.). (1985). *Roots in the sawdust: Writing to learn across the curriculum.* Urbana, IL: NCTE.

Gillet, J. W., & Kita, M. J. (1979). Words, kids, and categories. *The Reading Teacher, 32*, 538–546.

Gillet, J. W., & Temple, C. (1983). *Understanding reading problems: Assessment and instruction.* Boston: Little, Brown.

Graham, S., & Perin, D. (2007). *Writing next: Effective strategies to improve writing of adolescents in middle and high schools.* A Report to the Carnegie Corporation of New York. Washington, DC: Alliance for Excellent Education. Retrieved from www.all4ed.org/files/writingnext.pdf

Haggard, M. R. (1982). The vocabulary self-selection strategy: An active approach to word learning. *Journal of Reading, 26*, 203–207.

Hammond, W. D., & Raphael, T. E. (1999). *Early Literacy Instruction for the New Millennium.* Grand Rapids: Michigan Reading Association and Center for the Improvement of Early Reading Achievement.

Harmon, J. M., Wood, K. D., & Hedrick, W. B. (2006). *Instructional strategies for teaching content vocabulary, grades 4–12.* Westerville, OH: National Middle School Association.

Hart, B., & Risley, R. (1995). *Meaningful differences in everyday experiences of young American children.* Baltimore: Paul Brookes.

Heller, R. (2010). In praise of amateurism: A friendly critique of Moje's "Call for Change" in secondary literacy. *Journal of Adolescent & Adult Literacy, 54*(4), 267–273. doi:10.1598/JAAL.54.4.4

Herber, H. (1978). *Teaching reading in content areas* (2nd ed.). Englewood Cliffs, NJ: Prentice Hall.

Idol-Maestas, L. (1985). A critical thinking map to improve content-area comprehension of poor readers. *Remedial Reading and Special Education, 8*(4), 28–40.

# REFERENCES

International Reading Association (2009). New literacies and 21st century technologies. (Position Statement 1067). Retrieved June 17, 2013, from www.reading.org/general/AboutIRA/PositionStatement/21stcenturyliteracies.aspx

Irvin, J. L. (1998). *Reading and the middle school students: Strategies to enhance literacy.* Boston: Allyn & Bacon.

Israel, E. (2002). Examining multiple perspectives in literature. In J. Holden & J. S. Schmitt (Eds.), *Inquiry and the literary text: Constructing discussion in the English classroom* (89–103). Urbana, IL: National Council of Teachers of English.

Johnson, D. D., & Pearson, P. D. (1984). *Teaching reading vocabulary* (2nd ed.). New York: Holt, Rinehart, and Winston.

Kemper, D., Meyer, V., & Sebranek P. (1990). *Writers Inc.: A guide to writing, thinking, and learning.* Wilmington, MA: Great Source/Houghton Mifflin.

Kiuhara, S., Graham, S., & Hawken, L. (2009). Teaching writing to high school students: A national survey. *Journal of Educational Psychology, 101*, 136–60.

Knipper, K. J., & Duggan, T. J. (2006). Writing to learn across the curriculum: Tools for comprehension in content area classes. *The Reading Teacher, 59*(5), 462–470.

Langer, J. (1981). From theory to practice: A pre-reading plan. *Journal of Reading, 25*, 152–256.

Lannon, J. M., & Gurak, L. J. (2012). *Technical Communication* (12th ed.). Boston: Pearson/Longman.

Lehr, F., Osborn, J., & Hiebert, E. H. (2004). *A focus on vocabulary.* Honolulu, HI: Pacific Resources for Education and Learning.

LeMaster, J. (2009). *Critical reading: Deep reading strategies for expository texts, Teacher Guide 7–12.* San Diego, CA: AVID Press.

Lenski, S. D., & Niersheimer, S. L. (2002). Strategy instruction from a sociocognitive perspective. *Reading Psychology, 23*(2), 127–143.

Lewin, L. (2003). *Paving the way in Reading and Writing: Strategies and Activities to Support Struggling Students in Grades 6–12.* San Francisco, CA: Jossey-Bass.

Lewin, L. (2009). *Teaching comprehension with questioning strategies that motivate middle school readers.* New York: Scholastic.

Lewin, L., & Shoemaker, B. J. (1998). *Great performances: Creating classroom-based assessment tasks.* Alexandria, VA: ASCD.

Lewis, M., & Wray, D. (1999). Secondary teachers' views and actions concerning literacy and literacy teaching. *Educational Review, 51*(3), 273–281.

Lubliner, S. (2005). *Getting into words: Vocabulary instruction that strengthens comprehension.* Baltimore: Paul Brookes Publishing.

Lyman, F. T. (1981). The responsive classroom discussion: The inclusion of all students. In A. Anderson (Ed.), *Mainstreaming Digest.* College Park: University of Maryland.

Manzo, A., & Manzo, V. (1990). *Content area reading: A heuristic approach.* Columbus, OH: Merrill Publishing.

Manzo, A., Manzo, V., & Estes, T. (2001). *Content area literacy: Interactive teaching for interactive learning* (2nd ed.). New York: Wiley and Sons.

Marzano, R. J., Pickering, D. J., & Pollock, J. E. (2001). *Classroom instruction that works: Research-based strategies for increasing student achievement.* Alexandria, VA: ASCD.

McGinley, W., & Denner, P. (1987). Story impressions: A pre-reading/writing activity. *Journal of Reading, 31*, 248–253.

McTighe, J., & Lyman, F. T. (1988). Cueing thinking in the classroom: The promise of theory-embedded tools. *Educational Leadership, 45*(7), 18–24.

Middleton, J. L. (1991). Science generated analogies in biology. *The American Biology Teacher, 53*(1), 42–46.

Moje, E. B. (2008). Foregrounding the disciplines in secondary literacy teaching and learning: A call for change. *Journal of Adolescent and Adult Literacy, 52*(2), 96–107. doi: 10.1598/JAAL52.2.1

Morgan, B., & Smith, R. D. (2008). A wiki for classroom writing. *The Reading Teacher, 62*(1), 80–82.

National Center for Education Statistics (2004). *The condition of education, 2004.* Washington, DC: US Government Printing Office. Retrieved from http://nces.ed.gov/pubsearch/pubsinfo.asp?pubid=2004077

National Center for Education Statistics (2011). *NAEP 2009 Year in Review: A Compilation of Results from the 2009 Mathematics, Reading, Science, and High School Transcript Study Reports.* NCES 2011–471.

Ness, M. (2007). Reading comprehension strategies in secondary content-area classrooms. *Phi Delta Kappan, 89*(3), 229–231.

Ogle, D. (1986, February). The KWL: A teaching model that develops active reading of expository text. *The Reading Teacher, 39,* 564–570.

Olsen, M. W., & Gee, T. C. (1991). Content reading instruction in the primary grades: Perceptions and strategies. *The Reading Teacher, 45*(4), 298–307.

Palinscar, A. S., & Brown, A. L. (1984). Reciprocal teaching of comprehension-fostering and comprehension-monitoring activities. *Cognition and Instruction, 1,* 117–175.

Pauk, W. (1993). *How to study in college* (5th ed.). Boston: Houghton Mifflin.

Porter, C., & Cleland, J. (1995). *The portfolio as a learning strategy.* Portsmouth, NH: Heinemann.

Punch, M., & Robinson, M. (1992). Social studies vocabulary mnemonics. *Social Education, 56*(7), 402–403.

Raphael, T. (1986). Teaching question-answer relationships, revisited. *The Reading Teacher, 39,* 516–522.

Rasinski, T., & Padak, N. (1996). *Holistic reading strategies: Teaching children who find reading difficult.* Englewood Cliffs, NJ: Merrill/Prentice Hall.

Readence, J., Bean, T., & Baldwin, R. (1998). *Content area literacy: An integrated approach* (6th ed.). Dubuque, IA: Kendall Hunt.

Reeves, D. B. (2003). High performance in high poverty schools: 90/90/90 and beyond. Center for Performance Assessment. Retrieved from www.sj.boces.org/nisl/high

Ridgeway, V. G. (2004). One teacher's journey. *Journal of Adolescent and Adult Literacy, 47*(5) 364–368.

Robinson, F. (1961). *Effective study.* New York: Harper & Row.

Rose, A. (2000). Literacy strategies at the secondary level. *Leadership, 30* (2), 12–16.

Salinger, T. (2003). Helping older, struggling readers. *Preventing School Failure, 47*(2), 79–86.

Sanacore, J. (2000). Promoting effective literacy learning in minority students by focusing on teacher workshops and reflective practice: A comprehensive project supported by the Annenberg Foundation. *Reading Psychology, 21*(3), 233–255.

Santa, C. M. (1988). *Content reading including study systems.* Dubuque, IA: Kendall Hunt.

Schoenbach, R., Greenleaf C., Cziko, C., & Hurwitz, L. (1999). *Reading for understanding: A guide to improving reading in middle and high school classrooms.* San Francisco: Jossey-Bass.

Schwartz, R. M., & Raphael, T. E. (1985). Concept of definition: A key to improving students' vocabulary. *The Reading Teacher, 30*(2), 198–205.

Sevilla, R. (2012). Criteria for examining the credibility of information on the Internet. Project Look Sharp. Ithaca College. Retrieved June 17, 2013, from www.ithaca.edu/looksharp/criteria.pdf

Shanahan, T., & Shanahan, C. (2008). Teaching disciplinary literacy to adolescents: Rethinking content-area literacy. *Harvard Educational Review, 78*(1), 40–59.

Stauffer, R. G. (1969). *Developing reading maturity as a cognitive process.* New York: Harper and Row.

Strategic Literacy Initiative. (2004). Increasing student achievement through schoolwide reading apprenticeship, 2001–2004. Retrieved April 23, 2013, from www.wested.org/cs/print/docs/sli/wide reading.html

REFERENCES

Sturtevant, E. G. (2003). *The literacy coach: A key to improving teaching and learning in secondary schools.* Washington, DC: Alliance for Excellent Education.

Symonds, K. W. (2002). *Literacy coaching: How school districts can support a long-term strategy in a short-term world.* San Francisco: Bay Area School Reform Collaborative (ERIC Document Reproduction Service, NO. ED477297).

Tama, M. C., & McClain, A. B. (2007). *Guiding reading and writing in the content areas* (3rd ed.). Dubuque, IA: Kendall Hunt.

Tarasiuk, T. J. (2010). Combining traditional and contemporary texts: Moving my English class to the computer lab. *Journal of Adolescent and Adult Literacy, 53*(7), 543–552. doi: 10.1598/JAAL.53.7.2

Taylor, R., & Collins, V. D. (2003). *Literacy leadership for grades 5–12.* Alexandria, VA: ASCD.

Tierney, R. J., & Readence, J. E. (1999). *Reading strategies and practices: A compendium* (5th ed.). Boston: Allyn & Bacon.

Tierney, R. J., Readence, J. E., & Dishner, E. K. (1990). *Reading strategies and practices: A compendium.* Boston: Allyn and Bacon.

Tompkins, G. E., & Blanchfield, C. (2008). *Teaching vocabulary: 50 creative strategies grades 6–12* (2nd ed.). Upper Saddle River, NJ: Pearson/Merrill.

Tovani, C. (2000). *I read it, but I don't get it: Comprehension strategies for adolescent readers.* Portland, ME: Stenhouse.

Tragenza, J., & Lewis, M. (2008, December). Beyond simple comprehension. *Literacy Today,* 24–26.

US Department of Education, National Center for Education Statistics (2010). The nation's report card: Reading 2009 (NCES 2010–458). Washington, DC: US Government Printing Office.

Vacca, R. T., & Vacca, J. L. (1989). *Content area reading* (3rd ed.). Glenview, IL: Scott Foresman.

Vacca, R. T., & Vacca, J. L. (1993). *Content area reading* (4th ed.). New York: HarperCollins.

Vogt, M., & Shearer, B. A. (2003). *Reading specialists in the real world: A sociocultural view.* Boston: Pearson.

Vygotsky, L. (1978). *Mind in society.* Cambridge, MA: Harvard University Press.

Wood, K. (1988). Guiding students through informational text. *The Reading Teacher, 41,* 912–920.

Wood, K. D., & Endres, C. (2005). Motivating student interest with the imagine, elaborate, predict, and confirm strategy. *The Reading Teacher, 58,* 2–14.

Wray, D. (2001). Literacy in the secondary curriculum. *Reading, 35*(1), 12–17.

Zwiers, J. (2010). *Building reading comprehension habits in grades 6–12: A toolkit of classroom activities* (2nd ed.). Newark, DE: International Reading Association.

# INDEX

# ABOUT THE AUTHOR

**Gregory Berry** is currently an English teacher at South Salem High School in Salem, Oregon, where he has also served as teacher leader, instructional coach, and instructional coordinator. He has served on numerous school and district committees and leadership teams. He is also an adjunct instructor at Chemeketa Community College, teaching courses in English composition and technical writing, and is one of the state of Oregon's writing specialists for state writing assessment.

Dr. Berry has conducted teacher trainings and workshops on a variety of subjects and also taught courses in the Department of Education at Western Oregon University. Prior to coming to the Salem-Keizer School District, he taught English and drama at Ontario High School and Treasure Valley Community College in Ontario, Oregon.

Dr. Berry received his BA in English, BS in education, and MS in education from Eastern Oregon University (1986, 1990). He completed his doctorate in educational leadership, curriculum and instruction from Portland State University in 2009. His dissertation research focused on literacy leadership and literacy coaching in secondary schools. He enjoys spending time reading, writing, traveling, cooking, music, hiking, and gardening.